The Divine Archetype

The Sociobiology and Psychology of Religion

by
Brant Wenegrat

Lexington Books

D.C. Heath and Company/Lexington, Massachusetts/Toronto

Library of Congress Cataloging-in-Publication Data

Wenegrat, Brant.
The divine archetype : the sociobiology and psychology of religion
/ Brant Wenegrat.
p.   cm.
Bibliography: p.
ISBN 0–669–21457–4 (alk. paper).—ISBN 0–669–21471–X (pbk. :
alk. paper)
1. Religion and sociology.   2. Psychology, Religious.   I. Title.
BL60.W45   1989
306.6—dc20   89–12221
                                                                              CIP

Published simultaneously in Canada
Printed in the United States of America
Casebound International Standard Book Number: 0–669–21457–4
Paperbound International Standard Book Number: 0–669–21471–X
Library of Congress Catalog Card Number: 89–12221

The paper used in this publication meets the minimum requirements of
American National Standard for Information Sciences—Permanence of
Paper for Printed Library Materials, ANSI Z39.48–1984.

Year and number of this printing:

89 90 91 92 10 9 8 7 6 5 4 3 2 1

Contents

Preface

Early evolutionists considered distinctively human mental functions—such as moral and spiritual feelings and the capacities to speak and to reason—the critical litmus tests for an evolutionary account of the human species. Religious feelings especially seemed to demand an accounting by Darwinian theory if human institutions were ever to be understood in naturalistic terms. In spite of early efforts, however, Darwinian theory proved more easily applicable to anatomic structures than to psychological traits characteristic of humans. Religious psychology in particular developed without much input from Darwinian theory.

The past two decades have witnessed a resurgence of interest in the evolution of human behaviors and mental traits. Powerful new concepts, developed under the rubric of sociobiology, have widened the applicability of Darwinian (now called neo-Darwinian) theory. Sociobiologists have studied human sexual, affiliative, and aggressive behaviors and filial and parenting strategies. Anthropologists have applied sociobiologic concepts to cultural mores, and sociologists have applied them to social ills, such as murder and incest.

In this book, I return to one of the topics held in high regard by early Darwinian theorists: human religious feeling. I show how the data of religious psychology can be ordered and accounted for using sociobiologic concepts. In this way, I hope to overcome one more barrier standing in the way of a wholly naturalistic view of human mind. Of course, religious psychology is also intrinsically important. Religious beliefs play vital roles in life adaptations and social organization. I believe that a sociobiologic treatment of religious psychology illuminates some aspects of religious beliefs that previous treatments have left in relative darkness. These aspects are especially pertinent to predicting the future of religion in an age of science. Finally, a sociobiologic treatment of religious psychology increases our understanding of psychological systems that have previously been applied to religion. In particular, I hope that the reader will find new insights into Freudian theory and Jungian concepts in this book.

The book is written for students of human behavior and students of religious beliefs. I have not presupposed that the reader will have any particular background in psychology, sociobiology, or religion. Nevertheless, I have tried to keep introductory materials to a minimal length, so as to avoid boring more advanced readers.

Many people helped me while I wrote this book. Adolf Pfefferbaum, Walton Roth, and Bert Kopell created the circumstances that allowed me to study and write. Walton Roth and Peter Finkelstein critiqued earlier versions of this work, and many of their suggestions have been incorporated into the final text. Marc Galanter gave me many ideas, only some of which are cited in the bibliography; I certainly would not have written this book without the impetus provided by his work. Charles O'Reilly gave me sound advice. Paul Insel provided aid when it was needed most. Anne O'Reilly Wenegrat supported and encouraged me, and Jacob Wenegrat goodnaturedly provided me with material.

I am also indebted to Kathy Rodgers and to numerous Stanford University librarians, who assisted me in finding papers and other works.

Vocatus Atque Non Vocatus Deus Aderit.
("Summoned or not, the god will be there.")

—Answer given by the Delphic Oracle to the
Lacedaemonians, who sought advice concerning their
war against Athens. Carved by C.J. Jung above the
door of his house.

1
Introduction

Aims and Limitations

In this book, I will use sociobiologic concepts to explain religious beliefs. I will try to explain why people believe in gods and how they use religion in their everyday lives. The reader may know that sociobiologists have tried to account for social behavior, both animal and human, in evolutionary terms. Religion is an important facet of human social behavior. Later chapters and the appendix show that religious beliefs play pervasive roles in social adaptation. Therefore, it seems only fitting to include religious beliefs in the range of phenomena to which sociobiologic concepts might be applied.

In explaining religious beliefs, I will cite empirical studies, social and psychological theories, and numerous histories of individual persons. The empirical studies come from various disciplines, including anthropology, psychology, and sociology. Some of the histories are of historical figures; others are taken from case descriptions in clinical publications. In citing clinical cases, I do not presuppose a particular clinical interest on the reader's part. I cite them because clinical psychological and psychiatric publications are an especially rich source of information about religious psychology. Perhaps because of the opportunities they have to study individuals, clinical psychologists and psychiatrists have been keen observers in noting how religious beliefs may aid adaptation to difficult life conditions. Also, religious symptoms are prominent in some mental disorders. Readers interested in the relationships among religion, psychosocial adaptation, and mental illness are referred to the Appendix.

When they are applied to religious psychology, sociobiologic concepts shed incidental light on psychological theories familiar to most readers. For example, while examining religious beliefs, we will have occasion to reexamine Jung's theory of archetypes and to see how it might be stated in more modern terms. Jung's theory has played a prominent role in modern religious psychology. We will also have occasion to reexamine Freudian structural theory—Freud's theory that the mind is composed of three separate structures: id, ego, and superego. As it turns out, the superego can be viewed from a wholly new vantage point, which stands Freud's theory of God—as it is commonly understood—exactly on its head. This new vantage point alters Freudian structural theory nearly beyond recognition.

Although my agenda here is ambitious, the reader should be forewarned that my scope is definitely limited. This book is a study of religious psychology and of related theoretical issues. It is not, by any means, a complete account of religion. Insofar as particular religions are cited, they are mentioned only by way of illustration. Many equally important religions are not mentioned at all. Religious history, philosophy, and literature are mostly ignored. Little attention is given to the political functions of religious organizations or to the relationship of religion to secular cultural trends. Finally, though many authors are cited in later chapters, no attempt is made to present a comprehensive review of anthropological or sociological theories pertinent to religion (see, for example, Morris, 1987).

The plan of this book is as follows: In the following section, I will specify the types of belief under scrutiny here. In chapter 2, I will outline a sociobiologic model of human social behavior. According to this model, human social behaviors adhere to certain innately probable strategies. An innately probable strategy is a response rule—in this case, social—adherence to which is made more likely by species-typical genes. In chapter 3, I will show that the psychological functions of religious faith can be categorized by the few social strategies described in chapter 2. The seemingly infinite uses to which people put their faith can be ordered and simplified with the sociobiologic model. In chapter 4, I will examine the origin of religious belief in light of the model previously developed.

Religious beliefs reflect cognitive preferences that subserve adherence to innately probable strategies. They consequently reflect ancient selective pressures that have shaped human intellect. Chapter 5 discusses individual differences in beliefs about God. These differences, which are due to family and cultural factors, determine the functions that religious beliefs can serve for particular persons. A model of religion has to be capable of accounting for idiosyncrasies. Chapter 6 reexamines Freud's wish that religion would one day disappear, to be replaced by science and reason. For reasons that will become clear, Freud's wish is unlikely ever to be fully realized. The model developed here shows various ways in which religious beliefs aid psychosocial adaptation. It indicates why the mentally ill develop religious ideas. As I noted earlier, the relationships among religious faith, adaptation, and illness are reviewed in the Appendix.

Subject Matter

I will take as my subject matter any and all beliefs in imaginary beings with supernatural powers. Belief systems that fail to postulate imaginary beings with supernatural powers—regardless of their cosmic, metaphysical, or ethical content—will not be dealt with here.

By using the term *imaginary*, I run the risk of alienating religious believers. Those who are religious consider their deity real. Of course, for the purposes of this study, not every object of worship must be imaginary. As long as some deities are imaginary, then religious beliefs of the type I take as my subject matter do in fact exist. Religious readers might feel that their own deity has been wrongly considered imaginary in the following chapters. I intend no judgment on the relative evidence for any specific religious tradition. Religious readers should feel free to substitute other examples. For rather different reasons, nonreligious readers, too, might object to *imaginary*. It might seem to beg at least some of the questions that a study of religion is supposed to answer. However, the viewpoint here is purely psychological. A psychological inquiry into the origin and function of religious belief may reasonably assume that characteristics attributed to otherwordly beings are products of human imagination. In this way, interesting psychological (not theological) questions are cast in their clearest form. What is the function of belief in an imaginary being? Why are supernatural powers attributed to this being? What human attributes account for such beliefs? If these questions and their answers are psychologically interesting, then the assumption on which they are based should be thought through to its logical conclusion.

Similar remarks apply to my use of the term *supernatural*. I do not wish to imply an a priori link between religious belief and superstition or ignorance. However, beings with supernatural powers are able to accomplish seemingly impossible feats without apparent means that are visible to humans. To fulfill some of the functions described in chapter 3, deities must be able to act through incomprehensible paths.

Several issues should be kept in mind while reading the following chapters. First, because of the way I have defined my subject matter, potentially important aspects of religious psychology are given short shrift here. For example, many people believe that the most important feature of religious belief—and the one most in need of psychological research—is not its content, but its intensity. Insofar as strongly held beliefs of any kind play similar roles in adherents' lives, any intense belief system might seem akin to religion. Socialism, fascism, and psychoanalysis have each been likened to religions, even though their content appears entirely secular. It does seem that fervently held beliefs engender similar social forms. Adherents form clubs, insulate themselves from outsiders, read inspirational literature, and develop rituals almost regardless of exactly what they believe (see Wood, 1980, for a discussion of psychoanalysis in these terms).

Along the same lines, various authors have considered the following issues psychologically central to religious thinking: immortality of the soul, awareness of death, submission to higher powers, perception of the holy, the feeling of absolute dependence, the conservation of personal values, the wish for fellowship or justification in nature, the search for first principles, and the desire for moral perfection. This, of course, is a partial list. Like intensity of belief, these issues are given much less attention here than many might think they deserve.

Certain traditions, which are generally considered religious, even seem to disregard supernatural beings. Buddhism, for instance, is a doctrine concerning the cause of and remedy for human suffering, rather than a doctrine concerning higher beings (David-Neel, 1979).

On the other hand, there are precedents for the emphasis I am placing on supernatural beings. For example, Edward Tylor (1913), an important early anthropologist, distinguished religious from magical and scientific belief systems according to the role played by supernatural beings. James Frazer (1976), the best known religious ethnographer of this century, defined religion as an attempt to please supernatural agents. Freud's (1927) religious theory equates religious faith with faith in superior beings.

Second, even though they relate to unseen beings, certain beliefs and practices have symbolic significance beyond the scope of this study. For example, both Carl Jung (1927/1931) and Ernest Jones (1951) noted the Catholic legend that Jesus was conceived after the Holy Ghost breathed in Mary's ear. Jones—an early analyst who later became Sigmund Freud's biographer—argued that impregnation through the ear expressed a primitive notion concerning the fecundity of male intestinal gas! Similarly, baptismal and Communion rituals seem to exress primitive notions relating to birth and ingestion—and even to cannibalism. For the most part, such matters will not be dealt with here.

Finally, certain folkloric and mythical phenomena are marginally related to the types of beliefs I will try to explain. For example, in many societies, illness or misfortune may be ascribed to witches (see, for example, Senter, 1947; Wintrob, 1973). Though witches are thought to have supernatural powers, those believed to be witches are usually real persons. For instance, a spinster aunt or the recluse on the edge of town might be suspected of witchcraft. Consequently, beliefs of this type are marginal to those under study here. They share certain elements but differ in certain others.

The most important marginal cases are allegorical figures. Though they are imaginary and may have supernatural powers, allegorical figures are treated more as symbols than as real beings. For example, certain Balinese and Indian fables liken people to puppets (Coomaraswamy, 1945); Margaret Mead referred to these fables in explaining Balinese dances. But neither Indians nor Balinese really see themselves as puppets, any more than Plato did when he employed a similar analogy. The puppeteer of these fables is less object of belief than symbol of necessity or fate. Likewise, though no one believes they exist as beings, images of the goddesses Truth, Beauty, and Justice still adorn our public buildings. The Statue of Liberty in New York harbor has such sentimental value that millions of dollars were recently spent repairing it. It is safe to say, however, that not one contributor to this project believed in Liberty's literal existence. Sometimes the distinction between more narrowly defined religious objects and allegorical figures is blurred. The aforementioned goddesses once seemed real. And even as he was worshipped, Dionysius apparently served an allegorical function (Luyster, 1980). As Ernest Jones (1951) noted, several cultures have used essentially allegorical figures to represent the rebirth of nature and the return of the sun after the winter solstice. Because they represent renewal, such allegorical figures have generally been infants, or gods who have died and been reborn. Some of these figures were also objects of worship. According to Jones, the new-born Jesus serves such a function for Christian cultures, so that an object of religious faith is simultaneously occupied as an allegorical figure.

Allegorical figures and objects of devotion are sometimes confused in psychological studies. For example, some years ago, Fromm (1950) tried to reconcile religion and psychoanalysis. For this purpose, he distinguished "humanistic" from "authoritarian" faith. He thought that only the former was ethically acceptable in light of psychoanalysis. But Fromm's humanistic religion seemed to demote God to an allegorical figure. According to Fromm, a humanistic god is identical with the whole of the universe. He represents "the image of man's higher self." By contrast, authoritarian gods are considered real beings. Authoritarian gods are said to create the universe. They don't represent things; they simply exist. They are infinitely greater than "man's higher self." In what follows, the distinction between allegorical figures and objects of the type of religious belief under study here is carefully preserved. This is not to deny their linkage. To the contrary, distinguishing these two types of imaginary beings will later be helpful in tracing their common roots.

In summary, I will take as my subject matter belief systems that postulate imaginary beings with supernatural powers. As a result, certain aspects of religion that others may consider psychologically primary fall outside the purview of this study. Certain beliefs and practices of symbolic interest are also irrelevant here. Certain superstitions and allegorical figures are related but not identical to beliefs and deities of the type I will try to explain. These superstitions and figures are mentioned in later chapters.

2
A Sociobiologic Model

Innate Probability

The following model was described in a previous work (Wenegrat, 1984). Although some new material has been included, the model is developed here in a greatly simplified fashion. Readers who are unacquainted with biologic concepts may find the ideas here difficult to absorb in such brief form. They should not be too alarmed, however; later chapters will clarify how the model is used. Those who wish to learn more about sociobiology should read any of the excellent presentations currently available. E. O. Wilson (1975), Clutton-Brock and Harvey (1978), R.D. Alexander (1979), Breuer (1982), and Trivers (1985) are only a few of the first-rate sources easily accessible to the general reader.

In general, sociobiologists are interested in species-typical social life. They argue that social life is guided by various strategies, some of which are innately probable. Strategies are response rules; that is, they assign specific responses to environmental exigencies. Social strategies assign specific social responses to social exigencies. Innately probable strategies are those that are made more likely by the species' genes. By way of illustration, consider two strategies, A and B, which dictate different responses to the same social events. If the typical genetic endowment makes adherence to A more probable than adherence to B, then A is innately probable with respect to B. If other strategies exist, they, too, can be ranked with regard to innate probability. In general, when we say that a strategy is innately probable, without specifying the strategies with which it is compared, we imply that it is probable with respect to all potential alternative strategies.

In a previous work, I argued that two joint criteria can be used to identify social strategies that are innately probable (Wenegrat, 1984). I will describe these criteria here and explain why together they indicate that a strategy is innately probable in a particular setting. More sophisticated readers will recognize that the following argument invokes the Baldwin Effect, a concept invented to explain how acquired behavioral adaptations can become fixed in the genes through purely Darwinian processes (Baldwin, 1896; Mayr, 1963; Richards, 1987; Simpson, 1953).

The first criterion is *universality*. In the case of *Homo sapiens*, universal strategies will be found in all modern societies and in past societies about which we have information. These strategies should be evident in present-day human societies—such as hunter-gatherer tribes—that are thought to resemble the groups in which human beings evolved. Especially ancient strategies may even be evident in the behavior of nonhuman primates. Average persons everywhere, of the right age and sex, should be found to adhere to these strategies. Any exceptions—for example, a society in which typical individuals seem to follow a very different response rule—must in some way "prove the rule" if a given social strategy is truly universal. In such a society, either the true social exigencies or the average responses to them must be different from how they first appear.

The second criterion is *evolutionary stability*. A brief digression is needed to explain this concept: Adherence to a strategy will affect the actor's vitality and reproductive success as well as the vitality and reproductive success of other individuals who might share some of the actor's genes. Therefore, insofar as genes increase the probability of adherence to a strategy, they will affect their own prospects for propagation to the next generation. Consequently, to remain innately probable, an innately probable strategy must have a positive effect on the biologic success of the actor and his kin. In other words, innately probable strategies must be biologically adaptive. If they were maladaptive, the genes predisposing to them would be disadvantaged with respect to other genes and would gradually disappear. Sociobiologists measure the biologic adaptiveness of strategies in terms of "inclusive fitness" (Hamilton, 1964). *Inclusive fitness* is the number of copies of an individual's genes, both in direct descendants and in kin, that is lost or gained in the next generation as the result of adherence to a particular strategy.

Many factors determine whether a given strategy is biologically adaptive for the individual and his or her kin—that is, whether its inclusive fitness result is positive. For strategies governing social interactions, the most important factors determining their inclusive fitness results will be the social strategies adopted by other individuals. For example, if a social strategy dictates aggressive behavior in response to social frustration, its inclusive fitness result will be determined almost entirely by how others respond to aggression. If they band together to punish the aggressive individual, the strategy's inclusive fitness result will likely be negative. If they capitulate to the aggressive individual, its inclusive fitness result will likely be positive.

When they are used by a sufficient proportion of a population, some social strategies produce better inclusive fitness results than potential alternative strategies do (Davies, 1982; Maynard Smith, 1976, 1982a). These strategies are said to have evolutionary stability.

By way of illustration, imagine a response rule that says that an individual should do favors for others unless they have previously refused to do favors for him. This is a "tit-for-tat" rule, with a bias toward generosity in the absence of previous experience with an individual (see Axelrod, 1984). I assume here that favors cost little to perform but may be very valuable to their recipients. For example, throwing a rope to someone who is drowning costs the rescuer very little but benefits the potential drowning victim enormously. Sociobiologists call this tit-for-tat rule "reciprocal altruism" (Trivers, 1971). If virtually everyone in a population of interacting individuals adheres to this response rule, and if every individual is as likely to require as many favors as are requested from him, then reciprocal altruism will be evolutionarily stable. Individuals who depart from the reciprocal altruism rule by refusing to do favors may later be unable to obtain needed aid. Because the benefit of favors to recipients is assumed to be much greater than their cost to those who perform them, stingy individuals will lose more in the long run than they save by not helping others. Individuals who depart from the reciprocal altruism rule by aiding those who fail to do favors will incur the cost of a favor without increasing their chance of gaining future aid. By making their aid noncontingent, they may encourage others to withhold future favors. Finally, individuals who refuse both to do favors and to receive aid save the cost of the favors but lose the greater benefits of the aid. Therefore, in a population of reciprocal altruists, reciprocal altruism is always more adaptive than alternative strategies.

If a strategy is both universal and evolutionarily stable, it must be innately probable to some degree. By definition, a universal, evolutionarily stable strategy produces better inclusive fitness results than alternative strategies do. Consequently, insofar as particular genes predispose their bearers to adopt alternative strategies, they will tend to disappear from subsequent generations. This is true regardless of the actual pathways by which they affect behavior. I noted earlier that universal social strategies should be evident in known past societies, in societies resembling those in which human beings evolved, and, in some cases, in nonhuman primate behavior. If an evolutionarily stable strategy has been universal for a very long time—for example, throughout human history—the selective pressure against genes that promote alternative strategies has been maintained for numerous generations. Thus, rather few such genes are likely still extant. The genes that are common today must favor the stable strategy, which is therefore innately probable.

But how do genes affect strategic choices? How do they affect the likelihood of adhering to one or another response rule? Investigation of gene effects may clarify considerably the concept of innate probability. Consider reciprocal altruism. In all known cultures, past and present, typical individuals have practiced reciprocal altruism. Also, as noted earlier, reciprocal altruism is an evolutionarily stable social strategy. Thus, being both universal and evolutionarily stable, it must be innately probable. I will survey a few of the many paths by which gene activity makes reciprocal altruism a likely strategic choice.

First, adherence to a reciprocal altruistic strategy is more probable for a species if individual members of that species live for long periods of time in proximity to the same companions. Solitary or short-lived animals, or animals that fail to maintain contact with specific companions, would not tend to employ reciprocal altruism.

The human life span, of course, directly reflects genetic activity in particular environments, and human affiliative processes are known to depend on genetically determined mental mechanisms. From birth itself, human infants attend to and are attracted by social stimuli (Spitz, 1965). Young babies produce and interpret universal human gestures without benefit of learning experiences (Eibl-Eibesfeldt, 1973; Ekman, 1979; Trevarthen, 1979). They are able to distinguish vocalizations—requisite to language development—that have never been differentiated for them (Eimas et al., 1971; Marler, 1979). The syntactic structure of language itself is thought by many to be biologically encoded, rather than acquired during language development (H. H. Clark & Clark, 1977). Later, the social bonds created in the first days of life are succeeded by progressively wider and more differentiated social commitments. These later commitments depend on biologic factors—including sexual attractions, affective responses to children, and the capacity for emotional experiences—which themselves depend on genetic factors.

Second, pursuit of a reciprocal altruism strategy is more probable in species in which the individual can distinguish specific companions well enough to remember their behavior in previous interactions. In humans, recognition of others is dependent on genetically derived biologic mechanisms. Facial recognition mechanisms, for example, depend on inferior temporo-occipital lobe sites independent of those that subserve pattern recognition in general (Geshwind, 1979). Likewise, the ability to recall previous behaviors also requires cerebral mechanisms more or less closely dependent on genetic activity. There is some evidence, for example, that nonhuman primates are severely limited in this regard (Kummer, 1978).

Third, adherence to a reciprocal altruism strategy is more probable in species that have affective motivators for requisite behaviors. In humans, generous feelings motivate altruistic acts. Angry feelings are evoked when others are seen as selfish. These feelings motivate hostile acts and prevent further altruism. In humans and other mammals, chemically specific, genetically controlled nervous system pathways seem to influence socially relevant affects (see Barchas et al., 1977; Creese, 1985; Enna, 1985; Paul et al., 1985; Watson et al., 1985). Certain periodic psychotic disorders show very clearly how generous and aggressive motives in particular depend on factors under genetic control (Jenner, 1978). Mania, for example, is a familial illness. Manics are inclined to be markedly overgenerous; at the same time, they are quick to believe that others have failed them and to become excessively angry (Slater & Roth, 1969). A related pattern is sometimes evident in victims of temporal lobe epilepsy, who may display both exaggerated warmth and excessive anger (Bear et al., 1985; Blumer & Benson, 1975, 1982).

Finally, adherence to a reciprocal altruism strategy is more probable in species that are able to foresee the results of their actions in order to maximize their long-term welfare. This is because, in the setting in which it occurs, the tit-for-tat rule called reciprocal altruism optimizes the long-term benefit-to-cost ratio of individuals who adopt it (Axelrod, 1984). Like the capacity to remember how others have behaved, the human ability to foresee results and to maximize long-term welfare is dependent on cerebral structures that are closely linked with genetic activity.

Even this cursory examination of a single social strategy illustrates the complexity of innate probability, as the term is used here. Genetic activity produces perceptual mechanisms, memory capacities, somatic motives, cognitive and affective functions, and communicative and motor subroutines. These mechanisms, motives, capacities, functions, and subroutines enhance the probability that subsequent behavior will conform to a particular social strategy, which is then called innately probable.

As the reader might have noted from the foregoing particular examples, the concept developed here can also be expressed in terms of innate capabilities: Typical individuals are especially well-equipped for innately probable strategies that are characteristic of their species. In manifesting their innate capabilities—perceptual, cognitive, affective, and motoric—they fall into these strategies as if they were matters of course.

In this chapter, I will describe certain high-level social strategies that meet the criteria used here for innate probability; that is, they are both universal and evolutionarily stable. By *high-level*, I mean that these strategies subsume important behaviors that take up much of a person's time and energy. They account for common preoccupations and common affective responses. They also determine how people use religion. Eventually, I will try to show that intellectual processes that promote adherence to these highly advantageous strategies produce religious beliefs as incidental effects. Whatever selective disadvantage is incurred because of religion (see V. Reynolds & Tanner, 1983), if there is any, is more than outweighed by benefits conferred by adherence to the strategies described in the following sections.

Innately Probable Strategies

The remainder of this chapter is devoted to a survey of some strategies that meet the criteria used here for innate probability. Their universality and evolutionary stability will be treated very briefly. Readers who wish to pursue a more rigorous treatment of these and other strategies are referred to the sources cited herein. My aim here is strictly limited: Only as much will be said of specific strategies as will promote an understanding of religious beliefs.

The five social strategies discussed here include infant—caretaker proximity maintenance, sexual competition, mutualism, and two types of altruism. These strategies define behavioral systems that roughly correspond to various human potentials: to be parent or helpless child, a sexual being, a group member, a potential saint, or a narcissist. Their social importance is obvious. In fact, at one time or another, each of these systems has been considered the ultimate, or at least proper, source for all social behavior. Modern day "attachment theorists," for example, tend to see the infant—caretaker bond as the prototype and font for all social ties (see, for example, Hartog, 1980). According to this view, caretaking and being taken care of are the ultimate psychological functions of normal adult relationships. Even sexual motives have been treated in terms of attachment. Likewise, by making the Oedipal conflict the centerpiece of his theory, Freud portrayed sexual competition as the motive for many behaviors that are superficially unrelated to sex. It took many years before Freudian analysts recognized the importance of "pre-Oedipal" events—corresponding roughly to those described by attachment theorists—or of adaptive functions unrelated to sexuality (Blanck & Blanck, 1974, 1979; Eagle, 1984;

Greenberg & Mitchell, 1983). In a recent work, Corning (1983) attempted to derive virtually all social ties—including sexual, familial, and altruistic bonds—from motives related to mutualism. Although his argument seems overinclusive, Corning's work does show the ubiquitous role of "membership" in shaping human endeavors. Finally, insofar as they embody a psychological theory and prescribe a state of health, Christian doctrines dictate the primacy of altruism. The "well" Christian psyche is one that subordinates other motivational systems to the needs of selfless altruism. The Christian psyche falls "ill" precisely to the extent that altruism is no longer *primum mobile*.

There are other innately probable human social strategies—that define "contest" behaviors (see Maynard Smith, 1976, 1982a)—but they are conceptually incidental to the five discussed here. They are mentioned only in relation to sexual competition.

Infant–Caretaker Proximity Maintenance

Bowlby (1969, 1973, 1980) described complementary infant and adult behavior patterns that have as their predictable outcome the maintenance of proximity between infants and their adult caretakers. These behaviors are highly specific, in that infants aim for proximity to specific adults, or attachment figures, and caretakers aim for proximity to specific infants. Infants and attachment figures begin their mutual proximity maintenance shortly after the infant's birth. When the infant is very young, the attachment figure assumes most or all of the responsibility for proximity maintenance. As the infant matures, however, he or she assumes more of the responsibility and the caretaker correspondingly less.

Proximity maintenance is realized through diverse behaviors. Since the adaptive function of proximity maintenance is undoubtedly the ability of the caretaker to provide ready aid, the triggers for these behaviors are frequently situations of potential distress or danger. In response to hunger, cold, or other discomforts, young infants cry to their caretakers. Caretakers—particularly the principal attachment figure, who is usually the mother—respond by coming to them in order to relieve their distress. Older infants cry in response to the mother's absence, when they are injured, or in response to stimuli that may have signified danger for ancestral youngsters. Strangers, for example, might have been dangerous for ancestral primate infants, and today, infantile stranger anxiety is a particularly potent stimulus for proximity maintenance. Toddlers and young children are able to follow the mother or seek her out. Their responses are no longer limited to signals alone. Various proximity-maintaining responses are also evident on the caretaker's side.

Proximity-maintaining behaviors are evident in all human cultures. They are extraordinarily robust and can survive social arrangements—such as communal child rearing—that would superficially seem to thwart them. Evidence from contemporary hunter-gatherer societies, which are thought to resemble the social arrangements in which much of human behavioral evolution occurred, indicates that proximity maintenance strategies have been ubiquitous for a very long time. Similar strategies are even evident among nonhuman primates, such as chimpanzees and baboons, which genetically and ecologically resemble our likely protohominid ancestors. Therefore, what are now manifested as human proximity maintenance strategies may have been evolutionarily fixed before divergence of the hominid line.

Infant and caretaker strategies are also evolutionarily stable, though their stability depends on the frequency of helpless infants and caring adults, rather than on the frequency of proximity-maintaining behaviors per se. Given that infants will not take care of themselves, their adult relatives must provide them with aid. For the caretaker to be ready with aid when it is most timely, some degree of proximity must be maintained. Caretakers who fail to provide aid or who fail to maintain the proximity required for aid to be timely will be disadvantaged with respect to caretakers who do provide such aid. On the other hand, if the caretakers are to provide aid, the infants must notify them when aid is required. Insofar as they can, they, too, should maintain the proximity required for aid to be maximally effective. Infants who fail to notify caretakers of their needs, or who fail to maintain proximity, will be disadvantaged with respect to infants who do notify their caretakers and maintain proximity with them.

Proximity maintenance strategies, like the "kin altruistic" strategies they ultimately subserve, are not entirely harmonious. That is, infant and caretaker differ in the degree of proximity and the extent of aid they prefer. Moreover, this difference is greater at certain stages of development, during which it seems to play a critical role in psychological development (see the discussion of weaning conflicts in Wenegrat, 1984). Differences between infant and caretaker can be explicated in inclusive fitness terms, using a concept called "parental investment" (Trivers, 1974), which will be discussed later.

With advancing age, stimuli capable of eliciting infantile proximity-maintaining behaviors become more and more restricted. Proximity maintenance, in effect, becomes gradually less salient as an organizing principle of everyday behavior. By the time of maturity, events capable of eliciting childlike proximity maintenance to trusted attachment figures are very traumatic indeed. Major losses, injuries, and public disasters are among the triggers for adult behaviors of this kind. However, for some adults, childlike proximity maintenance strategies remain salient factors in everyday behavior (Wenegrat, 1984). For constitutional or developmental reasons, some adults—like normal children—are easily provoked into proximity-maintaining behaviors, even by everyday stresses. Because they cling to potential caretakers, such individuals appear to be dependent. They are also prone to certain psychological disorders, which can be treated as aberrant manifestations of excessively salient proximity maintenance strategies.

Sexual Strategies

Ethologists and sociobiologists have described interrelated sexual strategies characteristic of the separate sexes in a wide variety of mammalian and primate species, as well as in human beings (see, for example, Clutton-Brock & Harvey, 1976; Mellen, 1981; Symons, 1979; Trivers, 1978). Differences between male and female sexual strategies result from sex-related differences in the minimum "parental investment" (Trivers, 1974, 1978). Parental investments are contributions of time, energy, or physiologic resources on behalf of one offspring at the expense of other real or potential offspring. In mammals, the minimum parental investment required to reproduce differs enormously between the sexes. For males, the minimum parental investment is quite literally the time and energy of sexual intercourse. Anything more is optional. For females, the minimum parental investment is the time and energy of intercourse, pregnancy, and lactation.

Because his minimum parental investment is so much smaller, a male can potentially have many more offspring than a female of the same (mammalian) species. His reproductive success, in fact, is limited only by access to reproductive potential of the opposite sex. Striving for access to a limited number of females, males compete with each other. For one male to achieve anything near his maximal number of offspring, many other males must be deprived entirely of reproductive chances.

Because males compete for their reproductive potential, females can easily bear their maximal number of offspring. However, since this number is limited, they maximize their long-term success only by ensuring their offspring the best chance in life. They can do so in two ways. First, because male offspring might inherit from their fathers genes that promote success or failure in sexual competition, females can selectively mate with competitively successful males. Second, in circumstances such that male parental investments above and beyond the minimum are needed for successfully raising the young, females can selectively mate with males that are able and willing to make such investments. In some cases, the immediate object of male competition is control of the resources, such as territory, needed for parental investments. Thus, by selecting competitively successful mates, the female in these instances will obtain for her offspring both the best genes and the best care.

The foregoing strategies are widespread in nonhuman primates. They are also found in all human societies except those few in which women do not need paternal assistance in order to raise their children (see, for example, Betzig, 1982, 1986; Chagnon, 1974, 1977, 1979a, 1979b, 1980; Chagnon & Bugos, 1979; Chagnon et al., 1979; J. Hill, 1984; Irons, 1979, 1980, 1983; Mellen, 1981; Symons, 1979; cf. Leacock, 1978, 1980). Restricting our attention to humans: Men compete for resources that are useful for raising children. Sexual privileges—with the most fecund women—are among the prerogatives of successful men. Men compete with each other according to social rules, but male competition can take a violent form. Men court women more often than the reverse, and while they are courting they try to show that they have more than a sexual interest. Men who lack affection have probably always been unreliable fathers. Women prefer successful men to unsuccessful men.

In combination, male and female sexual strategies are evolutionarily stable. For instance, a woman who preferred to mate with competitively unsuccessful men, or with men who were unable or unwilling to commit more than the minimum parental investment, would penalize her own children. Insofar as his competitive failure was caused by genetic factors, a competitively unsuccessful father might pass on failure to his sons. In most societies, children who lack the advantages of male parental investments are handicapped in comparison with other children. A man who failed to compete with other men, whether directly or for resources useful for child rearing, would have trouble finding mates. Even if he did mate, his children would be penalized by his lack of resources and, possibly, by his genes.

Innate, gender-related differences in sexual arousal and drive and in aggressive behavior predispose men and women to adhere to their respective sexual competitive strategies in most societies (see Ehrhardt & Meyer-Bahlburg, 1981; Goy & McEwan, 1980; Maccoby & Jacklin, 1974; Schumacher & Balthazart, 1985; Schumacher et al., 1987).

Strategies that determine the form of resource competition, whether the resource is sex-related or otherwise, have also been studied in detail (Maynard Smith, 1976, 1982a). These strategies are important in their own right, because they determine the occurrence and extent of within-species violence. An important implication of these strategies is that individuals must compare themselves to those with whom they compete in order to assess their relative strength or resource-holding power (Parker, 1974). Among human beings, resource-holding power depends mostly on kinship, social and political connections, and intelligence, rather than on physical factors. Particularly in men, assessment of resource-holding power will directly determine the tactics used in sexual competition.

Elsewhere, I noted that the Freudian Oedipus complex can be related to sexual competitive strategies as they are understood by sociobiologists (Wenegrat, 1984; see, also, Badcock, 1986). On the one hand, the young boy's conflict with the father is only the first of many competitive relationships he will have with other men. On the other hand, the form the Oedipal conflict takes—and especially the opportunities it offers for identification with the father—may determine behavior in later sexual competitive interactions. In either case, men who are preoccupied with Oedipal issues are ultimately preoccupied with sexual competition.

Mutualism

Certain projects, though advantageous to individual organisms, require cooperation for their completion. Even lower animals are able to carry out such projects, which suggests that at least stereotypical cooperative behaviors evolved very early in evolutionary history. Certain spiders, for example, choreograph their spinning so as to build common web supports (Maynard Smith, 1982b). In this way, they can build their individual webs in especially advantageous positions. Animals that are higher on the phylogenetic ladder cooperate in less stereotypical ways. Baboons, for example, cooperate in defensive, foraging, and predatory expeditions. Every expedition is in some sense unique and requires that behavior be coordinated flexibly in light of common aims. In the case of spiders, the specific behaviors comprising common web building must have been selected for in their environment of adaptation. In the case of baboons, however, the relevant selective forces must have favored a cooperative tendency per se, rather than one or a few stereotypical behaviors. The readiness to take part in unstereotypical cooperative ventures that profit each participant reaches its limit in *Homo sapiens*. As found in humans, this readiness is an interactive strategy, which will be referred to here as *mutualism*. This use of the term *mutualism* differs slightly from its ethologic usage. In ethology, any cooperative endeavor is called mutualistic (Maynard Smith, 1982b; Wrangham, 1982), whereas here the term refers only to a readiness for unstereotypical cooperation.

A mutualistic social strategy—or a readiness to engage with

others in mutually profitable, highly varied cooperative ventures—requires two separate behavioral components. Each of these components is subserved, of course, by many behaviors and tendencies, but their distinction is nonetheless useful, at least for heuristic purposes.

The first component involves identification of the cooperating group. Many important cooperative endeavors interfere with the survival and reproduction of nonparticipants (Wrangham, 1982). For example, a group that cooperated to control a hunting territory would effectively deprive outsiders of access to game. Therefore, definition of the boundaries of the cooperating group—of in-group and out-group members, in other words—is an essential prerequisite of the most general sort of mutualism. Within the in-group, individuals should be prone to cooperate. Hostility should be muted and violent tendencies attenuated. With out-group members, cooperative tendencies should be weakened. Hostility may no longer be muted, and conflicts will more likely end in violence.

The second component involves acceptance of mutual goals and world views among in-group members. This is required for coordinated pursuit of highly variable common ventures. A hunting expedition, for example, can be coordinated successfully only if members of the expedition agree on the prey, on the terrain traversed, and on the respective roles to be played by each individual.

Among humans, both categories of mutualism-related behaviors are universally evident. Humans everywhere consider themselves members of one or another in-group, in which mutual cooperation and trust are at least the ideal, if not always realized (Pettigrew, 1978). An invidious distinction is always drawn between in-group members and other persons. Although the attitude toward outsiders may vary from benign interest to dehumanization and hatred, the gradient of hostility always favors its expression outside, rather than inside, the cooperating group. Avoidance of outsiders is probably highly correlated with positive feelings toward in-group members (R. A. LeVine & Campbell, 1972; Lopreato, 1984). Evidence from modern hunter-gatherer tribes and from nonhuman primates indicates that cooperating in-groups that are more or less hostile to outsiders are not the result of more advanced civilization and even antedate hominid evolution entirely (see, for example, Goodall, 1979; Mellen, 1981; P. C. Reynolds, 1981; Tinbergen, 1976; E. O. Wilson, 1978). Moreover, every human group has its consensual world view, acceptance of which is required for active membership (Berger & Luckmann, 1966). The consensual world view includes environmental maps, theories of specific events, moral and social values, and cosmological theories that place group life in a universal perspective.

Although group-living animals are able to share consensual world views (Breuer, 1982; Griffin, 1981; Maxwell, 1984; Menzel, 1975), the extent and nature of consensual information is highly constrained by the lack of real language in species other than *Homo sapiens*. Bees, for example, can share maps of their local topography, but would have no means, even if they had the desire, to share with each other theories on the formation of nectar. In human groups, by contrast, the subject matter and detail of potentially consensual ideas are virtually unlimited.

Flexible mutualism has many adaptive advantages. The advantages of common defense, initially against predators and later against other hominid groups, have probably played a major selective role (R.D. Alexander, 1979, 1987; R.D. Alexander et al., 1979). Coordinated expeditions allowed early hominids to hunt larger game (Fox, 1980). The increased productivity of these expeditions more than compensated for the need to share whatever was caught. Enduring mutualistic groups could also improve their technologies and pass them on to the next generation. Each individual in such a group benefits from the thinking of all present and previous group members, rather than just from that of his or her parents. Once established in a population, tendencies to form enduring mutualistic groups are also evolutionarily stable. An individual that failed to participate in such groups would forfeit the benefits of their common endeavors. Insofar as mutualistic groups interfere with the survival and reproduction of nonparticipants, an isolated individual would be doubly penalized. Insofar as these groups are unfriendly to outsiders, the individual would suffer even further.

To participate, however, the individual must desire to cooperate—must see himself as a working part of the group—and must share the consensual viewpoint on which group endeavors are founded. In other words, the individual must be "socialized" into the group whose consensual world view he takes as his own. Socialization has been studied extensively (see, for example, Luckmann, 1979) and will not be dealt with in detail here. In human groups, consensual world views are maintained by designated authority figures, who edify and correct other members (Berger & Luckmann, 1966). Authority figures are individuals whose thoughts about particular concerns are deemed consensually valid. This does not mean, of course, that everyone in the group knows what those thoughts might be, but simply that once spoken, these thoughts bear the mantle of consensual validity. With that mantle, their acceptance is virtually guaranteed. An individual who fails to accept the views of his or her group's authority figures would, in effect, refuse to accept the group's consensual reality. He or she would be opting out of the group. Means for the designation of authority figures, the method by which particular areas of knowledge are ceded to particular authority figures, the possibility of conflict between authority figures, and the certainty ascribed to various aspects of the consensual world view all differ greatly from culture to culture (see Berger & Luckmann, 1966; Lopreato, 1984; Sennett, 1981). These factors comprise particularly important differences among specific religious groups.

Altruism

Biologically altruistic behaviors differ from mutualistic behaviors in that they bear a net cost to the actor's survival or reproduction (Bertram, 1982; D.S. Wilson, 1980). Beginning with Darwin (1859), evolutionary theorists explained the evolution of altruistic tendencies in terms of group selection. They argued that altruistic behaviors contribute to group efficiency. More efficient social groups can outcompete less efficient groups and thereby avoid extinction. In recent years, however, the efficacy of selection pressures operative at the group level has been widely questioned (for discussions of this issue, see Brandon & Burian, 1984; Dawkins, 1982; D.S. Wilson, 1980). Also, certain theoretical difficulties—such as within-group cheating—have been raised with the group selection model. Therefore, other explanations have been sought for altruistic tendencies, and these have altered the way biologists think about behavior. For one thing, it is from the study of altruism that inclusive fitness, mentioned earlier, emerged to replace reproductive success as a measure of biologic adaptation (Hamilton, 1964). Inclusive fitness, the reader will recall, is the number of copies of an individual's genes, both in direct descendants and in relatives, that is lost or gained in the next generation as the result of a particular response type.

As it turns out, there are two situations in which altruistic behaviors—which, by definition, are paid for in reproductive success—will be associated with a positive inclusive fitness result. Genes that predispose individuals toward altruistic acts in these situations will outreproduce other genes. Also, tendencies to perform altruistic behaviors in these situations comprise social strategies. The first situation, widely discussed under the rubric *kin selection*, occurs when the potential beneficiaries are closely related to the altruist (Hamilton, 1964; Trivers, 1971). In this situation, beneficiary and altruist will likely share genes because of their common descent. In inclusive fitness terms, the beneficiary's improved well-being may then make up for costs borne by the altruist. Consider, for example, saving a sibling at the cost of losing an unborn child. Since the likelihood of sharing a specific gene by virtue of common descent is 50 percent for both sibling and child, this costly atruistic act will, on average, be neutral from the point of view of the genes that affect its probability. That is, its inclusive fitness consequence is, on average, nil. If the sibling can be saved at somewhat less cost, this altruistic act becomes advantageous to the genes that promote it. Saving a nephew at an average cost of less than half a child, or a cousin at an average cost of less than a quarter-child, is likewise advantageous. These figures, of course, follow from the fact that nephews and cousins have a one-quarter and one-eighth likelihood, respectively, of sharing the actor's genes by virtue of common descent. Also, although any given child is indivisible, it is still meaningful and convenient to speak of fractional children. Some altruists may lose nothing; others may lose everything. But the average will be a fractional child.

The second situation in which reproductively costly altruistic behaviors will be favored occurs when individuals live in social groups that are conducive to reciprocal altruism (see earlier discussion). The reader will recall that reciprocal altruism is basically a tit-for-tat rule, with a bias toward generosity in the absence of previous experience with a person. With reciprocal altruism, reproductive costs are repaid if each individual is as likely to be a beneficiary as an altruist and if the benefits of altruistic acts generally outweigh their costs. Reciprocal altruists protect themselves from exploitation by refusing favors to those who have not been generous and, perhaps, by punishing exploiters in order to discourage cheating. Group reciprocal altruism, in effect, is like group mutualism, but the costs and payoffs are no longer simultaneous. Thus, some will have to pay early and gain something later, whereas others will gain early and pay later.

Both kin-directed and reciprocal altruistic behaviors are ubiquitous in human societies (Fox, 1980; Gouldner, 1960; cf. Mauss, 1954). They are also shown by nonhuman primates. The advantages and evolutionary stability of kin-directed altruistic acts are obvious. Indeed, kin-directed altruistic tendencies will be favored regardless of their frequency in the population at large. The advantages and evolutionary stability of reciprocal altruism have already been discussed. Unlike kin-directed altruistic tendencies, reciprocal altruistic tendencies are evolutionarily stable only when they are shown by most of the population.

In order to adhere to a kin-directed altruistic strategy, individuals must be able to direct their aid accurately toward genetic kin. Mothers, of course, can identify their children. But other kin-directed altruists apparently utilize social cues that are predictive of relationships at the genetic level (see Dawkins, 1982). For example, children raised by the same mother are most likely genetic siblings. Therefore, individuals are likely to be aiding their genetic siblings if they aid those with whom they were raised. Children raised by siblings are most likely genetic nephews and nieces. Therefore, individuals are likely to be aiding their genetic nephews and nieces if they aid those raised by their siblings. Membership in a social group might also be utilized as a cue to kinship. Hunter-gatherer societies, which resemble the prehistoric societies in which much of human behavioral evolution occurred, inbreed sufficiently that all local tribe members are close genetic kin (Chagnon, 1979a; for similar findings in nonhuman primates, see Chepko-Sade, 1979).

Reciprocal altruists must remember the behavior of potential beneficiaries (cf. Kummer, 1978). They must distinguish real aid from aid that is only apparent, and they must assess the sincerity of those who claim to have changed by becoming more altruistic (cf. R.D. Alexander, 1987). These and other social demands resulting from reciprocal altruism undoubtedly contributed to selective pressures in early hominid groups. These pressures favored more highly developed communicative and social skills, which are dependent on cerebral structures. Trivers (1971) argued that the spread of reciprocal altruism led to the growth in human cortex during the Pleistocene epoch.

Selective Retention

In the previous section, I referred numerous times to aspects of human behavior that are everywhere the same. But human behavior is far from stereotypical. Although certain innately probable strategies are universally manifest, the specific behaviors associated with them vary greatly from one locale to another. Just as universal dietary needs are satisfied by very different foods in different societies, so universal strategies are satisfied by different actions in different cultures. For example, in one society, men fight for resources with clubs and poison darts; in another, they fight with attorneys. In societies that use clubs and darts, hiring an attorney would likely be ineffectual. Where attorneys are hired, physical assaults are usually not permitted.

How do people change their manner of adhering to innately probable strategies? How do cultures change while strategies remain the same? Beginning with William James, evolutionary theorists have answered questions like these by invoking various forms of selective retention theories (R.D. Alexander, 1979; Breuer, 1982; Campbell, 1960; Durham, 1978; Kurland, 1979; Langton, 1979; Lopreato, 1984; Lumsden & Wilson, 1981, 1983; V. Reynolds & Tanner, 1983; Richards, 1987). Selective retention theories suggest that new cultural artefacts—including ideas, ideologies, and social and technical innovations—are discarded or retained by individuals whose choices are influenced to a significant degree by certain innate dispositions. If innate biases make a particular artefact even slightly more pleasing or easier to use in a given environment, or if they make its promised effects even slightly more appealing, than the artefact in question is much more likely to be retained through repetitive and aggregate individual choices. Insofar as the biases affecting cultural choice also predispose individuals toward innately probable strategies, artefacts will be retained according to their apparent coherence with the aims of strategic functioning. Culture, in effect, will subserve social strategies, even as social strategies subserve culture.

There are several qualifications to selective retention theories. First, selective retention is a probabilistic process. That is, just as genetically influenced perceptual, cognitive, affective, and motoric dispositions only make adherence to certain strategies likely, genetically influenced dispositions only make it likely that culture will take a direction consistent with adherence to innately probable strategies. Consequently, short-term cultural fluctuations might work against adherence to these strategies. Second, in exploring the limits of selective retention theory, Boyd and Richerson (1985) suggest several mechanisms through which cultural evolution could, in effect, disrupt adherence to innately probable strategies. These mechanisms may be important in certain special circumstances. Finally, unselected effects of cultural change could well disrupt adherence to strategies in unforeseeable ways. An unanticipated effect of automobile use, for example, has been the attenuation of neighborly interactions. Such attenuated interactions have sometimes proved insufficient for maintaining reciprocal altruistic and other innately probable social strategies that previously governed relations among people living in close proximity. However, neither random fluctuations, the mechanisms discussed by Boyd and Richerson, nor the unforeseen effects of cultural change wholly vitiate a social strategic approach. Outcomes like those described by Boyd and Richerson can be viewed as "overhead" costs for mutualistic strategies. Random fluctuations and unforeseen disruptive effects of cultural change are probably self-limited and characterize only transitional cultural phases. They mobilize restitutive forces, consequent to the continued influence of innate biases. Such restitutive forces are often religious (see the discussion of cults in chapter 3).

Selective retention theories have especially interesting implications for ethical ideologies. These ideologies are presumably retained or discarded like all other cultural products (see, for example, Markl, 1978; Reynolds & Tanner, 1983; Wolff, 1978). However, since the adoption of ethical mores also implies their enforcement, those with the greatest power in any given society have a disproportionate influence on new ethical rules. Conversely, those with the greatest power are frequently able to discard older mores without fear of punishment. Therefore, the choice of whether to selectively retain or discard ethical mores will be primarily for the powerful to make and will reflect their preferences concerning others' behavior (see, for example, R.D. Alexander, 1979, 1987; Badcock, 1986; Breuer, 1982; Kurland, 1979; Trivers, 1981). Insofar as these preferences are consistent with their innately probable strategies, ethical mores will promote the strategic interests of those with power. The weak, by contrast, usually can neither impose ethics on the powerful nor disregard the ethics imposed on them. It is consequently less likely that ethical mores will faithfully promote their social strategic interests.

I have assumed (chapter 1) that religious beliefs are factually erroneous—that is, that religious beliefs are cultural inventions. Insofar as this is correct, selective retention theories require that these beliefs subserve, or promise to subserve, innately probable strategies of either the faithful or their masters. Otherwise, they would more or less quickly be changed or discarded. If the bewildering variety of religious beliefs actually subserve or promise to subserve just a few social strategies, then these strategies can be used to categorize the otherwise seemingly infinite psychological functions of the religious beliefs. This categorization is found in the next chapter.

3

The Strategic Functions of Religious Beliefs

Four innately probable social strategies were described in the preceding chapter. The sociobiologic model predicts that genetic activity will produce perceptual, cognitive, affective, and motoric dispositions that have, as their combined effect, adherence to these strategies. Cultural innovations, including religious beliefs, are likely to be retained only insofar as they promise to be useful to individuals who are pursuing these strategies.

In this chapter, I will show how religious beliefs promote, or promise to promote, adherence to the social strategies described in the preceding chapter. In doing so, I will parcel diverse psychologically significant functions served by religion into categories that correspond to the innately probable strategies. In looking at religious beliefs from this point of view, I am continuing a project started by V. Reynolds and Tanner (1983), who used selective retention theory to explain religious rules pertaining to matters of health and reproduction. Their work is described later in this chapter.

Proximity Maintenance

Attachment to God

Infants spend much of their time and energy maintaining proximity to caretakers. For constitutional or developmental reasons, certain adults, too, are easily provoked into proximity-maintaining behaviors modeled on those of the infant. As noted in the preceding chapter, these individuals, because of the way they cling to potential caretakers, often appear dependent.

A number of studies have shown an association between dependent personality traits and religious belief (Dreger, 1952; Graff & Ladd, 1971; Rokeach, 1960). Stressful life events play an important role in this association. For example, Ostow (1980) observed that dependent persons adopt religious beliefs as a means of coping with loss. Stern (1985) described a patient whose history illustrates Ostow's point. Sects or cults, in particular, may attract dependent persons who are unable to cope with their lives. For example, Halperin (1983a) found that families of religious cult members described them as passive, unable to cope, and dependent on structure provided by others. Simmonds (1977) studied ninety-six members of a fundamentalist sect and found that they had had poor adjustments prior to their conversion. To Simmonds, the high frequency of depression, suicidal ideation, and drug use among them suggested underlying problems with dependency. Some of the case histories cited later in this chapter describe individuals with dependent traits or with psychological disorders related to dependency and proximity maintenance (see Wenegrat, 1984).

Like dependent persons, religious persons tend to be obedient, conforming, and anxious to obtain external approval (Black & London, 1966; Fisher, 1964; Goldsen et al., 1960). For many of the religious, however, these traits may be more closely associated with group-related than with proximity-maintaining strategies. These traits are discussed later in regard to "extrinsic" religion.

If dependence and religiosity are sometimes related, it must be because religious beliefs promise to serve attachment needs, whenever these needs are salient in adult life. How is this promise made? First, and most obviously, some prayers and rituals depict God as an attachment figure. Those who believe in such a god imagine that they are never far from a caretaking figure. The Twenty-third Psalm, for instance, depicts God fulfilling the watchful, protective, and nurturant functions of the ideal mother. According to this popular psalm, which plays a prominent role in modern liturgies, the Lord is a "shepherd." He leads his flock to "green pastures" and beside "still waters." Protected by the Lord, the worshipper "fear

[s] no evil." Nor does he fear his "enemies." The worshipper's "cup runneth over" and a "table" is always prepared for him. The worshipper is promised that he may live "in the house of the Lord" as long as he cares to stay.

The psychological model employed here suggests that believers most attracted to prayers like the Twenty-third Psalm are those with the greatest dependency needs, in whose lives proximity-maintaining strategies play the most salient roles.

Since childhood caretakers are most often female, it may surprise some readers to hear that the masculine Old Testament God may be an attachment figure. However, psychotherapists are accustomed to the fact that childhood attitudes toward one or the other parent may be directed later, in more or less disguised form, toward individuals of either sex. Patients in psychotherapy, for instance, develop maternal tranferences to male therapists as well as the common father transferences. In the grip of maternal transferences, they see male therapists as being like their mothers, at least in certain ways.

In many religions, though, feminine deities permit attachment themes to emerge undisguised. The oldest known religions all have maternal deities. In these religions, the divine mother is particularly associated with the provision of food, and the ground in which crops grow may even be called her breast. Burial in the ground is thought to ensure rebirth. Gaia, the earth goddess of ancient Greece, was said to bear all living things, to feed them, and to receive from them their fertile seed (Eliade, 1958)—a formula applicable to all goddesses of her type. Weigert-Vowinkel (1938) discussed the cult of the great mother manifested in rites of Cybele, Artemis, Isis, and Astarte, among many others, at various times and places in the ancient world. In every case, the feminine deity embodied death and fertility and was closely associated with the life-giving forces of nature.

Present-day Catholics, particularly in Latin American and Eastern European countries, frequently direct their attachment wishes toward the Virgin Mary, a semidivine, desexualized maternal figure.

In writing about God, Jung, James, and Freud each observed what we would call God's attachment functions. Jung (1939/1954), for example, wrote that "the faithful try to remain children" with respect to their various deities. In his account of "healthy-minded" believers, James (1902) described a form of childlike dependency. According to James, the healthy-minded are optimistic believers. They think of God as a loving parent. He seems to them the personification of kindness. His strength, they believe, will always protect them. In short, they see in God an attachment figure. James's terminology is still used today. For example, Shaver et al. (1980) analyzed survey data from 2,500 American women. According to these authors, the majority of nonconverted believers agreed with statements indicative of what James would have called healthy-minded religious faith.

Freud (1927) considered the childhood wish for nurturance and protection to be at the very root of religious beliefs. According to Freud, these functions are initially served in life by the mother, who is gradually replaced by the father, with whom the (male) child has an ambivalent relationship. By inventing God, and by relating to him in the same ambivalent way as they relate to the human father, adults deny their helplessness. Lorand (1962) and Vergote (1988) have emphasized similar themes.

The relation between proximity maintenance and religious beliefs can be studied by various methods. Spiro and D'Andrade (1958) used ethnographic data from eleven societies to study the relation of child-rearing methods to the form of religious belief. Their results—expressed in a series of Pearson product-moment correlations—underline the great importance of attachment dynamics to religious beliefs and to relationships with supernatural beings. For example, societies that satisfy early childhood dependency and oral needs believe in supernatural beings who can be compelled, through performance of specific rituals, to lend their aid whenever it is required. Societies in which children must solicit assistance from their parents believe in supernatural beings whose aid must be solicited. Similar results were obtained by Lambert et al. (1959). In general, parallels exist between parental responses to childhood needs and how adults expect to be treated by supernatural beings.

Attachment to Religious Leaders

Religious leaders can also be attachment figures, particularly if their belief system promotes them in this role. Charismatic religious leaders such as Maharaj Ji, the Reverend Moon, and Baghwan Shree Rajneesh undoubtedly serve this function for many of their followers. Gurus of every faith may become attachment figures to their close devotees. Smaller sects in particular may predispose to the formation of fantasied infantlike attachments. V.P. Gay (1980) described a young woman, Jane, who entered such a sect; her history illustrates the attachment function of charismatic religious leaders.

Jane was the youngest of three children. She had been an unhappy child, but she had pleasant memories of attending church with her father. After a difficult adolescence, she married impulsively and became pregnant. She left her husband and young child to run off with a musician. The musician abandoned her, and Jane joined a cult. The leader of the cult, an older man called Thomas, had messianic delusions. Though she became his lover, Jane thought of him as a nurturant father figure. Eventually, Thomas's wife forced Jane out of the cult. Jane was depressed until she discovered Jesus, whom she saw as a loving parent. She felt quite a bit better, being in Jesus' care.

Jane had psychological problems—including poor reality testing, impaired social judgment, inadequate self-control, and abnormal interpersonal relationships—typical of patients with borderline personalities. Borderline personalities may result from miscarriage of proximity maintenance strategies (Wenegrat, 1984). Features suggestive of borderline personality are frequently mentioned in case reports of cult members (see, for example, Halperin, 1983b; Olsson, 1983; Spero, 1983). In Jane's case, there is evidence that her attachment relationships began to go wrong early, leading to her unhappiness even as a child. Like most patients with borderline personalities, Jane had strong dependency wishes. She saw herself as a child in need of adult aid. She had sought this first from Thomas and later from Jesus.

Deutsch (1975, 1980, 1983) also emphasized what we would call attachment to the cult leader. Deutsch described a cult led by a man called Baba. Baba was psychotic and eventually left his followers (see Appendix). Deutsch recounted the history of "Sandra," one of the members of Baba's cult. At age two or three, she learned that she had been adopted. She was always at odds with her adopted mother, and she believed that her real mother lived in a Catholic nursing home visible from her window. She felt that her adopted father was arrogant and distant. He was always sickly, and he died when she was thirteen. She feared being abandoned by her adopted mother. Because of depression, Sandra dropped out of school for a time. At fourteen she was hospitalized after attempting to kill herself. Sandra's fear of abandonment spoiled all her relationships. She couldn't stand it when others were weak or in any way unreliable. When she met Baba, she felt calmed by his loving manner. She was impressed by the certainty with which he held his beliefs. Around Baba, Sandra felt, for the first time, that she no longer needed others. As Deutsch observed, disappointments in Sandra's earliest relationships seemed to have set her on a lifelong search for the perfect parental figure, which she thought she had found in Baba. Whether Sandra resumed her search following Baba's departure or whether, like Jane, she found in religion another attachment figure, is not indicated in Deutsch's later papers.

Breaking Attachments

Religious beliefs are also frequently involved when attachment bonds must be broken. One such situation occurs when dependent persons must separate themselves from their parents. In most societies, adult status requires at least a semblance of independence from parents. This may pose a particular problem for dependent adolescents, who become anxious if their ties to attachment figures are weakened. Dependent persons also tend to form ambivalent relationships with their caretakers, so the conflict of the dependent adolescent is frequently accompanied by angry feelings toward the very persons from whom separation seems impossible.

By providing real or imaginary substitute attachment figures, religious beliefs may help young people break ties with their parents without giving up their attachment needs. If nothing else, religious attachments are socially more acceptable than continued dependence on parents. Ostow (1980) described this dynamic. He noted the hostility dependent believers express toward their parents. For example, adolescents sometimes become more orthodox and pious than their parents. They honor their parents' religion, but in a fashion that emphasizes their parents' shortcomings.

In cases of apostasy, poor parental relations are more directly expressed (see Caplovitz & Sherrow, 1977; Dudley, 1978; Hunsberger, 1980). For example, Ostow (1980) described a twenty-year-old woman who had been raised in a New York Jewish family. In high school she was promiscuous. After being thrown out of school for drug trafficking, she left home to work as a nude model. While traveling in Mexico, she met a young peasant who took her to live with his family. She felt like a family member. She took hallucinogenic mushrooms and saw Jesus. He seemed loving and kind, and he urged her to convert to Catholicism. The local priest considered her motives abnormal, but she nonetheless managed to be baptized into the Church. She then returned to New York to visit her parents. By flaunting her apostasy, she upset her parents even more effectively than she had with her previous promiscuity and drug use. She went back to Mexico to live with her newfound family.

Spero (1982) described some cases illustrating the link between piety and defiance. Isaac, for example, was the twenty-two-year-old son of alcoholic parents. The father was feeble-minded and had never managed to support his family. The mother was violent. She had frequently been hospitalized following fights with her husband or at local bars. The only reliable people in Isaac's early life were his maternal aunt and her husband, who were both religious Jews. At age eighteen, Isaac began to adopt their faith. His parents objected violently. Isaac defied them by joining a Hasidic youth hostel and becoming more orthodox. He criticized his parents for being poor Jews. But Isaac's increasing fervor alarmed his religious friends. Soon he became so orthodox that he criticized them as well. They persuaded him to have treatment. In treatment, Isaac proved to be obsessed with various Jewish heroes. These heroes had become for him highly idealized figures, which probably served his dependency needs. Isaac believed literally in their superhuman powers. In treatment, Isaac apparently realized that he was angry at his parents, but Spero provided no follow-up data.

Levin and Zegans (1974) described a similar patient, Phil. Phil's parents were nonreligious Jews. His mother was critical and excessively protective. When Phil was young, she had frequently lost her temper. Phil's father was quiet and introspective. He followed his wife's lead in all matters related to their children. He favored Phil's younger brother. Like Isaac, Phil had an intensely religious (maternal) uncle, whom his mother despised for his orthodoxy. A a young child, Phil had been angry and finicky. He fought with his brother and with other children. He had been a loner in elementary school. Later, he was sent to boarding school, where he developed food fetishes and a preoccupation with weight loss. Concerns like these are common in adolescence, and they are frequently associated with problems in separating from overcontrolling parents (Bruch, 1973; Crisp, 1984; Yager & Strober, 1985). Phil developed grandiose delusions, but his mother signed him out of a hospital against medical advice. At home again, his delusions remitted. He was able to finish high school and entered an Ivy League college. In college, he became an Orthodox Jew. He believed that he might fall ill for failing in any observance. By the time he returned home for his first summer vacation, his behavior had become bizarre and ritualistic. He spent hours cleaning his food, which had to be both organic and kosher. When his father insisted that he stop, Phil became mute. He was taken to a hospital, where he was diagnosed as schizophrenic.

By adopting his uncle's faith, Phil defied his excessively powerful mother. Phil's mother didn't control Phil's uncle as she controlled Phil's father, and Phil knew that his mother despised his uncle's religion. By identifying with his uncle, Phil was behaving like a man who wasn't controlled by women. Also, Orthodox Judaism is patriarchal and male-oriented. It devalues women, who are not even counted as full members of the congregation. Men like Phil, who have grown up dominated by an overly powerful female attachment figure, might feel bolstered by its patriarchal orientation in pursuing their own separation. A similar dynamic might have been important for Spero's patient, Isaac, who also had a powerful mother and a weak father and became an Orthodox Jew.

Religious conversion can have the opposite meaning, too. That is, conversion may be a way of maintaining relations with parents from whom the young adult is unable to separate. Roberts (1965) studied forty-three students from a conservative evangelical college. They were all in their twenties, and all but one was male. The students were interviewed and, on a separate occasion, were given the Minnesota Multiphasic Personality Inventory (MMPI). Roberts found that the ten students who had experienced a sudden conversion to the faith of their parents were significantly more neurotic than the remainder of his sample. On the basis of interview and test data, Roberts concluded that sudden conversions of this kind signify capitulations to the parents and are regressive solutions to adolescent emancipation problems. The sudden convert, in effect, gives up and returns to the parental fold. By contrast, those who had gradually adopted their parents' faith seemed to have had fewer problems with emancipation. For these students, faith signified neither rebellion nor capitulation.

Attachment bonds may also need to be loosened following death of a loved one. Bowlby (1980) treated grief responses in attachment terms and showed that many aspects of mourning have as their raison d'être maintenance of proximity with the dead person (see, also, Wenegrat, 1984). Presumably, recovery from mourning entails loosening or redirection of proximity maintenance bonds. Religion seems to be helpful in grief and bereavement (Glick et al., 1974; Haun, 1977; Loveland, 1968; Parkes, 1972), and this beneficial effect may be partly due to potential attachment uses of religious belief. I have already referred to Ostow's (1980) finding that dependent persons may adopt religious beliefs following major losses. In many cases, the newly religious adopt religious attachment figures (see earlier discussion). In other cases, doctrines of soul or spirit are used to nullify loss. People everywhere seem to believe that they can still relate to kin who have died (see, for example, Swanson, 1960). Hallucinatory experiences during the grieving process (see Raphael, 1983) probably foster such beliefs, which are then reinforced by religious justifications.

Yap (1960) studied sixty-six Hong Kong mental patients who complained of possession. The souls of dead relatives play an important role in Chinese folk beliefs, so it is not surprising that thirty-nine of these patients believed themselves possessed by deceased family members. One case in particular illustrates how fantasied interactions with the souls of dead relatives are used to maintain attachments and to express conflicts that arise as the result of loss. The patient, an illiterate twenty-seven-year-old peasant woman, believed herself possessed by the spirits of her dead husband and mother. As a child, she had been given to her eldest uncle, because he had no children of his own. It was considered important for the eldest son in the family to have children who could carry on the rites of ancestor worship. Later, she was given away to her future husband's family and raised with him until their marriage. The traditional Chinese practice of rearing together children who would one day marry has been shown to promote marital problems and sexual dissatisfaction (Wolf, 1966, 1968; Wolf & Huang, 1980), though Yap (1960) gave no information concerning the quality of this particular patient's marriage. Her husband had died of typhoid fever two years previously, leaving her with three children, one of whom she could not feed and had had to give away. She worked as a coolie and vegetable hawker. Because she received aid from a Catholic welfare agency, she had recently converted to Catholicism. She was not entirely happy with this change, which her neighbors had criticized, and she felt guilty for neglecting her husband's grave. She had received a marriage proposal but had refused it because she thought it was improper for a widow to remarry. Six days before her hospital admission, her employer had cheated her of her salary.

In the hospital, she was agitated and tearful and expressed fears that she would lose her remaining children. She had nightmares in which her dead relatives reproved her for becoming Catholic and neglecting their graves. She believed that she was having intercourse with her husband's ghost, who told her that he did not want her to remarry. Her mother possessed her and complained about her change of religion. The patient, who feared that abandoning her new religion would offend the Virgin Mary, attempted to take her life. As Yap pointed out, her dreams and possessions clearly expressed the conflict she felt between starting a new life, with a new husband and new religion, and remaining loyal to lost relations. Although she improved somewhat in the hospital, the difficult conditions of her life precluded a full recovery.

Fear of Death

The religious believer also frequently believes in his or her own survival after death. Those who do believe in their own survival expect that things will be fine for them. Dixon and Kinlaw (1982), for example, administered a questionnaire to 534 normal subjects from many different religious faiths. Of the 439 who believed in an afterlife, only one subject expected her situation after death to be unfavorable. Apparently, everyone else expected to go to heaven. Spilka et al. (1985) reported that twenty-four of thirty-six studies they surveyed on the relationship between death anxiety and religious belief or belief in an afterlife confirmed that such beliefs reduce death concerns. Negative findings (see, for example, Williams & Cole, 1968) may come from extrinsically religious subjects, who in certain respects don't believe in religion but merely honor its forms. Intrinsically religious subjects do seem to show less death fear (Kahoe & Dunn, 1975; Spilka et al., 1977). (Differences between extrinsically and intrinsically religious persons are discussed later in this chapter.) The equanimity with which at least some religious believers contemplate their own death has suggested to many that reducing death anxiety is the prime motive for religious belief (cf. Malinowski, 1974).

Studies have shown that death fears are multidimensional, not of a single type (Hoelter & Epley, 1979; Minton & Spilka, 1976; Spilka et al., 1977). However, it seems likely that at least one component of what is felt as death fear is separation anxiety. This is because the earliest interpretation of death is as an attachment loss. Lifton (1979; cf. Freud, 1923a, 1926) noted that children learn of death at a time when they are fearful of separation from others. In the terms used here: Children learn of death while they are pursuing proximity maintenance strategies. Children interpret death as a form of "going away." Consequently, according to Lifton, the very first significance likely to be ascribed to death is as an enforced separation from potential caretakers.

Classic studies by Nagy (1948), Anthony (1972), and Furman (1974) are indeed remarkable for the attachment concerns they uncover beneath the child's idea of death. When questioned, children often equate death with vanishing, becoming lost, or being trapped or kidnapped. These fears, which are of losing valued contact and protection, take the same form as other childhood separation fears described by attachment theorists (Bowlby, 1969, 1973, 1980).

Children with serious illnesses and children whose parents have died show the same preoccupations in even more poignant form. For example, Spinetta et al. (1974) provided leukemic children with toy hospital rooms in which they were asked to place dolls representing themselves and others. Comparisons were made with a control group of hospitalized children with nonfatal illnesses. The children with leukemia placed dolls representing hospital staff and parents at a greater distance from dolls representing themselves than the children with nonfatal illnesses did. With subsequent admissions, as the leukemic children grew sicker, the differences became even more pronounced. The authors concluded that dying children feel themselves separated from their parents and caretakers. With respect to bereaved children, Raphael (1983) found little evidence that they understand death in its abstract meaning. What they were aware of was that their dead parent had left and could no longer provide for them.

If death fear is initially an expression of separation anxiety, and if it retains this character in adult life, then the defenses used against it might betray its attachment origin. Yalom (1980) cited two patterns of adult defenses against death anxiety. The first, involvement with an "ultimate rescuer," is nothing other than the direct enactment of attachment strategies. A caretaker is sought whose powers seemingly can protect against all harm. For the believer, religion provides such a rescuer; nonbelievers must find real persons with whom they can form dependent relationships. The second pattern, a near-delusional belief in one's own specialness, closely resembles pseudo–self-sufficiency of the kind described by Bowlby (1969, 1973, 1980). For example, one patient described by Yalom (1980) was said to have cultivated "consummate self-reliance." He could not tolerate even minor degrees of dependency.

Therefore, to the extent that religious beliefs decrease death anxiety, they may do so in large part by reducing separation fears—mainly for those with salient proximity maintenance needs. However, I am unaware of any studies relating death anxiety, religiosity, and personality attributes related to attachment needs, such as dependency.

Parental Investment Strategies

V. Reynolds and Tanner (1983) applied selective retention theory to account for religious rules pertaining to matters of health and reproduction. Their subject matter—alternative strategies for making parental investments—pertains to kin-directed altruism. However, since the purpose of proximity maintenance is timely parental investment, their work can also logically be described here. Reynolds and Tanner argued as follows: Depending on ecological factors, parents may maximize their reproductive success by having many children, and giving them minimal care, or by having few children, and caring for them intensively. In other words, there are two alternative strategies for dividing parental investment among potential offspring, and ecological factors determine which is superior. Ecological factors that produce stable supplies favor intense investment in fewer children. Ecological factors that lead to instability favor minimal investment in larger numbers of children. Reynolds and Tanner assumed that parents will prefer the superior strategy in any given geographic region and that this preference will be reflected in whatever religious choices they make in their lifetimes. If regional ecological factors are more or less constant for many generations, religious rules will be shaped by successive parental choices: They will come to promote the strategy that is superior in that region.

Reynolds and Tanner surveyed religious beliefs that seem to promote one or the other strategy. They argued that regions of low material stability do, in fact, produce beliefs that promote larger families. In various ways, these beliefs discourage intense investment in caring for individuals; they are pronatal and anticare. Regions of high stability, according to Reynolds and Tanner, produce religious beliefs that promote smaller families. These beliefs encourage intense individual care; they are antinatal and procare.

In general, Reynolds and Tanner succeeded in showing the extent of religious control over decisions that affect parental investment. But their explanatory scheme may be overly simple. First, in some cases, pronatal beliefs have further impoverished regions, making them more ecologically unstable. Conversely, both by stabilizing population and by emphasizing the value of individual health, antinatal beliefs may produce material wealth. The relationship between ecology and belief may be circular, rather than one-way, as Reynolds and Tanner seemed to imply.

Second, religious rules and proscriptions that control parental investments may not be chosen by parents at all. Instead, they may reflect the strategic preferences of more powerful persons who are able to impose their choices on parents. Such situations were mentioned in chapter 2. An example cited by Reynolds and Tanner illustrates this point with regard to parental investments: In the fourth century B.C., Carthaginian priests required that aristocrats sacrifice their first-born children. At least some Carthaginian nobles purchased lower-class children to sacrifice in place of their own. To put the matter in technical terms, these nobles must have wished to continue parental investments in the children who were to be sacrificed. As punishment, the priests imposed a levy of 500 additional children to be given to Bal Hammon, the Carthaginian god. This is clearly a case in which parental investment decisions actively evaded by parents were enforced by a more powerful group to serve its own political needs.

More recent power elites with control of religious institutions have likewise had their own interests at stake in controlling or promoting lower-class fertility and in dampening discontent with conditions of life that produce high mortality rates. Pronatal, anticare religions in particular may owe their form to historical powers-that-be. Parental strategies preferred by those who actually suffer material insufficiency, the lower classes, may have little effect on religious dogma.

Sexual Competition

Chastity, Permissiveness, and Disavowal

In the preceding chapter, I argued that genetically determined dispositions cause men and women to adhere to certain sexual strategies. These dispositions predictably lead males to compete with each other for a maximal share of female reproductive potential. They predictably lead females to seek mates who have the best genes and are able and willing to help raise their children. Both male and female sexual strategies entail the risk of potential anxiety-provoking conflicts with other persons. These conflicts might occur not only with competitors of the same sex but also with objects of sexual interest and with parents and authority figures who have a stake in reproductive arrangements (see Wenegrat, 1984).

Just as they decrease anxiety related to attachment, religious beliefs may decrease fear related to sexual strategies. They ease sexual fears by providing hard and fast—and ostensibly divine—guides to sexual decision making. Religion may be used to flee from conflict-ridden sexual feelings, or it may provide a guide to sexual activity for which one cannot be blamed (Vergote, 1988). By prescribing the nature and circumstances of acceptable sexual activity, religious rules can relieve the sexually fearful person of the need to make anxiety-provoking social decisions.

Religious rules concerning sex can relieve anxiety only insofar as people adhere to them more or less automatically. Insofar as people perceive a choice with regard to sexual dictates, they are once again confronted with difficult social decisions. The difficulty of these decisions might even be magnified, because the fear of divine retribution will have been added to anxieties inherent in sexual strategies. Fears related to violating sexual taboos have been obvious to psychologists since Freud called attention to them. Sources of anxiety inherent in sexual strategies have largely been overlooked, leading to the impression that sexual activity could be anxiety-free if religious taboos were only dropped. Freud, of course, knew that biology rendered sexual choices inherently conflict-ridden, but his thoughts on sexual taboos attracted wider attention. In fact, Freud saw taboos and inherent conflicts as closely interwoven, not independent at all. This is the position I have taken here in por-traying ideology as a tool of social control shaped by powers-that-be to serve their own interests, including, presumably, their inclu-sive fitness interests (see chapter 2). Ideological conflicts are there-fore, ultimately, interpersonal conflicts. On the other hand, the post-Freudian emphasis on the cultural-religious source of sexual fear is the opposite position to that suggested here: that religious sexual mores can also alleviate fears inherent to sexual strategies (cf. Vergote, 1988).

At least in some societies, religious sexual rules do affect behavior. Some individuals in these societies must be adhering to religious sexual rules more or less conscientiously, consequently avoiding conflict-ridden decisions. For example, numerous studies have shown decreased rates of premarital intercourse among religious subjects (see, for example, Herold & Goodwin, 1981; Kinsey et al., 1948; Kinsey et al., 1953; Middleton & Putney, 1962; Reiss, 1969; Tavris & Sadd, 1975). Lower rates of premarital intercourse are reflected in fewer premarital conceptions. H.T. Christensen (1953, 1960), for example, studied the rates of early live births following religious and civil weddings. In Indiana, less than 10 percent of religious weddings but more than 20 percent of civil weddings were followed by the birth of a child within seven months. Only 1 percent of religious weddings but more than 16 percent of civil weddings in Utah were followed by the birth of a child within seven months. Comparable figures from Denmark were 13 and 37 percent! Blood (1969) found similar rates in Detroit. Comparable data exist regarding other indices of sexual behavior (see, for example, Hassett, 1981).

Many cultlike religious groups have extreme antisexual norms, which could help them attract sexually anxious recruits (Galanter, 1982). Studies of cult recruits sometimes mention that sexual fears contributed to conversion. For example, Deutsch and Miller (1983) studied four women who were former members of the Unification Church. All four had joined in their early twenties. Three of them had been members for more than five years. Each woman was interviewed and given various tests. Interview material and test results showed prominent sexual fears and problems relating to men. Defenses were used to ward off sex-related stimuli. Apparently, the strict mores of the Unification Church had provided these women relief from social and sexual pressures. In the church, there had been no need to form heterosexual partnerships.

Converts to an antisexual cult described by Lofland and Stark (1965) were also notably anxious concerning sexual matters. To avoid sexual intercourse, one such convert had locked herself in the bathroom on her wedding night. She continued to abhor intercourse through nearly ten years of married life. A homosexual encounter with a neighbor woman upset her so much that she made her family move. Shortly thereafter, she converted to the cult studied by Lofland and Stark.

Psychological histories occasionally show religion in the service of sexual phobias. For example, Ostow (1980) described a young man who was made extremely anxious by nongenital intimacies with his fiancée. He thought his anxiety resulted from guilt. However, when his rabbi reassured him that such intimacies were proper for an engaged couple, he questioned the rabbi's authority. He wanted religion to keep him from the sexual acts he feared.

Kutty et al. (1979) described a fifteen-year-old male member of the Hare Krishna movement. After unsuccessful efforts to have a heterosexual relationship, he had lost all confidence in his abilities with the opposite sex. He found sexual abstinence, as promoted by the Hare Krishna movement, more and more appealing. The authors considered that the denial of sexuality preached by the Hare Krishna movement allowed this young man to phobically avoid heterosexual relationships and the narcissistic blows he expected from them. Lubin (1958) and Sexton and Maddock (1980) argued that unconscious anxieties related to sexuality can likewise promote religious beliefs with antisexual functions.

Mahatma Gandhi's religious beliefs illustrate some of these points (see Erikson, 1969; Mehta, 1976; Shirer, 1979). Gandhi married when he was only thirteen. When he was sixteen, his father fell ill. Gandhi's relationship with his father was highly ambivalent. One night, Gandhi left off nursing the ailing man and went to his own room. There he woke up his pregnant wife for the purpose of sexual intercourse. While he was gone, his father died. Although her pregnancy was very advanced, his wife miscarried several weeks later. Gandhi felt guilty for leaving his father at the moment of his death and for his wife's miscarriage. Four decades later, Gandhi wrote in his autobiography that he still felt shame for his "animal passion" on the night of his father's death. When he was thirty-one, Gandhi resolved, with his wife's consent, to abstain from sexual acts. Actually, as Erikson (1969) noted, it was not just the sexual act that Gandhi resolved to avoid, but male aggression, too. In this sense, his resolution extended to the whole of what we would consider masculine competitive actions. Gandhi struggled for five years to suppress his sexual urges. Then he took a religious vow and gave up sex for good.

Gandhi's account of events on the night of his father's death, and of his emotional response to them, implies that his sexual shame derived from a filial conflict. His mixed feelings toward his father are evident in his autobiography. Yet Gandhi gave up sex only after taking a religious vow, and he chose to explain his celibacy in traditional Hindu terms. According to Hindu scriptures, conservation of semen increases spiritual strength and brings one closer to God.

Although he took a religious vow, Gandhi disregarded Hindu scriptural injunctions to quiet the sexual drive by avoiding contact with women. He apparently had to keep proving he had risen above temptation. Women bathed and massaged him and, eventually, slept with him, naked. Orthodox Hindus were outraged by Gandhi's apparent hypocrisy. Yet Gandhi was consciously truthful in his claim to be merely testing himself. Sleeping with naked women in order to test restraint was advocated by Christians, too, in the early years of the Church. A nocturnal emission in his sixty-seventh year seemed to horrify Gandhi:

> My darkest hour was when I was in Bombay a few months ago. It was the hour of my temptation. Whilst I was sleep I suddenly felt as though I wanted to see a woman. Well, a man who had tried to rise superior to the instinct for nearly forty years was bound to be intensely pained when he had this frightful experience. I ultimately conquered the feeling, but I was face to face with the blackest moment of my life and if I had succumbed to it, it would have been my absolute undoing. (Shirer, 1979, p.238)

Gandhi's language leaves no doubt concerning his anxiety: He is "pained." He must "conquer" his thoughts or "succumb" to them. The hour is "dark" and "frightful." He is faced with his "undoing." It seems that Gandhi went through life disturbed by sexual thoughts (and by aggressive thoughts, as well), with the religious formulas he used against them providing him only a partial peace.

Of course, religions do more than forbid sex; they also permit certain sexual acts. In this way, they provide a guide to conflict-free sexuality (cf. Vergote, 1988). Jewish tradition, for instance, sanctions lawful intercourse between man and wife. The frequency of intercourse is specified in the marriage contract. In marriage, Jewish men and women may have sexual relations free from risk of disapprobation. Religions sometimes promote sex outside monogamous marriage. For example, certain Semitic and Greco-Roman shrines offered male worshippers access to sacred prostitutes. Priestesses in some cults were highly valued courtesans. On special festival days, rules of sexual conduct were partially suspended.

Although Christianity on the whole has been antisexual, splinter groups have permitted sexual activity forbidden by mainstream churches (see, for example, Garvey, 1983; B.Z. Goldberg, 1958; Shneidman & Levine-Shneidman, 1983; V. Weber, 1983). For example, as early as the third century, a Persian dualist named Manes established a sexually promiscuous community on the shores of the Jordan River. The Manichaean heresy was important in early Church history. Augustine turned to this doctrine to ease his sense of sexual guilt (Bokenkotter, 1979). As late as the nineteenth century, Christian sects in the United States practiced communal marriage, and communal marriage is still practiced by some present-day cults.

Finally, some religious beliefs help the faithful disavow their sexual aims. Once disavowed, sexual wishes may be expressed without risk of retribution. For example, Galvin and Ludwig (1961) described a seventeen-year-old Mexican-American girl who claimed to be bewitched. Her history, and that of her mother and stepfather, illustrates nicely how disavowed impulses that are inconsistent with existing social arrangements can achieve partial fulfillment. Disavowal was furthered here by ideas regarding witchcraft, which were related to religion in the patient's ethnic group (Senter, 1947). Galvin and Ludwig's patient fell into trances attributed to witchcraft. During these trances, she acted out varied sexual themes. On one occasion, for instance, she seemed to be in labor. She moaned and writhed and claimed she was having contractions. She said a witch had put something in her vagina in order to discredit her. On other occasions, she hit and scratched her parents or called them abusive names. Her stepfather could end her trances by stretching out on top of her as she lay supine. But the mother began to grow jealous. She thought she saw a "man in black." He said that her daughter and husband were making love behind her back. Not to be outdone by her daughter, she, too, fell under a spell and tried to attack her husband. Fortunately, he was able to douse her with salt, which brought her to her senses. The witchery touched him, too, though: He awoke for no reason in the middle of the night. His wife was sleeping next to him. He reached over and touched her breast, but it felt to him like his stepdaughter's. Clearly, Galvin and Ludwig's patient, and her mother and step-father, expressed their sexual preoccupations under the guise of being bewitched. This relieved them of any attendant blame and allowed them to say and do things that would otherwise occasion considerable anxiety.

Vergote (1988) described several mystics, including Teresa of Avila, Agnes Blannbekin, and Marie Alacoque, who gave voice to sexual fantasies in their ecstatic visions.

Oedipal Themes in Male Religious Belief

Freudian psychoanalysts believe that early experiences with the parents motivate adult sexual competition. The sociobiologic model described in the preceding chapter suggests that early experiences with the parents only adumbrate adult attitudes. Precocious experiences with intrafamilial sexual competition may color later expectations and in this way may determine adult competitive styles, but they do not truly motivate the competition. The sociobiologic model also implies that early competitive experiences will be less important for females, except in special circumstances. This is because inclusive fitness considerations dictate that sexual competition should be less fierce among females than among males and should be accorded correspondingly less time and energy. Psychoanalysts, too, have found Oedipal formulations less powerful when applied to female patients, but this clinical observation has failed to have much effect on psychoanalytic theory.

Regardless of their differences, both the psychoanalytic and the sociobiologic models suggest that, at least for the adult male, sexual competitive concerns should be closely intertwined with Oedipal-type fantasies. Insofar as religious beliefs address masculine concerns that are directly or indirectly related to sexual competition, they should manifest these fantasies. Religious beliefs should express and reconcile the ambivalent filial attitudes—pushing toward both submission and defiance of the father—that preoccupy many males.

According to Freud (1907, 1913, 1927, 1939), God is modeled on the childhood notion of the all-powerful father. Religious rituals appease this heavenly father figure, while religious customs define safe circumstances for instinctual gratification. In a later chapter, I will review studies pertaining to Freud's formulation. As the reader might suspect on the basis of previous sections, Freud's formulation turns out to be overly simple. There are persons—including some men—for whom God is a predominantly maternal figure or for whom God has characteristics borrowed from both parents. Other objections, too, have been made to Freud's theory, even by psychoanalysts (see V.P. Gay, 1975, 1982; Zilboorg, 1962). Yet Freud's treatment of religion has proved exceptionally valuable as a starting point for psychological inquiries. Gandhi's history, which contains obvious Oedipal themes, has already been described. Aside from the cases to be presented here, cases for which the Freudian view is indispensable have been described by Kutty et al. (1979), by Ostow (1980), and by Salzman (1953, 1966), among many others. Ernest Jones's (1951) applications of the Freudian viewpoint to understanding Christian theology will also be mentioned here. J.W. Miller (1982, 1983) provided an interesting, if perhaps oversimplified, viewpoint closely related to the Freudian model. Its chief defect seems to lie in its lack of attention to cultural factors.

Perhaps the most influential man to see his father in God, and to work out filial conflicts in relation to a divine father figure, was Martin Luther. Oedipal aspects of Luther's religious life have been well summarized by Erikson (1962), whose account I will follow. Readers who desire a fuller description are referred to Erikson's work. Luther's father Hans—in whose image the Christian God was to be remade—was the oldest son in a fifteenth-century Thuringian peasant family. In accordance with local customs, the family farm went to his younger brother. Hans moved to Mansfeld, a copper and silver center, and went to work in the copper mines.

Ambitious, hard-working, and penurious, he rose eventually into the class of small capitalists who held shares in the mines and foundries. He was known for his bad temper; he may even have killed a man in a fit of violent rage. He beat his children for minor offenses but was seldom satisfied by their efforts to please him. Luther's mother Margareta, a downtrodden and superstitious woman, seemed to have been completely overshadowed by Hans's stronger personality. Erikson surmised that Hans formed a wedge between Martin and his mother, from whom Martin was expected to be precociously independent. Young Martin was said to be sad and anxious and a thoroughly browbeaten child.

Hans wanted his son to study law, so at age seventeen Martin enrolled in the university at Erfurt. On a visit home in 1505, he found that his father had arranged a lucrative marriage for him. Erikson surmised that Luther was troubled by his father's plans but was afraid to confront him. On his way back to school, Luther was caught in a thunderstorm. A bolt of lightning struck nearby, throwing him into a panic. He vowed to become a monk if his life was spared. This was his "road to Damascus." Rather than going back to school, he entered a monastery. His father was enraged when he heard of his son's decision.

Throughout his life, various symptoms betrayed Luther's neuroticism. He was given to crying and fainting spells, to fits of melancholy, and to rages reminiscent of his father's. He had scatological preoccupations like those that characterize modern-day neurotics. Numerous anecdotes show that he was also preoccupied with filial conflicts. For example, while he was a novice in the monastery choir, Luther once fell to the ground and shouted, "It isn't me." According to Erikson, Luther's fit had followed the reading of Mark 9:17, which describes how Christ cast devils from a possessed son. In his fury at Martin's becoming a monk, Hans had suggested that Martin had made his sacred vow under the devil's sway.

Later, visiting Rome, Luther climbed the Lateran steps. On each step, he said a prayer to save a soul in purgatory. According to his own report, however, on each step he compulsively wished his parents dead, so that he could save their souls as well! Reciting his first Mass, Luther reported that he suddenly felt that he was speaking directly to God. The thought so terrified him that he had to restrain himself to keep from running away.

The god Luther feared—and later impressed on Christendom—strongly resembled his father. Unlike the Roman God, but like Luther's father, Luther's God could accept or reject arbitrarily. No scrupulosity could ensure his grace nor protect those without it from his terrible anger. Sins, however, were still to be punished, just as in Luther's youth. God, according to Luther, could be a "gluttonous fire" for those who had displeased him. In the monastery, one of Luther's instructors had found it necessary to remind him that God does not hate and that malice is a purely human emotion.

Psychologically, one of Luther's most important theological arguments concerned the Virgin Mary. By denying her the godlike status she had gained in Roman worship, Luther further glorified the reigning paternal deity. He also recreated his family constellation: The children are ruled by the powerful father; the mother is forced to the sidelines.

Some background would be helpful here: In an essay on the Virgin Mary, Ernest Jones (1951) argued that the Holy Ghost in the Trinity had replaced a primal mother-goddess. According to Jones, submissive Oedipal wishes are at the heart of Christian doctrine and distinguish it from its ancient rival, Mithraism, which was favored by the Roman Army. Unlike Christ, who sacrificed himself to appease his father's wrath, Mithra slew his father and reigned in his father's place. Essentially, by ceasing to worship the mother, the Christian male further renounced his patricidal wishes and strengthened his ties with God the Father. This left a gap in the divine triad, which was filled by the Holy Ghost, a somewhat shadowy figure. But the mother returned, according to Jones, in the guise of Mary, desexualized by Saint Jerome. Consistent with the importance of her psychological functions, which subserve what we have called proximity maintenance strategies, the Virgin Mary gradually gained importance. By the time of the Reformation, she was virtually divine. Lutherans and later Protestants, according to Jones, denounced the mother in her new form in order to better worship the father.

To reshape God in his father's image, Luther had to defy the Pope, a father figure himself. Roman Catholics still refer to the Pope as the Holy Father. By assaulting the worldly incarnation of paternal authority and the ideology on which it rested, Luther made possible the eventual worldwide triumph of his own father's materialist values (see M. Weber, 1930). Luther perhaps thought that he had rebelled against these values by leaving the university and by spoiling his father's plans for a well-connected marriage. But for Luther, it was always easier to deify his father than to defy him. Ironically, so-called Social Darwinism owed more to Luther and those who followed him than to anything Darwin wrote (see Lopreato, 1984).

Men who see God as a father figure may have ideas about him that suggest passive homosexual wishes. Freud (1923a) believed that passive homosexual wishes result from an unresolved "negative" Oedipus complex: Rather than wishing to defeat the father and marry the mother, the young boy wishes to take the mother's place. In doing so, he denies his love for his mother and symbolically submits to the father instead. Ernest Jones's (1951) remarks on the Virgin Mary refer to this dynamic.

Male paranoid patients are frequently preoccupied with negative Oedipal themes (see Wenegrat, 1984, for a sociobiologic discussion of this issue). They are also prone to religious delusions, with homosexual overtones (see Appendix). The most famous such patient was Schreber, whose published memoirs were studied by Freud (1911). More recently, Niederland (1959a, 1959b) reexamined the Schreber case in light of data previously unavailable. Schreber was born in 1842, the son of a well-known but probably psychotic pedagogue. The elder Schreber was delusionally preoccupied with his childrens' posture and upbringing. Starting in their infancy, he made a habit of restraining them with grotesque clamps and corsets. One of his devices, for example, attached to the child's hair and body, so as to pull the hair if the head were not held absolutely upright. Another, a harness with an iron bar, pressed painfully on the collarbones if the child slouched at all. From the time they were three months old, the elder Schreber insisted that his children be bathed in cold water. He believed that this would toughen their moral fiber.

The younger Schreber became an eminent jurist. He first became psychotic in 1884. After a number of months, he recovered sufficiently to resume his duties, but eight years later he suffered a second collapse. From 1893 to 1902, he was held in an asylum against his will. His memoirs, which he wrote toward the end of his stay, were published in 1903. These memoirs describe his psychotic delusions. Schreber believed himself in contact with God, who performed painful "miracles" by means of rays on Schreber's body. Niederland demonstrated the point-by-point correspondence of Schreber's delusional "miracles" and the actual treatments he had suffered at his father's hand. There is no doubt that Schreber's delusional God was modeled on his real father.

The core of Schreber's delusion was that God would make him a woman and then impregnate him by means of divine rays. Schreber believed that his emasculation would give God pleasure. He also believed that after divine coitus, he would give birth to a new race. Schreber's delusion, which he maintained until his death, led Freud to theorize that passive homosexual wishes play an etiologic role in paranoid psychoses.

Kaufman (1939) described a patient much like Schreber. A paranoid schizophrenic, the patient had believed for many years that he was the Messiah. His delusion had formed on the way to the mental hospital, while sharing a berth with his father. Kaufman summarized the filial and homosexual aspects of his patient's religious beliefs.

Thomas, the apparently psychotic cult leader to whom V.P. Gay's (1980) patient, Jane, was attracted (see earlier discussion), displayed the same combination of filial and homosexual elements. Thomas claimed to have participated in an initiation rite strikingly similar to Ezekiel's appointment as messenger of God (see Appendix).

Religious autocastration is the most extreme expression of the negative Oedipus complex. Here the worshipper quite literally emasculates himself in order to please the parental deities. Autocastration was common in the worship of ancient mother goddesses. The followers of Aphrodite, for example, severed their genitals and carried them through the streets. When they could go no further, they threw their severed parts into the nearest house; the occupants of the house were thereby obliged to furnish them female garb. Weigert-Vowinkel (1938) concluded that autocastration in the service of mother goddesses had two symbolic meanings. First, by castrating himself, the male worshipper renounced his phallic intentions toward the goddess, in relation to whom he then was like a child. Second, autocastration was a punishment for the Oedipal wishes intrinsic to these ancient religions. The Skopzis, a Russian sect that achieved a wide following at one time, practiced the most gruesome sexual mutilations, citing Origen for justification. Kushner (1967) summarized the history of autocastration in religion and presented two interesting cases. Both were male paranoid psychotics, with religious delusions and passive homosexual impulses, who had severed their genitals in order to please their obviously paternal gods.

Thomas (1932) described a famous case of a female with religious delusions. Brenner (1939) pointed out certain homosexual elements in her case history, but they are more subtle than the corresponding themes in the delusions of male patients. In any event, they present no obstacle to the view adopted here: that male religious beliefs in particular are prone to contain Oedipal elements; and when these elements take the negative form, submissive homosexual themes will be prominent.

Mutualism

A Historic View

In the preceding chapter, I defined mutualism as a readiness to engage in unstereotypical, mutually profitable cooperative endeavors. Insofar as these endeavors interfere with the survival and reproduction of noncooperating individuals—such as would be the case, for example, when a group of individuals cooperate to monopolize food supplies—they require two separate behavioral components. The first is a tendency to form stable cooperative social groups whose members are distinguished from outsiders and accorded preferential treatment. The second is a tendency for members of a cooperative group to adopt consensual world views, which in human groups are embodied in authority figures. The results of these strategies are cognitively cohesive groups of cooperating individuals who are potentially hostile to others.

Religious beliefs may serve both of these mutualistic strategies.

Social scientists have noted the extent to which religious beliefs define group boundaries and provide consensual world views (see, for example, Berger & Luckmann, 1966; Durkheim, 1912; Gluckman, 1963; Johnson, 1963; Lopreato, 1984; Radcliffe-Brown, 1952; Troeltsch, 1931; Turner, 1968; M. Weber, 1930). They promote cooperation within the group and, frequently, hatred and violence without. They define the roots of in-group authority and penalties for failure to accept it.

In what follows, the relationships between religious beliefs and mutualistic social strategies are discussed in two parts: First, in this section, I will note historic correlations between mutualistic endeavors and religious beliefs. Then, in the following section, I will discuss the methods and circumstances of religious recruitment, the means by which religious beliefs are maintained, and the means and consequences of religious apostasy, in order to relate them to mutualistic strategies.

First, new religious enthusiasms frequently trigger large-scale common endeavors. Because these endeavors are typically disadvantageous to nonbelievers, they are legitimately categorized with mutualistic projects of the type discussed in the preceding chapter. Consider, for instance, how the Arabs conquered the Middle East in the early seventh century (see Lippman, 1982; Rodinson, 1971; Sabini, 1981). During the sixth century, the Arabs were split into numerous camps. The average Arab owed loyalty to his clan, tribe, or town, but not to a larger group. Neighboring clans fought blood feuds, towns and tribes waged wars, and robber bands harassed trade routes. Even within the small group, cooperation was limited. Men were judged less by their contribution to what we would call the common good than by their seeming recklessness. The ideal sixth-century Arab would sacrifice everything, including the well-being of loved ones, for the sake of revenge or passion or to play the extravagant host.

At the time of Mohammed's birth, around 571 A.D., most Arabs were practicing henotheists. That is, they acknowledged a supreme creator God, Allah, but considered everyday affairs more the concern of lesser deities, to whom prayers were more effectively addressed. These lesser deities were local gods and were worshipped in competing shrines, such as the Kaaba in Mecca, that depended on more or less local patronage. Jews, Christians, and indigenous monotheists formed a minority of the Arabs. Jews were allied with Persia, Christians with Byzantium. Indigenous monotheists, called *hanifs*, from the Arabic word for infidel, worshipped the supreme creator God but not the lesser gods found in Arab shrines.

Mohammed's revelations, recorded in the Koran, laid the basis for a common Arab identity, a common Arab ideology, and a new cooperative ethic. They released Arab energies in unforeseen ways. First, Mohammed told the Arabs that they were all descendants of Ishmael and, through him, of Abraham. Allah, the supreme being already acknowledged by Arab henotheists and monotheists alike, had now sent them a prophet equal in dignity to those he had sent the Jews. Second, Mohammed revealed a universal God; the local cults and shrines were ruthlessly eliminated. Mecca became the center of Arab religious identity: Gabriel had saved Ishmael's life at Mecca. Abraham himself had built the Kaaba there. Every Muslim prayed facing Mecca. Every Muslim visited Mecca. Finally, Mohammed devised a new standard of conduct: Men would be judged according to God's cause. Those who put private or tribal concerns ahead of God's kingdom could expect eternal torments. Those who made the greatest sacrifices—dying, for instance, in a holy war—could expect to live in paradise.

Although he was persecuted by his own clan, who saw him as a threat to the lucrative Meccan shrines and forced him, in 622, into exile in Medina, Mohammed lived to see his religion triumphant. First, the Hejaz, then the peninsula as a whole, and finally Syria, the Holy Lands, and Egypt fell under the power of the newly united Arabs. Eventually, Byzantium itself, the whole of North Africa, Persia, India and Spain were controlled by these once-despised peoples. Yet, in numbers, Arabs formed only a small part of even their own empire, much less of the whole world. Arab scholars preserved classical literature, invented the modern alphabet, and laid the foundations for mathematics and science. Their artistic and architectural achievements are emulated to this day, and copies of their inventions can be found on every continent. Muslims today live throughout the world and are the majority or a sizable minority in countries from Indonesia to Morocco, from Pakistan to equatorial Africa. They recite the Koran in Arabic, pray toward Mecca, and—if they are able—travel to the Hejaz once in their lifetime. All this was triggered by Mohammed's new religion.

Not only can religion promote mutual action; the need for mutual action can produce new religions. Consider an example from another age: the Ghost Dance of 1890 (see Ewing, 1983; D.H. Miller, 1959). In the late nineteenth century, most Native Americans, particularly the Plains tribes, were poverty-stricken and semistarved. Driven from their land, they were settled on reservations without means of survival. Either by intent or by oversight, food supplies promised by government treaties proved to be unreliable. Children were forced into government schools, and missionaries had free reign to undermine tribal leaders. Indian police answered to the white man. Nor was there any recourse: The tribes had scant experience with intertribal cooperation or with large-scale military actions, they lacked weapons, and they were greatly outnumbered by the onrushing white men. Few of their leaders understood the white man's system of government.

The Ghost Dance originated around 1870 with a Paiute shaman, Tavibo. His son Wovoka revived the dance in the late 1880s. Wovoka predicted the imminent beginning of a new age, which the Indian could hasten by performance of the Ghost Dance. In the new age, the earth would be renewed. Game would again be plentiful. The white man would be gone.

From across the Plains, tribal emissaries traveled to Nevada to meet Wovoka and learn the sacred dance. Previously hostile tribes gathered together to dance and sing. The seditious sentiments expressed on these occasions, reported by government spies, alarmed the white authorities. Steps were taken to prevent free travel. Ghost Dance leaders were imprisoned. In the summer of 1890, a Sioux outbreak occurred at the Pine Ridge Agency, where the Ghost Dance had reached a fever pitch. Though the outbreak had resulted from incompetent government agents, broken promises, and hunger, most whites preferred to blame the Ghost Dance. A band of Sioux, attempting to surrender, were slaughtered at Wounded Knee.

Wovoka later claimed that the Sioux had twisted his doctrine. Whether he really renounced his teaching or was pressured by government agents will probably never be known. In any event, the massacre at Wounded Knee turned native opinion against the Ghost Dance religion. Insofar as it did survive, the Ghost Dance lost its millenial fervor: Performance of Wovoka's dance might assure eventual happiness, but not the imminent overthrow of the white man's world.

Other religions soon replaced the Ghost Dance. Although its distribution had been prohibited by Congress in 1887, within ten years of Wounded Knee, peyote enjoyed an increasing popularity in native rituals (see Preston & Hammerschlag, 1983). The Native American Church—members of which now enjoy the legal right to use peyote ritually—was formed less than thirty years after Wounded Knee.

The historical relationship between mutualistic endeavors and religious beliefs can also be demonstrated in specific religious doctrines that take the form best suited to achieve mutual goals. As noted previously, Mohammed's theology was ideally suited to promote large-scale cooperation among Arabs who had no previous experience with it. Wovoka's Ghost Dance, like other millenarian religious movements (see Bellah, 1964; Fabian, 1983; Worsley, 1959), was doctrinally suited to increase the unity and self-esteem of a group that had been divided and repressed. The most enduring religious belief systems are flexible enough to remain useful when the group's situation and needs change. The history of the Jews, for example, shows how religious faiths can become sufficiently flexible to endure any exigency, including defeat and exile.

In summary, religious beliefs can trigger mutualistic endeavors, mutualistic needs can spur development of religious beliefs, and some fit seems evident between mutualistic needs and specific religious doctrines. Doctrines that are sufficiently flexible to remain mutualistically useful in spite of changing circumstances are more likely to survive changing group fortunes. This is the macroscopic, historical view of the relationship between religiosity and mutualism. In the following section, the relationship is examined from a microscopic view, as it actually evolves in modern religious groups.

A Closer Look

If religious beliefs subserve mutualistic social strategies, then those whose group-related tactics have failed might find them especially helpful. That is, individuals who for one reason or another do not feel part of a cooperating, cognitively cohesive group should be prone to religious enthusiasms. In recent years, rapidly growing religious cults have focused attention on the predisposition to religious involvement in general and to cult involvement in particular. Therefore, ample evidence now exists that this prediction is largely true.

Except for subtle dependency and attachment problems, those who join religious cults show no characteristic personality traits that distinguish them from nonjoiners (see Halperin, 1983b; Maleson, 1981; Olsson, 1983; Ross, 1983; Spero, 1983; Ullman, 1988). In an earlier section, I discussed the motives that might lead dependent individuals toward religious involvement. Religious cult joiners do differ from nonjoiners, however, in their social integration and in the degree to which they are affiliated with nonreligious social groups. In their study of conversion to a religious cult, Lofland and Stark (1965) found that converts were generally alienated from family, spouses, or friends. Where positive attachments did exist, geographic distance made close contact impossible. Converts were frequently so unintegrated, that, in Lofland and Stark's words, "they could, for the most part, simply fall out of relatively conventional society unnoticed." S.V. Levine (1979) interviewed members of the Hare Krishna movement, the Unification Church, the Divine Light Mission, the Church of God, the Jesus People, and the Scientology, Process, and Foundation Churches, among others. He reported that alienation and loneliness were key factors in the predisposition to join these groups. Later studies of diaspora Jews who had joined ultraorthodox cults in Israel revealed the same factors (S.V. Levine, 1983). Their recruitment into these cults had been facilitated by their being away from home and, therefore, from the social ties that might otherwise have prevented their joining.

Galanter (1980) prospectively studied participants in Unification Church workshops intended to recruit new members. Of the 104 subjects Galanter studied, 77 percent were male, 77 percent were Caucasian, and 95 percent were single. The average age was twenty-one years. The major differences between those who did and did not become Unification Church members were in regard to social ties. Those who dropped out of the workshops, whether early on or at the end, had much stronger outside social affiliations than those who ultimately joined the church. Even when potential recruits felt considerable enthusiasm for the church, previously developed outside social ties seemed to exert a protective effect against actual membership.

Not only social scientists but proselytizers, too, know that socially isolated persons are the best potential religious recruits. Cults direct their recruiting efforts toward those who appear to be alone. In Western societies, there has historically been a gap—occurring in adolescence—between what Luckmann (1979) refers to as primary and secondary socialization. Primary socialization takes place in the family. Secondary socialization occurs in the larger group. Factors in modern life that make it harder to feel part of the larger group have probably widened this gap (see, for example, Bellah et al., 1985). As a result, adolescents and young adults today may be disaffiliated from their families on the one hand and from peer or adult groups on the other. Consequently, when cults direct their recruiting efforts toward the disaffiliated, they concentrate on young adults, especially those just leaving home. Since Starbuck's (1897) classic study (see, also, C.W. Christensen, 1963), adolescents and young adults have been known to be prone to religious conversion. Modern cults merely take advantage of preexisting vulnerabilities. University campuses are particular targets of cult recruiters, especially at the beginning of new academic terms. The Israeli cults studied by S.V. Levine (1983) look for potential recruits among young people who don't seem to be at home. Recruiters from these groups approach youths at tourist spots, at airports, or at hostels.

In modern society, the elderly, too, are especially prone to loneliness. Recently, isolated elderly—especially the bereaved, those living alone, and residents of nursing homes—have also become favored targets for religious cult recruitment (Brooks, 1986).

Once in contact with the isolated person, religious recruiters concentrate their efforts on making him or her feel part of the group. Etemad (1978) pointed out that although every religious cult has its own style, virtually all cults recruit by offering camaraderie. Potential members are asked to visit the cult meetinghouse. There they are surrounded by concerned new friends. They are fed and coddled and made to feel special. Practical help may be offered, especially to the elderly (Brooks, 1986). They may be invited to a country retreat, where they meet more friendly people; they are never left alone. Use of affection to make the potential recruit feel part of the religious community has been called "love bombing" (Halperin, 1983c), perhaps to emphasize the force it exerts. The ultraorthodox cult members studied by Levine (1983) were subjected to the same technique.

Religious dogma is mentioned only after the potential recruit has become attached to the group. By that time, adopting the dogma is merely, in Lofland and Stark's (1965) words, "coming to accept the opinions of one's friends." In terms of the model developed here, adopting the dogma is something that comes naturally: accepting the consensual reality of what is now one's social group. The importance of the social group to acceptance of dogma is illustrated by Unification Church recruiting efforts in the late 1960s (Long & Hadden, 1983). At that time, rather than "love bombing" potential recruits, the church offered public lectures in order to sell its beliefs. Few people came to these lectures and even fewer converted. Only after the introduction of "love bombing"—when ideology was put on the back burner until group affiliations could be formed—was the Unification Church able to recruit American youths.

Outside observers, including mental health professionals, are frequently surprised by sudden changes in beliefs following induction into religious cults (Galanter & Westermeyer, 1980). Suddenly acquired beliefs may seem ludicrous to the observer or may appear to be at odds with the cult member's previous life. Students of cults and conversion, however, have stressed the malleability of beliefs and the extent to which they reflect powerful social settings and social needs (J.G. Clark, 1983; Galper, 1983; Halperin, 1983c). It is worthwhile to remember that under the influence of their religious and social group, mentally normal persons in many different societies act as if they were possessed (see, for example, Alland, 1962; Boisen, 1939; Chandrashekar, 1981; W. Davis, 1985; Hine, 1969) or have hallucinations (Al-Issa, 1977; Andrade et al., 1988; Buckley & Galanter, 1979; Schwab, 1977; O.M. Stone, 1962; Young et al., 1987).

If a major psychological function of religious involvement is to achieve membership in a cognitively cohesive social group, then subjective benefits of religious activity and subjective feelings of belonging should be correlated. Galanter and Buckley (1978; also, Galanter, 1978) asked 119 recent converts to the Divine Light Mission to rate retrospectively neurotic symptoms experienced during two-month periods immediately before and after their conversion. The extent of reported relief was, in fact, strongly correlated with measures of perceived group cohesion. Converts who felt most tied to the religious group reported the greatest improvements in their well-being. These findings were so dramatic that they prompted Galanter (1978) to propose a model nearly identical to the one proposed here: Affiliation with large groups is an innate need, frustration of which leads to neurotic distress and enhances vulnerability to cult recruitment. In a later study, Galanter et al. (1980) reported that for both Divine Light Mission and Unification Church converts, feelings of membership in a cohesive group predicted decreased drug use. Simmonds (1977) also reported decreased drug use in those who had joined a closeknit fundamentalist group. Drug use also declines in certain closeknit secular communities (Rebhan, 1983). As is the case with religious groups, drug users who reformed in secular, therapeutic communities may never be able to really leave. It is of some interest that group affiliations originally intended for therapeutic purposes (for example, Scientology) or for drug rehabilitation (for example, Synanon) have assumed religious colorations (Ofshe, 1980; West & Singer, 1980). Although tax incentives are certainly instrumental in effecting this change, the trappings of religion may also strengthen the sense of in-group unity. They extend group ideology in such a way as to place the group in a cosmic perspective, which Berger and Luckmann (1966) considered essential to successful socialization. Sometimes, even converts themselves become aware of the secondary role played by specific religious doctrines and the primary role played by newfound group affiliations in their own conversions. S.V. Levine and Salter (1976) reported that when asked about the benefits of cult membership, devotees from a wide variety of cults all mentioned a sense of group belonging. Closeness to God and ideological issues were mentioned only secondarily, and not at all by a third of Levine and Salter's subjects.

Individuals who are discriminated against by society at large, and consequently are denied access to culturally approved in-groups, might benefit particularly by the sense of belonging that comes with sect involvement. Kiev (1964), Griffith et al. (1980), and Smith (1981), among many others, have noted the importance of church group solidarity to the mental health of minority persons living in a hostile or indifferent larger society. Kumasaka (1966) made a similar point with respect to the Soka Gakkai, a Japanese religio-political organization with chapters in the United States. Sociocultural upheavals that produce large numbers of culturally displaced persons have long been known to lead to religious revivals (see Durkheim, 1912).

The importance of the group to conversion phenomena suggests that continued group interactions will be necessary to maintain and strengthen faith. For this reason, contemporary cults almost uniformly encourage communal living (Galanter, 1982). Lofland and Stark (1965) considered residential interactions among cult members essential to the consolidation of newly acquired religious beliefs. According to Lofland and Stark, living together with others of the faithful turns merely intellectual acceptors into totally committed cult members. In the 1960s, before they had perfected their recruitment methods, Unification Church proselytizers were in the practice of giving new converts work assignments that would result in their isolation from other church members (Long & Hadden, 1983). Once isolated, a large proportion of these converts quickly reverted to their old beliefs. The lesson was not lost on church recruiters. Galanter et al. (1979) found that the 237 Unification Church members they studied spent 94 percent of their nights in commmunal living arrangements.

Historically, the importance of residential isolation to growing or minority religious movements is easily documented. As I noted earlier, Mohammed went to Medina in 622 A.D. Medina, a small town north of Mecca, proved the ideal environment in which early Islam could flourish. Certain nineteenth-century sects, such as the Amish and the Hutterites, have survived in large part because they have their own settlements. Some American sects achieved such strict endogamy that they now differ genetically from surrounding populations (see Reynolds & Tanner, 1983). Joseph Smith and

Brigham Young led the early Mormons to one of the most isolated areas in the country. Protected from the incredulous surrounding culture, in Utah the new sect found the breathing room to become a stable religion. More recently, Jim Jones moved his People's Temple from San Francisco to Guyana. As noted in the Appendix, the move was made for reasons that were likely psychotic. However, the residential isolation Jones thereby achieved gave him greater control over his followers' beliefs, so that most of them took cyanide without coercion. Before his deportation, Bhagwan Shree Rajneesh established a city in Oregon. He lived there in luxury, surrounded by hard-working followers (see Gordon, 1987). It seems unlikely that the Bhagwan's enterprise could have worked had it not been isolated.

In spite of social group pressure, reinforced by isolation, a certain proportion of converts ultimately break free of their respective religious cults. As predicted from the importance of group dynamics, these are individuals who, for various reasons, feel less integrated in the social-religious group. Ungerleider and Wellisch (1979), for example, found that subjects who had voluntarily departed from religious cults differed from current cult members and from successfully or unsuccessfully "deprogrammed" members in that they saw themselves as less emotionally affiliated while they were actively in the cult. Ungerleider and Wellisch also reported that forcible deprogramming was likely to be successful only with members who had joined their cults less than one year previously. Presumably, individuals who had been in their cults for longer periods of time were too thoroughly integrated into the cult group to keep them from returning later. Similar phenomena are noted in mainstream religions: A.M. Wallace (1985) observed that Catholic priests with poor community lives are prone to break their sexual vows. After Vatican II, when Roman Catholic orders became less socially isolated, they began to have trouble maintaining their numbers (see Ebaugh, 1977).

Religious cult members who do leave their cults suffer emotional symptoms. Significantly, one prominent symptom is paranoia, which may generally be secondary to dysfunction of group-related social strategies (Wenegrat, 1984). Ungerleider and Wellisch (1979) and Galanter (1983) both mentioned paranoia as a common sequel to abrupt cult departures. Halperin (1983b) described a paranoid patient who had recently left a religious cult. Predictably, the emotional distress of recently separated cult members is most effectively treated with group therapy, in which several cult members who have shared the same experiences can discuss what they have in common (Galanter, 1982).

The affiliative needs met by cults may be important to mainstream religion, too. For example, attitudinal studies during the civil rights movement uncovered something surprising: Although churches taught brotherly love, religiously active sample populations evinced greater prejudice than equivalent samples of nonreligious subjects (Allport, 1954; Allport, 1966; Allport & Ross, 1967; L.B. Brown, 1962; Martin & Nichols, 1962). Allport and his co-workers (Allport, 1966; Allport & Ross, 1967) found that mainstream religious samples were actually bimodal with respect to degree of tolerance. Some religious subjects were less ethnically and racially prejudiced than the average nonreligious. Allport called these subjects, who seemed really to believe in the doctrine of brotherly love, "intrinsically" religious. Other religious subjects, whom Allport called "extrinsically" religious, were far more prejudiced than the average nonreligious. In large samples of religiously active subjects, extrinsically religious subjects usually outweighed the intrinsically religious, making the religious population appear to be generally bigoted. Allport's distinction, which is the major discovery of modern religious psychology, has been extensively validated (see Spilka et al., 1985). Allen and Spilka (1967) defined another dichotomy—"committed" versus "consensual" faith—which for all practical purposes is identical to Allport's. Committed faith is intrinsic faith; consensual faith is extrinsic.

Most significantly, intrinsically and extrinsically religious individuals turned out to differ on many measures besides prejudice. As Allen and Spilka implied by using the term *consensual,* ethnically and racially prejudiced extrinsically religious persons—a substantial proportion of mainstream congregations—appear to be seeking an in-group experience. In terms of the model developed in chapter 2, the motivations and fears of extrinsically religious persons relate to group mutualism: They are generally conformists, and they are highly attuned to rules (Hunt & King, 1971). They are sensitive to social rank and envy persons above them on the social ladder (Pargament et al., 1979; Spilka, 1977). They are chauvinistic and ethnocentric, and their religion is often exclusionary. Intrinsic religion, by contrast, stresses universalism and respect for other faiths. Extrinsically religious persons tend toward authoritarianism. In religious or nonreligious persons, authoritarian traits (Adorno et al., 1950) may manifest group-related strategies (Wenegrat, 1984).

Significantly, Shaver et al. (1980) found that female respondents to a questionnaire were especially likely to respond in a manner consistent with extrinsic faith if they had changed their religion from that in which they were raised. For example, converts were especially likely to doubt that people from other faiths had a chance of salvation. They were also more likely to proselytize for their group, to believe that everyone should belong to the same faith, and to feel that leaders deserve blind obedience. Most of the converts had joined a Protestant church. Obviously, group-related social strategies may be major factors behind religious conversion, whether to cults or to mainstream faiths.

Extrinsically religious persons generally have fewer religious or mystical visions, spontaneous or induced, than their intrinsically religious counterparts (Hood, 1972, 1973; Hood & Morris, 1981). Apart from its group function, religious faith per se may not really interest them as it appears to interest intrinsically religious persons.

Finally, although I have described how religious activity may promote group affiliation, in a few cases it can serve the opposite function. Some individuals—many of them no doubt mentally ill—find in religion an excuse for withdrawal from human company and from the pressures of the human group. This is the theme of anchoritic monasticism. Anchorites are rare in the modern world, of course, though many would-be anchorites are found in modern mental hospitals. Also, some religions go out of their way, or so it seems, to prevent worship from being used for group-related or, in Allport's term, extrinsic purposes. One Hindu rite, for example, assigns to every young worshipper a private name for God. A teacher chooses this name to reflect the young person's character. It is kept secret and is used only in private prayers. As Allport (1950) pointed out, we find here "an institutional religion recognizing the . . . individuality of the religious sentiment."

Altruism

Reciprocity with God

Many religions favor altruistic behavior. Particularly in the West, many humane practices essential to modern life were first organized as a consequence of religious faith. For example, I currently work in a large public hospital. Such hospitals are descendants of the fifth-century *hospitium,* a home for the poor established by Roman Catholic bishops in accordance with canon law (Bokenkotter, 1979), which required that a certain proportion of the revenue of each diocese be spent on relief for those in need. Nearly 900 years later, at the height of the Black Death, the mission of the hospitium changed to that of the hospital. It is of some interest that the original mission of the hospitium, provision of food and lodging to the needy, is still in large part dependent on the activities of religious groups (see later discussion). The reader undoubtedly knows of many other good works done in the name of faith.

Many studies have been performed to determine whether believers are really more altruistic when called upon individually. In general, these studies support the commonsense view that religious people will try to be helpful, but the issue is very complex. First, altruistic tendencies are difficult to measure. Although some studies have used paper-and-pencil tests, there is little evidence that written responses correlate with actual behavior. Subjects who are given these tests may merely be giving socially appropriate answers to hypothetical questions. Batson and his colleagues (Batson, 1976; Batson & Gray, 1981; Darley & Batson, 1973) have pioneered the use of experimental setups to measure real behavior. In one famous experiment, for instance, seminary students were observed to see whether they would aid an individual lying in a doorway in apparent distress (Darley & Batson, 1973).

A second problem is that readiness to help may differ from situation to situation. Readiness to help in each situation may depend on different factors, personal or religious (see Nelson & Dynes, 1976). Finally, readiness to help may reflect religious style. In particular, extrinsically religious subjects may be less altruistic than their intrinsically religious counterparts (see Batson & Gray, 1981; Benson et al., 1980). Insofar as their religion serves group-related needs, their altruism might depend on whether they perceive the beneficiary to be an in-group member.

Egocentric acts are obviously inconsistent with altruistic tendencies. Therefore, insofar as crimes are egocentric and antisocial, the crime rate could provide still another measure of individual altruism. There is no doubt that religion per se fails to prevent criminality (see Spilka et al., 1985). But the studies in this area are methodologically flawed and use simplistic measures of crime and religious faith. In the matter of conscience, too, extrinsically and intrinsically religious persons seem to be different populations (Weibe & Fleck, 1980).

The religiously inspired altruist believes, in effect, that he has a reciprocal altruistic relationship with God, and that what God wants from him is for him to aid other people. Readers will not be surprised to hear that believers imagine themselves to be in reciprocal altruistic relationships with God. The idea that the creator God is a reciprocal altruist—that is, that God wants "assistance" from people and is willing to help them to the extent that they provide it—is a major theme in monotheistic religions. The Book of Job, for instance, accounts for personal tragedies that are seemingly incompatible with divine adherence to reciprocal altruism. Christians, especially, viewed God as adhering to reciprocal altruism, at least until Martin Luther. The New Testament, for instance, promises that faith and purity will be rewarded in heaven, if not on earth. As for Luther, the reader will recall that his father punished his children but failed to reward reliably their efforts to please him. Luther's God, accordingly, could punish those who displeased him but would not necessarily save those who did good works.

But why do believers think that God wants assistance in caring for other people? Why do they think that this is the aid that God wants them to give him? The answer probably lies in God's role as an attachment figure.

Human parents, as Trivers (1974) pointed out, are involved in a conflict with their children over the level of selflessness the children direct toward their siblings. Basically, inclusive fitness considerations predict that parents—following their own kin-directed altruist strategies—will encourage more intersibling altruism than children are ready to give and that parents will discourage intersibling egocentrism that the children might otherwise indulge in. Differences in child and parental preferences will result in ubiquitous pressures on the child and will affect every aspect of the parent–child relationship. Concerning altruism, for example, kinship considerations predict that a child will be altruistic toward a full sibling when the sibling's probable benefits are at least twice as great—measured in terms of future reproductive success—as the child's probable costs. Full siblings share half their genes by direct descent. Consequently, the child kin-directed altruist must depreciate benefits received by the sibling by a factor of one-half before comparing them to the costs he or she will bear. The parent, on the other hand, has a different viewpoint. When his or her offspring are involved, the parent shares an equal proportion of genes with both the potential altruist and the beneficiary. Therefore, the parent should prefer to see altruistic acts occur between his or her children whenever the probable benefits exceed the probable costs, not just when they are twice the probable costs. The parent, unlike the child, does not depreciate potential benefits. With regard to egocentric acts, a child might act so as to harm a sibling whenever the benefits he or she anticipates exceed half the harm imposed on the sibling. The harm done, in other words, is depreciated according to the sibling's degree of genetic relationship. The parent, sharing an equal proportion of genes with the child and the sibling, should not wish to see the child harm the sibling unless the benefits of doing so exceed the harm done.

Insofar as God plays the role of supreme attachment figure—and, consequently, universal parent—worshippers should attribute to God a desire for human altruism. In this, they are modeling God on the basis of real caretakers, whose kin-directed altruistic preferences exert a continuous influence on the child's moral upbringing. In numerous religious texts, unrelated persons, being all children of God, are described as brothers and sisters. As such, they are held responsible for each other, as in the story of Cain and Abel.

As I will illustrate later, the dual perception of God as reciprocal altruist and universal parent directs beneficent acts beyond the interpersonal limits predicted by the two sociobiologic theories, kin-directed and reciprocal altruism. This is the moral advance in the monotheistic religions, and it is the only way—the reader will no doubt note—in which religious beliefs produce large-scale deviations from behaviors predicted by sociobiologic models (see, also, Bellah, 1964).

Several authors (for example, Batson, 1983; Campbell, 1979; Lopreato, 1984) have noted that religious beliefs extend altruism beyond the narrow confines predicted by sociobiologic theories. Campbell (1979) and Lopreato (1984) attempted to explain this effect by reference to needs of the social group. Batson's (1983) account is closer to mine. According to Batson, by using kinship language that encourages "brotherly love," religions extend the range of kin-directed altruism. By contrast, the model outlined here suggests that the effect of religion develops from reciprocal altruism with the deity, rather than from kin-directed feelings, however extended. Of course, something called brotherly love might develop as a result of mutualistic feelings encouraged by religion, but this differs both conceptually and qualitatively from true kinship feeling. Although members of hunter-gatherer tribes—which are probably like the small groups in which humans evolved—are so highly related that in-group camaraderie and kin-directed altruistic feelings necessarily overlap (Chagnon, 1979a), even in these societies a distinction is apparent between kin and comrade.

Here is an example to show how religion extends altruistic behavior beyond the limits predicted by sociobiologic theories: At the beginning of this section, reference was made to provision of food and shelter to needy persons. In recent years, increasing numbers of homeless people have appeared in American cities (Bassuk, 1984; Koegel et al., 1988). There is general agreement that governmental responses to homelessness have been inadequate, so that many of the homeless go without food or shelter on a more or less regular basis. Religious groups have tried to provide for those not otherwise cared for. By late 1983, for example, there were sixty religiously sponsored shelters operating in New York City alone (Bassuk, 1984). This compared with only sixteen public shelters available at that time. Shelter beds require a considerable outlay; janitorial services, laundry, food, supervision, and sometimes guards are required to provide bed and board to the homeless, many of whom are disabled or severely mentally ill (Koegel et al., 1988). So the part played by religious groups is especially striking. How can we account for this?

First, sociobiologic models of altruism and mutualism, together with particular facts of social life in modern America, predict that provision of aid to the homeless would be tenuous at best. One basis of altruism, for example, is perceived kinship. Undoubtedly, many persons who would otherwise be homeless are currently cared for by concerned and loving kin. This is not always possible, though. For example, one chronic mental patient described by Bassuk (1984) had been cared for by his mother following his release from a state hospital. When she herself developed severe depression, he took to the streets. He was obviously psychotic by the time Bassuk encountered him. In another case described by Bassuk, one parent was dead and the other was in a nursing home. In our society, furthermore, easily available transportation, together with mores that encourage mobility, frequently results in separations between mentally ill or disabled persons and kin who are willing to help them. Kin may not know that the disabled person is homeless, and the mentally ill person may be too confused to seek out family members.

Another basis of altruism is reciprocal ties. However, the homeless are generally neither known to those who can help them nor conceivably able to reciprocate any favors done for them. In seeming rather unsavory, in fact, the homeless may exude—with culturally specific signals—the very unreliability that is likely to discourage continued reciprocal altruism.

A third basis for generous acts is a perceived mutualistic relationship. Insofar as the more fortunate saw themselves as "in it together" with the homeless, they might be more willing to extend them aid. In other words, the fact that some are homeless might be seen as a common problem to be solved by society at large, with every person shouldering his or her share of the burden. However, the innately probable strategies that govern the formation of cooperative groups most likely depend on processes evolved so as to be active only on a small scale. Throughout the Pleistocene epoch, for example, protohominid groups probably consisted of no more than fifty individuals (Mellen, 1981). Hunter-gatherer tribes still fission when their size begins to preclude personal relationships among all members (see Chagnon, 1979a).

Cognitive factors can work to expand the scope of these evolved processes. Systematic education, together with symbols of common interest, can expand group feeling even to the level of the modern state. Someday, it is hoped, education and symbols will expand this feeling to include the whole of humanity. In America today, however, the feeling frequently stops at the next-door neighbor's fence. Because of the emphasis on individualism, and an economic system in which the highest values are placed on individual interests, cooperative group feelings are highly attenuated (see Bellah et al., 1985). They are easily mobilized only in the face of external, or out-group, threats, which seem to have retained their emotional power. Since so many of the homeless are also deviant, affluent Americans are even less likely to see themselves as having anything in common with them or to experience their plight as a personal problem.

A final basis for aiding the homeless is simple egocentrism. This is the very opposite of altruism, even though it might result, at least momentarily, in beneficent acts. The Chamber of Commerce, for example, might consider it bad for business to have transients sleeping on subway grates. Beggars on the sidewalks change the urban environment in ways detrimental to those who work and live there.

Because kin are frequently absent and little prospect exists for reciprocity, and because American culture produces only weak mutual feelings, the sociobiologic model predicts that efforts to help the homeless would be desultory at best and tinged with egocentric, rather than humane, motives. Although certain persons who have helped the homeless are apparently motivated by unusually strong mutualistic or altruistic feelings, most individuals who have made a greater effort than the sociobiologic model predicts have been motivated by their religious beliefs. They are individuals, as noted earlier, who believe that they are involved in a reciprocal altruistic relationship with a deity they perceive as a universal parent, who has asked them to be their brother's keeper.

In practice, unusual mutualistic or altruistic motives, on the one hand, and religious motives, on the other, may be hard to distinguish quickly. Persons who are driven by each of these motives may express their intentions in very similar terms. An obviously reciprocal relationship with a parental deity indicates a religious motivation, but, as discussed in the following chapter, individuals frequently disavow their own religious beliefs. Those who disavow their religious beliefs may nonetheless act on them but give other—perhaps mutualistic—reasons for their behavior. In each case, details of personal history and fantasy life might elucidate the role played by conscious or subconscious religious beliefs. The study of unusually helpful persons could possibly yield socially useful results.

Unfortunately, all this is only half the story. Some religions are indifferent to altruism or militate against it (see V. Reynolds & Tanner, 1983). In Buddhism, for instance, salvation and social interests are wholly disconnected. Accordingly, Buddhism makes no provision for any form of social work. Hindus once believed that victims of illness or deformity had been guilty of crimes in their previous lives. Thus, lepers were thought to have stolen clothes; the blind were thought to have stolen lamps; the dumb were thought to have stolen the words of the Veda. Such victims were "despised by the virtuous" and forbidden from temple sacrifice. Hindu beliefs with regard to these victims were totally incompatible with altruistic behavior. The Christian Aladuras, along with some other modern African sects, also consider illness a punishment for sin. They eschew even palliative measures, in the belief that efforts to relieve suffering interfere with God's judgment. Likewise, ancient Jews believed that leprosy resulted from commission of various sins. Segregation of lepers was as much a moral act as a hygienic practice.

Nor does a reciprocal altruistic relationship with a parental deity guarantee socially desirable behavior. Religious believers have again and again proved ingenious in finding reasons not to be generous, even when their own beliefs naively seem to demand it. Believers find it all too easy to selectively exclude people from the divine parent's family. The American slaveholder, for example, was far from eager to convert his African slaves, thereby making them "brothers in Christ" (B.Z. Goldberg, 1958). The Kingdom of God, apparently, had to wait on the convenience of agricultural labor. In some areas, Negro churches were specifically outlawed. It was only after ingenious theologians had justified holding other Christians in bondage that efforts to convert the black man met with less resistance. Even then, these efforts were sponsored by Christian groups—such as the Baptists—that generally held no slaves. According to some historians (see Lippman, 1982), the early Islamic caliphs—who, like Christians, were devoted to spreading the word of God—had once faced a similar problem. Conquered peoples were allowed to keep their religion, but only if they paid heavier taxes. When too many became Muslims, the caliphs had to discourage further conversions just to preserve their tax base.

The reciprocal altruistic relationship with God has another effect, too, which should be mentioned for the sake of completeness. Insofar as believers expect divine rewards for compliance with divine laws, it profits the ruling class in any society, or those with the power of selective cultural retention (see chapter 2), to promote religions whose divine laws encourage social docility. Such selection may be hypocritical or it may be quite sincere, since ethical dispositions often adhere closely to perceived self-interest. But quite aside from their own beliefs, ruling classes have generally known that religion can promote lower-class tranquility. According to Gibbon, for example:

> The various modes of worship which prevailed in the ancient world were all considered by the people as equally true; by the philosophers as equally false; and by the magistrates as equally useful. (Harrington, 1983, pg. 26)

Or according to Napoleon, on the "mystery of religion":

> This mystery is not that of the Incarnation. . . . I see in religion the whole mystery of society. I hold . . . that apart from the precepts and doctrines of the Gospel there is no society that can flourish, nor any real civilization. What is it that makes the poor man take it for granted that ten chimneys smoke in my palace while he dies of cold—that I have ten changes of raiment in my wardrobe while he is naked—that on my table at any meal there is enough to sustain a family for a week? It is religion which says to him that in another life I shall be his equal, indeed that he has a better chance of being happy than I. (Harrington, 1983, pg. 25)

The most famous formulation of this principle, of course, is Marx's treatment of religion as the "opium of the people" (Mc-Lellan, 1973). Modern readers, raised on news accounts of Martin Luther King and "liberation theology," may doubt the validity of the Marxist, or even the present, formula. Obviously, this topic is too vast to treat fully here (see, for example, Harrington, 1983), but it would be a great mistake to underestimate the pervasive conservative social role of supposedly divine laws just because these same laws are occasionally invoked to topple the social order. In their famous treatise, Berger and Luckmann (1966) argued that majority religious views necessarily support the status quo; and Johnson (1963) defined the difference between churches and sects according to the degree to which they support the social order. Religious support seems most salient when the social order is least egalitarian. The most extraordinary inequalities have historically leaned on religious crutches, to keep the lower classes from overthrowing their masters. The Hindu caste system, for example, leans on the notion of *dharma,* or duty. The highest achievement in any caste is performance of social duty.

In the West, Saint Paul considered social evils—including slavery, war, and poverty—the result of individual sin. Rather than worry about these evils, the Christian was advised to seek his own salvation. In the feudal age, a concept of divinely ordained duty—similar to that of Hinduism—was added to the Pauline formula and used to prop up the social order. The social condition was ordained by God. The challenge to each person was to perform the role in life to which he or she had been born.

In more egalitarian modern societies, religious support is less salient, but it contributes nonetheless to the status quo. In the United States, observers long ago noticed that religious groups that formed in response to hardship evinced little interest in changing social conditions (see, for example, Boisen, 1939). Millenial sects in particular, by deflecting the poor from political action, have more than once served the interest of the upper class. Stark (1964) found that English churchgoers were more likely to favor the social status quo than nonattenders were, even when social class was controlled. Radicals, on the other hand, expressed religious disinterest. The situation is no doubt much the same in the United States today.

4
The Origin of Religious Belief

Theoretical Considerations

In the preceding chapter, I categorized psychological functions served by religious beliefs according to innately probable social strategies. The conceptual importance of these strategies follows from the model of human social behavior outlined in chapter 2. But as Freud and Jung apparently realized (see later discussion), religion is not "explained" by showing how it is used. A theory of religion must account for its origin as well as for its uses. In this chapter, I discuss the psychological mechanisms that produce religious beliefs. I will argue that the psychological mechanisms that produce religious beliefs are the cognitive processes people need to adhere to innately probable strategies. These psychological processes ground religious beliefs in the presumed evolutionary history of human mental life.

To begin with, the model described in chapter 2 is a model of social behavior. The strategies discussed there are all social strategies. Modern-day humans, according to chapter 2, have innate mental attributes that predispose them to adhere to these social strategies. Therefore, previous social exigencies must have exerted selective pressures sufficient to mold mental attributes.

In particular, selective pressures from the social arena were probably major factors driving evolution of intellectual functions. Darwin and Spencer expressed this view in the nineteenth century (Richards, 1987). Chance (1962) argued that human intellectual abilities evolved because of advantages they conferred in dealing with people rather than because of advantages they conferred in dealing with nature. According to Chance, superior intellectual abilities produced more complex social environments, which exerted selective pressures in favor of greater intelligence. No such feedback loop could form with natural forces. Humphrey (1976) made a similar point. He noted, too, that technologies acquired very early in hominid evolution further reduced the advantages conferred by creative intelligence outside the social arena.

In recent years, cognitive psychologists have begun to stress the importance of understanding the social functions of intellectual processes, which led to their evolution, in order to avoid misleading conclusions about human mental capacities (see, for example, Cole et al., 1982; Cooper, 1987; Cosmides & Tooby, 1987; Neisser, 1982; Wyer & Srull, 1984, 1986). Most recently, Cosmides and Tooby (Cosmides, 1989; Cosmides & Tooby, 1989; Tooby & Cosmides, 1989) have shown how apparent logical errors elicited by certain tasks may be accounted for by the social origin of intellectual processes.

Which specific social problems might have exerted selective pressure on human mental capacities? One set of problems involves reciprocal altruism. Trivers (1971) argued that cognitive demands created by reciprocal altruism strategies may have contributed to the extraordinary increase in human cerebral volume that occurred during the Pleistocene epoch. The advantages of successful reciprocal altruism are enormous, as indicated by Axelrod's (1984) recent theoretical work, and there is some evidence that the specific cognitive capacities required to pursue such strategies are lacking in nonhuman primates (Kummer, 1978).

Another set of problems results from sexual competition, especially between males. Studies of primitive tribes leave little doubt as to the selective efficacy of within-sex competition (Chagnon, 1979a, 1979b; Symons, 1979). Success depends more on cognitive skills than on merely physical attributes. Charismatic, articulate men with above-normal intelligence attain positions of power in primitive societies and take more than their share of available mates. They control less intelligent men through a network of social restraints.

Yet a third set of problems results from in-group strategies. The ability to absorb complex consensual world models, particularly when they were linguistically encoded, and to play flexibly coordinated roles in group activities undoubtedly required intellectual abilities that were lacking in protohominids (see Konner, 1982). Finally, keeping track of complex kin relationships and caring for immature young through longer and longer dependent stages—requisite for kin-directed altruistic and attachment strategies, respectively—likely created burdens more cognitive than physical (see Konner, 1982).

Insofar as mental processes have been shaped to produce skilled adherence to social strategies, rather than to deal with less specific exigencies arising from natural events, the human mind is better conceptualized as a dedicated than as a general-purpose computer. That is, the human mind, is akin to an electronic chess player (see Humphrey, 1976; see, also, Cosmides & Tooby, 1987), but the games it is made to play are the innately probable social strategies outlined in chapter 2. To say that computer hardware is dedicated to a specific purpose is not to say that it cannot be programmed to perform other tasks. It simply means that its design is such as to run certain programs with maximal efficiency or to be maximally efficient with a given type of program. Other programs may be run, but only with inefficient modifications or at a suboptimal speed. General-purpose computers, by contrast, are made to run several different types of program with more or less equal efficiency. Their design reflects a compromise between the requirements for efficient operation with several different types of programs. Their efficiency with any given program may be less than that achievable with dedicated devices, but their flexibility compensates for their lack of optimal functioning. Therefore, to say that human mental processes are dedicated to social strategies, rather than general-purpose, is to say that social analyses—needed to support those strategies—are what the mind does best. These same processes may be used to perform other analyses, but perhaps not with the same ease.

What analyses are required for social strategic functioning? What types of problems do human minds—insofar as they are socially dedicated computers—approach with the greatest ease? Some of these analyses follow from specific problems cited earlier. With an eye on their cultural norms, humans must be able to categorize others as reliable or not according to their past actions, to judge power and dominance relations, to perceive degrees of similarity and foreignness, to learn new models from those in positions of group authority, and to trace kinship relations. Other analyses are more general and are required for several strategic problems. For example, individuals must see their own actions from the viewpoints of others and calculate the responses these others may make to them. They must identify actors responsible for complex events, perceive hidden intentions, and creatively compromise when interests are in conflict.

When applied to nonsocial events, the more general social analyses lead to religious beliefs. In particular, the tendency to surmise actors and intentions from complex events will lead to religious beliefs when the events in question are outside the social realm. Because such surmises come naturally to humans, an attempt to apprehend the natural world with the human mind will inevitably lead to religious beliefs. For example, social events are instigated; when social analyses are applied to natural events, the result is inevitably belief in a hidden instigator. Social events have social meaning; when social analyses are applied to natural events, the result is inevitably assignment of social meaning. Social events can be influenced; when social analyses are applied to natural events, the result is inevitably an attempt at social influence.

Actually, the propensity to assimilate nonsocial problems to readily invoked social-analytical schemata can be observed most easily outside the formal religious sphere, in the realm, for example, of idiosyncratic superstitions. From the present point of view, some of these superstitions are spontaneous, unsystematized, ephemeral, and sometimes disguised religions. Since they lack cultural validation, idiosyncratic superstitions can be taken as products of individual thinking. In fact, such superstitions resist education and, therefore, the influence of cultural authority, as if they were particularly easy to acquire and difficult to give up. Gamblers, for example, often seem to believe that their luck has to change: If they have been winning, they expect to start losing. If they have been losing, they expect to start winning. This has been called the "Monte Carlo fallacy," because it manifests a fallacy about probability theory, which holds that random trials should be independent. But close study of gamblers' behavior and fantasies usually reveals more than a fallacy about probability theory. To forestall losing, winning gamblers often make magical gestures, pleas, or oaths addressed to unseen agents. They think that they have done something right, or that an agent has been good to them, and they take steps to ensure the agent's continued favor. Losers, on the other hand, make new magical gestures, pleas, or oaths in order to change their luck. They believe that they have done something wrong, or that an agent has been depriving them, and they take steps to change that agent's mind. They may think that something is owed to them.

An extraterrestrial being who was able to read minds might be thoroughly confused by the thoughts of human gamblers. If he himself thought in nonsocial terms, he would probably get the impression that humans are insane. At the very least, he would think that something about gambling makes humans delusional, so that they begin negotiating with and appeasing agents who aren't really present. Nor would he fail to notice how widespread the disorder is: Gambling is one of the world's major commercial activities (see Lopreato, 1984), and superstitious behaviors are thoroughly intermixed with it. Only if the observer came from a species, like humans, whose cognitive evolution had occurred in response to social pressures, might he understand what was going on. If we ever encounter aliens, their ability to sympathize with our social thought patterns will no doubt determine the impression we make, at least at church and while gambling!

All of this, of course, is not to say why gamblers gamble or to comment on the causes of compulsive betting behavior. Very simple behaviorist notions might account for that very nicely. Games of chance create random reinforcement schedules, which can lead to expectations that are difficult to break. Real or perceived rewards at some critical juncture might therefore be followed by persistent maladaptive behaviors. However, though reinforcement schedules might account for why people gamble, knowing intellectually that they will probably lose, they do not account for what Humphrey (1976) felicitously termed the "transactional" quality of the accompanying fantasies and behaviors. The transactional quality is the result of ad hoc religious beliefs, as I have defined them here, which are generated when social-cognitive schemata are applied to interpreting indifferent natural events.

Other sources of inchoate religious beliefs are found in the thought and play of children. These often reveal quite strikingly the socialization of nature that results from human cognitive biases. Perhaps this is because children are freer to express what is on their minds or have not yet learned the consensual religious beliefs, with their limits and boundaries, to which normal adults adhere. To take just one example: A two-year-old boy was lying in bed while his mother read him stories. Without warning, the house was shaken by a sustained moderate earthquake. The windows rattled loudly, and the wooden house frame creaked and groaned. Quickly, his mother scooped the boy up and ran to the nearest doorway, where they would be safe from falling debris. She told him that there was an earthquake. As soon as the shaking stopped, he said that the earthquake had gone. It was not immediately obvious that he had personified the earthquake, but later that day, he described the earthquake as a being who had come and shaken the windows. His mother explained that the ground had moved. He told his father that the earthquake had come and shaken the windows and then had gone down beneath the ground. His father replied that the earthquake was not a person but a shaking of the ground. Over the next several weeks, the boy described what the earthquake looked like and decided that it lived beneath the ground. At various times, he seemed to think that he had scared off the earthquake, or that his mother had, or that the earthquake had simply gone away because the windows were closed. Many months later, he still occasionally played at scaring away the earthquake, which he said was very big and lived beneath the ground. He ran toward the window in the room where he had been when the earthquake occurred and shouted "Go away, earthquake! Don't come here anymore!"

There are several noteworthy aspects to this simple sequence of events. Clinical psychologists, for example, might note this child's compulsive repetition and his projection of his own fear, both of which indicate the alarm he experienced and his attempts to neutralize it. The most salient feature of all, however, is the rapid and fixed personification of the anxiety-provoking event. In spite of his parents' attempts to educate him, the child evolved an elaborate notion of who had caused the shaking, what he looked like, where he lived, and what sort of rituals might keep him from coming again. As far as this child was concerned, events must be caused by willful agents. If the windows shook, someone must have been shaking them. If the ground shook, someone must have been shaking it. If someone was doing these things, then he must—like a human being—live somewhere and be capable of fright or discouragement. It must be possible to communicate with him and to persuade him not to return. Thus, in trying to understand what had happened, the boy invented a nature god and a rudimentary liturgy.

Natural events might be especially likely to evoke social explanations—even from adults—because they are frightening and unpredictable. Other events that evoke social thought patterns are also generally traumatic, and social perceptions generally reduce the uncertainty associated with them. Noyes (1980), for example, studied 138 persons who had come close to death. Most of the subjects had experienced falls, drownings, or motor vehicle accidents, but a minority had come close to death as a result of illness. Twenty-one percent of the subjects studied by Noyes believed that they had survived as the result of destiny, and five out of six of these believed that a supernatural agent had rescued them, usually for some specific purpose. It stands to reason, the reader should note, that if some deity rescued them, they didn't have to worry that it would happen again soon, particularly if they fulfilled the purpose for which they had been rescued. It is not clear from Noyes's report whether those who gave their experience a religious interpretation were religiously inclined before their brush with death, but several other studies have suggested changes in religious and spiritual orientations in similar situations (Greyson, 1983; Greyson & Stevenson, 1980; Sabom, 1980). As later sections will illustrate, the issue may be less real than apparent, since overt religiosity is only a partial guide to the scope of religious thought patterns.

The aforementioned two-year-old, like all children his age, also showed his tendency to personify in his nonanxious play. There, however, compulsive repetition and defensive projection were considerably less salient. He had several toy trucks, for example, to which he assigned essentially social roles. The small, or "baby," truck rode around his room looking for the larger, "mommy" truck. When the larger truck drove over, the "baby" truck rushed to greet it. Sometimes, an even larger truck played the part of "daddy." Likewise, smaller and larger toy trains were sometimes "baby" and "mommy" trains, or "baby" and "daddy" on occasion. Admittedly, this type of personification differs in its function from that following the earthquake. In play, inanimate objects are assigned social roles in order to vivify fantasies. In the case of the earthquake, a social agent was invoked in order to account for an otherwise incomprehensible real event. But despite their differing functions, both types of personification demonstrate the child's readiness—uninhibited by cultural norms concerning the boundaries of social phenomena—to apply social categories to nonhuman objects or nonhuman events.

Childhood personifications bring up the so-called transitional realm. According to Winnicott, whose theories are summarized in accessible form by M. Davis and Wallbridge (1981), the transitional realm is the broad area of psychological life that is neither wholly internal nor wholly external and objective. This is an area, neither completely private nor consensual, in which real objects assume idiosyncratic meanings. They become "transitional objects," which, though they exist in the consensual physical world, assume a personal meaning quite unrelated to the facts of their physical existence. Winnicott called such objects transitional because, he believed, they form a bridge from the autistic, internal life of the infant to the consensual, external life of the older child. The transitional realm and transitional objects have been thought highly relevant to religious beliefs (M. Davis & Wallbridge, 1981; Eigen, 1981; Joyce, 1985; Meissner, 1984; Rizzuto, 1979). Religious beliefs, in effect, are susceptible to analysis as superordinate transitional phenomena. In light of religious beliefs, the whole external world, in both its human and its natural aspects, assumes a meaning that is inner-derived. Actually, accounts of religious beliefs as transitional realm phenomena are closely related, if not identical, to the sociobiologic account given here.

Consider, for example, the earliest transitional objects. Typically, these are pacifiers, blankets, teddy bears, or other artifacts of civilized life with some morphologic or textural resemblance to the mother's body. The odor of well-used transitional objects is sometimes also important, so that children will reject the object once it has been cleaned. Children suck on, cling to, or simply cuddle these objects, particularly when they are tired, ill, or anxious. Children of a certain age will sometimes not leave home without their transitional objects, or, if they discover that the object has been left behind, they might become very upset. Bowlby (1969) suggested that physical resemblance allows certain attachment-related behaviors—such as nonnutritive sucking, clinging, or cuddling—to be directed toward the transitional object, rather than toward the mother. That is why play with transitional objects varies according to the same factors that elicit or inhibit attachment behaviors, and why cuddling, clinging, or sucking with transitional objects appears to relieve anxiety.

These early transitional objects, therefore, result from the imposition of social features on inanimate objects, leading to their psychosocial enlivenment. Perhaps because of the morphologic or textural resemblance, the young child acts toward the transitional object as he or she would act toward the mother. The object is seen as protective and nurturant, and the child wants to be near it. Insofar as later transitional objects resemble these early ones, they, too, might result when external objects are brought to life by internal social processes. If so, the transitional realm will be populated, so to speak, with dead objects conjured into social life by inner perceptual biases and corresponding preoccupations.

According to the theory developed here, religious beliefs result when natural events or the natural world as a whole are brought to life by being perceived in social terms. In this case, the objects of social perceptions are no longer isolated entities but comprise the whole of experience. Consequently, religious beliefs are aptly treated as potentially superordinate transitional phenomena, as several authors have noted (see M. Davis & Wallbridge, 1981; Eigen, 1981; Joyce, 1985; Meissner, 1984; Rizzuto, 1979), but this treatment is really the same as that proposed here on entirely different grounds. Sociobiologic concepts have the advantage, in comparison to Winnicott's, of being more naturalistic, less ambiguous, and less tainted with dualism, but when the two concepts are applied to the origin of religious beliefs, both may point down a similar path.

The account given here is also consistent with the recent emphasis on attribution theory among psychologists studying religion (see Spilka et al., 1985). According to attribution theorists, individuals actively try to account for each of their varied experiences and for events they observe. They are not merely passive observers. If an individual has an incomprehensible experience or witnesses an incomprehensible event in a setting that suggests a religious explanation, then it is more than likely that he or she will attribute it to religious causes. Most events in the world, and many private experiences, are in fact incomprehensible, so religious beliefs flourish wherever they gain a foothold. The sociobiologic model is consistent with this view, but it tries to show why religious beliefs are credible in the first place. That is, the model explains why social attributions—even in the absence of an observable being—appear so readily plausible that human beings might seize on them in seeking an explanation for events they can't comprehend.

Finally, the model developed here is consistent with viewpoints expressed by Feuerbach (1957), Bergson (1935), and Godelier (1977) on the essence of religious beliefs. These authors and others (see Morris, 1987) observed that in religion, human nature is projected onto the world. Volition and purpose are ascribed to events that lack subjectivity in the human sense.

Religion and Intellect

Humans think socially as naturally and spontaneously as they walk on two legs. Insofar as religious beliefs result from the application of social-analytical schemata to nonsocial problems, they manifest the most deeply ingrained and unselfconscious type of mental activity. Many people, of course, are satisfied with the fruit of social thought. In chapter 3, I showed how religious beliefs can meet certain needs not readily met in any other fashion. But there are also many people who simply lack the wherewithal to think in any but the most spontaneous ways about the nonhuman world. They are unable to attend to their failures or inconsistencies, think critically, or reflect on their own ideas sufficiently to discard intuitively appealing social ideas about the world in favor of functional thinking. Insofar as these individuals gravitate toward religion, the ranks of the religious might contain a disproportionate number of persons with poor education or intellect or with poorly developed skills needed for critical thinking.

Many empirical studies seem to confirm this prediction. For example, L.B. Brown (1966) studied 398 boys and 703 girls between the ages of twelve and seventeen. Brown's subjects came from the United States, New Zealand, and South Australia and included large numbers of both Roman Catholics and Protestants. Subjects were given a questionnaire concerning the appropriateness and efficacy of prayer for several purposes, both selfish and altruistic. Brown found a clear inverse relation between advancing age and belief in the efficacy of prayer, even when prayers were thought to be morally appropriate. There can be no question here that the effect of advancing age or education was an artefact of socioeconomic class, because both younger and older children came from the same backgrounds.

Elsewhere, L.B. Brown (1968) reported findings from a similar questionnaire administered to 267 adolescent schoolboys and to 57 adult males enrolled in church schools or seminaries. Another 40 adult male subjects were university students. Once again, Brown found a clear inverse relation between advancing age or education and belief in the efficacy of morally appropriate prayers. Not surprisingly, the seminary students continued to have more faith than their university counterparts. As in Brown's earlier study, the effect of advancing age or education cannot be attributed to socioeconomic factors.

D.G. Brown and Lowe (1951) administered an inventory of religious beliefs to 887 American university students enrolled in liberal arts courses. Data from 622 Protestant students were analyzed. A significant decline in religious belief was found in conjunction with advancing educational status. Freshman students tended to be more religious than sophomores, who in turn were more religious than juniors and seniors. When students who scored more than 1.4 standard deviations above the average on the belief inventory (believers) were compared with students who scored more than 1.4 standard deviations below the average (nonbelievers), the effect of advancing education became even more apparent. Eighty-one percent of the believers were freshmen and sophomores, in comparison to 54 percent of the nonbelievers. Studies of college students before World War II reported the same phenomenon (Dudycha, 1933; E.S. Jones, 1926; E. Nelson, 1940).

Studies of the personalities and thought patterns of religious believers have shown an association with decreased intelligence and academic achievement, on the one hand, and with increased hysterical traits, denial, repression, and unrealistic thinking, on the other. Actually, given the methods by which intelligence is usually measured, intelligence and academic achievement can hardly be meaningfully differentiated, so I will discuss them here together.

In L.B. Brown's (1968) study of boys and young men enrolled in church-affiliated schools, described earlier, the boys ranged in age from twelve to seventeen years. Brown defined two samples of thirteen- and fourteen-year-olds according to their levels of academic ability, as assessed by their schools. Although the more able boys frequently endorsed the nonspecific effects of prayer—for example, the effects of prayer on morale—significantly fewer evinced belief in the material efficacy of prayer, as compared to their less able counterparts. The youngest, low-ability group expressed greater confidence in the material efficacy of prayer than any other subject group. Since high- and low-ability subjects came from the same schools, socioeconomic status was unlikely to account for differences in their beliefs.

In the D.G. Brown and Lowe (1951) study described earlier, the researchers administered an academic achievement test to the "believers" and "nonbelievers" culled from their larger sample of college students. As the reader will recall, believers and nonbelievers were subjects whose degree of religious belief was 1.4 standard deviations above and below the sample average, respectively. Mean achievement scores for nonbelievers were approximately 20 percent higher than those of believers. An outside sample of Bible students scored at the same level as the believers. Eighty-seven percent of the nonbelievers were above the fiftieth percentile for college freshmen, in comparison with 57 percent of believers. Conversely, there were more than twice as many believers as nonbelievers below the fiftieth percentile. The reader will recall that believers tended to be freshmen, but Brown and Lowe demonstrated that the difference between believers and nonbelievers in academic achievement persisted even when college class was controlled for. Before World War II, Howells (1928, cited in D.G. Brown & Lowe, 1951) administered the Thorndike Intelligence Test to religious and nonreligious undergraduate students and noted the same phenomenon.

Particular forms of religious activity may be especially likely for those with lower intelligence. Kildahl (1965) administered an academic achievement test to forty first-year students at a "middle-of-the-road" denominational Christian seminary. All of these students considered themselves religious, but twenty of them had had sudden religious conversions and the other twenty had not. The two groups were matched for age, socioeconomic status, rural or urban upbringing, and family, military, and marital status. The seminary must have had good academic credentials, because achievement scores from both groups of students were above national norms for male college freshmen. Nevertheless, when students were compared to each other, scores obtained by the students with histories of sudden conversions were significantly lower than those of the students who lacked such experiences.

Along with the achievement test, Kildahl (1965) administered tests of personality style. Students with and without sudden conversion experiences did not differ in their perceptions of authority figures or in their levels of authoritarianism or depression. However, the students who had had sudden conversions did score significantly higher on the MMPI Hysteria scale. Elevated scores on the Hysteria scale suggest the use of repression and denial and the potential for manifesting hysterical personality traits.

D.G. Brown and Lowe (1951) also administered the MMPI to their groups of believers and nonbelievers. Nonbelieving males had significantly lower scores on the Hysteria scale than those of male Bible students, which were not significantly different from those obtained by believing male university students.

Pattison et al. (1973) studied forty-three fundamentalist Christians who reported faith-healing experiences. These subjects had modestly elevated scores on the MMPI Hysteria scale and were found to rely heavily on denial and repression. Their cognitive functioning was said to manifest a disregard for reality.

Deutsch and Miller (1983) administered a battery of personality tests to four female members of the Unification Church. These subjects were found to have sexual conflicts and mixed personality styles, with prominent hysterical and obsessional features. Extreme denial of problems and wishful thinking were evident in their responses to projective tests.

As described earlier, sudden conversion experiences most often indicate lesser degrees of academic achievement. They frequently might also indicate a lesser regard for reality than religious beliefs in general do. Allison (1968) studied twenty male divinity students. Ten of Allison's subjects reported intense religious experiences motivating them to enter the ministry and ten of them did not report such experiences. The subjects were administered Rorschach tests, and replies were scored for evidence of nonlogical, unrealistic elements in both form and content. Replies by the students who had had intense religious experiences were more unrealistic in form than replies by the students who had not had such experiences, although replies by the two groups did not differ with regard to psychologically "primitive" content. As examples of formally unrealistic replies, Allison cites "a crab with bat's wings" and "a lion egg"; the latter interpretation, for example, might be given to an egg-shaped, lion-colored inkblot. Allison noted that students who have had intense religious experiences are able to integrate formally incompatible elements to produce socially appropriate responses, which is hardly a sign of ill health. For our purposes, though, the important point is not whether the ability to disregard reality temporarily is a sign of health but merely that it seems to be associated with compelling religious experiences.

Like diminished intelligence, increased hysterical traits, tendencies toward denial and wishful thinking, and disregard for reality evident among many religious believers point toward the spontaneous nature of religious thinking. In a well-known monograph, Shapiro (1965) observed that hysterical personality styles and predispositions toward repression, denial, and wishful thinking reflect certain cognitive failures. The hysteric thinks, for example, in overly global, impressionistic terms. Therefore, he or she is most often swept away by the superficial, intuitive, or obvious solution. Satisfied with his or her hunches, the hysteric never really attends to particulars or checks the veracity of quickly reached conclusions. According to Shapiro, hysterics are incapable of sustained curiosity and are disinterested in sustained intellectual enquiries. Denial and wishful thinking are easily maintained when facts are so easily put aside. Difficult and highly cultivated alternatives to readily invoked social schemata would hardly hold much attraction for the person described by Shapiro.

Significantly, clinical studies of hysterical patients led to the first psychiatric critique of religion, by the nineteenth-century French neurologist Jean-Martin Charcot (see Drinka, 1984). Charcot directed La Salpetriere, the Paris asylum for women. There he observed so-called grand hysteria, a hysterical syndrome that Charcot considered a neurologic illness but is now thought to have been the result of subtle suggestion. Women with grand hysteria fell into trances, suffered apparent seizures, and even seemed to hallucinate given the proper stimulus. The stimulus was frequently pressure on body parts. During their fits, these patients sometimes assumed ecstatic religious postures resembling prayer or crucifixion. Coincident with their posturing, they reported religious visions. Charcot and his followers concluded from their observations that historical religious ecstasies, such as that of Saint Catherine of Siena, were manifestations of brain disease like those of their patients. Freud was a student of Charcot, and Charcot's attack on religion no doubt added impetus to Freud's own skepticism (see chapters 3 and 6).

In the Appendix, I present evidence that religious beliefs become more salient in the presence of mental illness, in which, however, they play no etiologic role. I also present evidence that religious beliefs affect psychological adaptation and relieve psychological distress. The pervasive effects of religion on psychological adaptation are easily understood in light of the strategic uses discussed in the preceding chapter. These uses also account, in part, for the salience of religious ideation among the mentally ill. It stands to reason, for example, that patients who are profoundly distressed by attachment or sexual competitive issues, or by egocentric impulses, would turn to the tactics offered by their culture in order to manage their conflict. Religious beliefs are among these tactics and may thus be elevated from the periphery of mental life to its center when mental illness develops. The model developed in this chapter suggests that the severely mentally ill may also be prone to religious thinking as a result of mental regression. Suffering as they do from impaired concentration, disorganized thinking, and disruptive affects, patients may be unable to maintain a critical attitude toward their own social hypotheses. They are prone to becoming swept away by their social-cognitive schemata.

Some Remarks on Disbelief

It may be worthwhile to recapitulate the model developed thus far: Because the bulk of selective pressures in human cognitive evolution occurred in the social arena, intellectual processes evolved so as to apply social-analytical schemata with the greatest possible ease. That is, the human mind is dedicated to carrying out complex social analyses. Religious beliefs result from application of social-analytical schemata to nonsocial events. They result, therefore, from doing what comes most easily. Studies concerning personality styles and intellectual achievements of religious believers are consistent with the notion that religious beliefs manifest the most spontaneous forms of mental activity. Specifically, individuals who are poorly equipped to question seemingly obvious ideas are found in excessive numbers among religious believers. Specific religious activities, including some conversion experiences, may especially indicate poor critical faculties.

Although specific social ideas may be criticized or rejected, social schemata themselves are probably irrepressible. Even persons who are capable of doubting their own ideas may first think in social terms when they are faced with a nonsocial problem. The durability of social thought is due, of course, to the ease with which it occurs, but also to its utility for everyday life. Even persons who are most concerned with events outside the social realm live in a human world that taxes their social skills. It seems most unlikely that readily invoked and constantly exercised analytical schemata that are appropriate to the social realm could ever be kept entirely out of nonsocial problem solving.

This is in contrast to the position taken by some anthropologists: that social interpretations of natural events typify the thinking only of primitive peoples (see, for example, Douglas, 1975;

Godelier, 1977; Levy-Bruhl, 1926). In fact, not only do moderns interpret natural events in social terms, but primitives think in other terms, just as moderns do. They merely lack the data base to apply functional thinking to more of their everyday life (cf. Malinowski, 1974).

Actually, social interpretations of natural events are analogous to what Freud called *primary process thinking*. According to Freud, primary process thinking occurs in very young children. It is illogical, depends on symbols and imagery, and lacks certain indicators, such as indicators of time and negation. Primary process thinking is obscured in later life by less spontaneous modes of thinking, which effectively censor it, at least in the waking state (see Fenichel, 1945). But primary process thinking is never completely abandoned. Creative acts in particular may betray the primary process thought stream flowing beneath the surface of apparent adult rationality (see Kris, 1952).

Social and functional ideas concerning nonsocial events are frequently interwoven to produce a composite product (cf. Evans-Pritchard, 1937, on Azande beliefs about witchcraft). For example, V. Reynolds and Tanner (1983) described an African man who worked in a modern hospital. He attributed his dysentery to contaminated water, but he felt that a magic spell must have caused him to drink it! Along the same lines, many people today profess to believe in a God who established natural laws that now determine events in a purely functional manner. Others mix alternative modes of thought by thinking of God as a symbol, not an actual being. Intellectually atheist, they pray to an allegorical God and get some comfort from him. They avoid asking themselves why they are praying at all. As the reader might recall, Fromm (1950) went so far as to advocate allegorical gods. He distinguished between authoritarian religions, which treat God as a real being, and humanistic religions, which treat God as a symbol. In humanistic religions, according to Fromm, God might be the "image of man's higher self" or a symbol of the universe. Only humanistic religions, according to Fromm, might be made compatible with a scientific world view.

Taken to their extreme, Fromm's humanistic religions might begin to look like Philanthropic Deism, the official state religion after the French Revolution. The French Revolution was to be the triumph of reasoning man. Its values and world view were inimical to those of the Church. But the masses were uneducated; they could not be asked to live without gods. Consequently, in 1793, churches throughout France, including Notre Dame, were converted to "temples of Reason." Figures of Reason replaced the crucified Jesus. Statues of Brutus, a Republican saint, replaced the Virgin Mary. Saint-Simon later proposed forming a "council of Newton." Led by a mathematician, the council would answer moral questions once left to the Church. A shrine—presumably some sort of rationalist Kaaba—would be erected to Newton, the hero of human intellect.

The power of social thinking and the consequent readiness to acquire religious beliefs are sometimes underestimated because of the apparently large numbers of agnostics or nonbelievers. However, many of those who have apparently freed themselves of religious thinking actually reject or avoid religion for reasons extrinsic to whether they really believe in God. Freud (1928), for instance, discussed a letter written to him by an American doctor. This letter described the doctor's religious experience consequent to seeing an elderly female corpse prepared for dissection. Freud hypothesized that the doctor's previous religious doubt was due to animosity toward his father, on whom his image of God was based. The image of God, in other words, was such as to cause rebellion, manifested as doubt.

The origin of specific images of God, and their relation to real figures, is discussed in the next chapter. Since Freud, several investigators have agreed that antireligious sentiments or religious indifference may reflect ambivalent and conflictual feelings concerning religious concepts, not simply disbelief (Allport & Ross, 1967; Hood, 1978; Rizzuto, 1976, 1979; Vergote, 1988; Vernon, 1968; Vitz, 1988).

A case described by Rizzuto (1979) shows how a punitive image of God can be masked by apparent disinterest, which serves a defensive function: "Daniel Miller" was the elder of two children born to a middle-class Jewish family. Daniel's father was a pharmaceutical salesman who was away from home much of the time. When he was at home, he had rage attacks, and he seemed pleased that his wife and children feared him. He expressed derision for his family, and especially for Daniel. Daniel's mother had been an elementary school teacher before her marriage. She was anxious, fearful, and unable to handle even minor crises. In the Miller household, decisions of any importance were always made by the father. Daniel was a shy, lonely child. His only friend was his younger sister. His school performance was mediocre, and he seemed to suffer from phobias.

Daniel's religious education began with his bar mitzvah preparation. He disliked the Old Testament God, who seemed to him to be lacking in compassion. His father ridiculed religion, but his mother expressed no opinion. Daniel assumed that she was a secret believer.

Daniel's father pressured him to get good high school grades. He did Daniel's homework. He forced Daniel to take unneeded achievement tests. School counsellors noted Daniel's shyness and social isolation and recommended that he have psychiatric treatment. His father reluctantly agreed, but only for the purpose of improving Daniel's grades. He broke off Daniel's treatment after just two months. Daniel began to have chest pains, which he thought were caused by heart disease. The family physician discounted their importance.

Spurred on by his father, Daniel gained admission to a reputable college. He left home for four years and developed some social relationships, but his grades were mediocre and he could not decide what he wanted to do after graduation. Unwilling to wait for Daniel to make up his mind, his father took matters into his own hands. He filled out medical school applications for Daniel and drove him to interviews. He forced him to memorize answers to questions he knew would be asked. Daniel was admitted to a local medical school and continued to live with his parents. He performed poorly in school, he was socially isolated, and he began to develop more and more physical symptoms. Lower abdominal pain, back pain, and burning urination gradually convinced him that he had a fatal illness. On graduating, he failed to look for work and began to see a psychiatrist.

In treatment, Daniel's depression and anger quickly came to the surface. The anger was aimed at his father. His hypochondriasis worsened until it became delusional. When he demanded further evaluations for what he believed to be a fatal illness, he was hospitalized for more intensive psychiatric treatment.

While Daniel was in the hospital, Rizzuto gave him a questionnaire designed to elicit information about his image of God. Daniel doubted that God really exists, but like other agnostics, he was able to describe the God whose existence he doubted. Daniel's image of God closely resembled the image he held of his hostile father. God, according to Daniel, epitomizes masculine power. He is vengeful and distant and lacking in compassion. He despises those in need and the unsuccessful. Furthermore, Daniel thought, if God exists, worship is nonetheless pointless. God cannot be satisfied, so why bother trying? Daniel thought he could be more religious only if he felt that God could be more loving.

The reader may have noticed that Daniel resembles Luther in certain important respects (see chapter 3). Like Luther, Daniel was the eldest son of a domineering, hostile father. Daniel's mother was unable to restrain the father's behavior or to protect her children from his rage. Her role in the family was apparently highly circumscribed. Like Luther's, Daniel's image of God was squarely modeled on that of the powerful father, to the exclusion of other elements. In this respect, Daniel's case, too, seems to confirm Freud's (1907, 1913, 1927, 1939) theory that God is modeled on the Oedipal father. Both Luther and Daniel defied their father's plans for them: Luther entered the monastery, and Daniel dropped his medical career. But whereas Luther defied his real father in order to worship God, Daniel doubted God's existence or the value of worshipping him.

Rizzuto provided data to show that Daniel's agnosticism served psychological functions related to feelings he held about his father. By doubting God's existence or the need to worship, Daniel defied the God who so resembled his father. At the same time, he denied the fear that would ordinarily result from belief in such a malevolent deity. This was the fear he felt with his father. Luther suffered a life-long fear of God, who was modeled on his father. On the other hand, by not entirely denying God's existence and by making religious observance contingent on a loving God, Daniel maintained the hope that God might really change. He might become the loving father Daniel had always wished for. He maintained his ties to his real father for much the same reason.

Daniel's agnosticism, in other words, may be more apparent than real. He readily describes a God modeled on his father and, no doubt, on the more fearsome aspects of the Old Testament God, to whom he maintains a studied indifference. The reasons for this indifference are likely defensive, wishful, and defiant and recreate with God his filial ambivalence. Neither a rational assessment of the uses of religion nor a rational disbelief in the concept of God necessarily plays a significant role in Daniel's religious disinterest. In fact, Daniel could be highly religious and still play out in avowed agnosticism his personal feelings toward God. For Daniel to actually worship, however, his image of God would have to change. Alternatively, he would have to adopt a God whose image differed from that of his father, thereby defying his father and the God modeled on him together. Neither of these conditions—a change in his own God image or conversion to another God—is likely to be met, so Daniel will remain without whatever comfort religion might provide him.

Religious beliefs may also be disavowed for social reasons incidental to religious affiliation. In the preceding chapter, young people were described who used their religious conversions to escape parental influence. In many other cases, seemingly agnostic or atheistic rejections of parental religious affiliations, or of religious affiliations of any kind, serve the same purpose. Parents may be defied equally well with avowed agnosticism or atheism as with conversion to a new religion. In such cases, inquiries and observations will reveal the social function of avowed disbelief and the lack of rational reasons for it. Alternatively, avowed disbelief may serve social functions beyond the family circle. For example, in the past hundred years, European Jews who have desired full integration into the larger culture have been faced with the choice of conversion or atheism. Many of them chose Christian conversion, which Heine (quoted in Bakan, 1958) once called "the admission ticket to European Civilization." Others, feeling in part that Christian conversion had the smell of treason, chose instead to be atheists. In doing so, they allied themselves with the secular, scientific, and humanistic movements, as opposed to the dominant religious culture.

Bakan (1958) and Meissner (1984) presented evidence that Sigmund Freud's atheism was at least partially conditioned by extrinsic factors that belong in this second category. I will not specifically discuss these factors as they apply to Freud, but I will review Freud's religious interests (see, also, P. Gay, 1987). They illustrate the point that apparently straightforward atheism may be very complex. Although Freud claimed to be "godless," he was deeply preoccupied with matters of religion. No less than three of his books—*Totem and Taboo* (1913), *The Future of an Illusion* (1927), and *Moses and Monotheism* (1939)—and several of his important papers concerned religious beliefs more or less directly. Although he never attended synagogue services and indulged in activities—such as collecting primitive idols—uncharacteristic of religious Jews, Freud nonetheless maintained his Jewish identity. He attended the B'nai Brith lodge, where he played in a weekly card game. He refused royalties on Hebrew and Yiddish translations of his work, and he wrote special prefaces for them. He enjoyed Jewish humor and collected Jewish stories. Freud was dogged throughout his life by fateful superstitions. These were referred to in many of his works and concerned, for the most part, the date of his own death. In an earlier section, such superstitions were seen to manifest powerful social-cognitive schemata.

Freud was raised in a free-thinking Jewish family. Although his parents were not especially religious, they introduced him to the Bible at an early age. According to Ernest Jones (1957), the child Freud was conversant with both Old and New Testaments. During his first two-and-a-half years, Freud also had a Catholic nanny, who often took him with her to church. Shortly after the birth of Freud's younger sister, this woman was fired for stealing. Zilboorg (1958) suggested that the loss of his nanny—to whom he was strongly attached—affected Freud's view of religion and of Catholicism in particular. Vitz (1988) presented evidence supporting Zilboorg's theory.

Freud's early exposure to the Old Testament may have led to his long-lasting interest in Moses, with whom he strongly identified. In Jewish folklore, Moses was the model for the Messiah ben Joseph, the long-awaited leader who will vanquish Israel's enemies. Identification with Moses implies messianic fantasies of a militant kind. In correspondence and conversation, Freud frequently compared himself to Moses: With his new science, he would lead his followers to the Promised Land, which he himself could not enter. References to the Promised Land appear in his published dreams. In a letter written before their rift, Freud compared Jung to Joshua, the younger man who completed Moses' work. In his early years, Freud lived and worked mostly in company with Jews. Jung was virtually the only Christian among Freud's early followers, and Freud saw him as a conduit to the wider Christian world.

Between 1895 and 1898, Freud traveled to Italy no fewer than five times, but each time, in spite of his conscious intentions, he failed to visit Rome. He referred to this inhibition as his "Roman neurosis" and eventually related it to his boyhood worship of Hannibal. Hannibal, like Moses, was associated for Freud with militant messianism. Like Moses, Hannibal had reached the very threshold of the land he would conquer before being turned back. Of course, Rome was also the seat of the Catholic Church, associated for Freud with his lost nanny. According to Jewish mystics, the Messiah ben Joseph would first appear in Rome. In his published dreams, Freud linked Rome with Jerusalem.

When he finally reached Rome in 1901, Freud became fascinated by Michelangelo's Moses, which moved him so strongly that he wrote a paper about it thirteen years later (Freud, 1914). Freud himself reported that in September 1913, he stood daily before this statue, which adorns the tomb of Pope Julius II, for a period of nearly three weeks. Freud published his paper anonymously, with an extraordinary dissembling preface intended to hide his authorship. Significantly, Michelangelo's Moses has horns, as the Messiah ben Joseph is supposed to have. As Bakan (1958) and Meissner (1984) pointed out, Freud's interpretation of Michelangelo's statue had more to do with Freud than with Michelangelo's Moses. Freud seemed particularly intent on restraining Moses' anger, as if he were fearful of the father figure he wished to emulate. Alternatively, Freud may have been preoccupied in 1914 with restraining his own anger, since Jung, like the Israelites who waited for Moses at the foot of Mount Sinai, had begun to worship what seemed to Freud to be a Golden Calf (see E. Jones, 1958).

In the late 1930s, nearing the end of his life, Freud (1939) returned again to the study of Moses. By all accounts, *Moses and Monotheism* is one of Freud's most idiosyncratic works. Freud himself acknowledged that his argument was arbitrary and speculative, and he showed the same reticence to publish that had earlier preceded his paper on Michelangelo's statue. In *Moses and Monotheism* (1939), Freud portrayed Moses as the victim of his followers, who had risen up and slain him on the threshold of victory. Freud's portrayal of the man he identified with is partly an autobiography; in the late 1930s Freud was physically ill and still deeply troubled by the defections of former followers.

It is of some interest that for several years, Freud lived almost across the street from the famous Zionist Theodor Herzl yet never met him in person (see Meissner, 1984). Herzl, at least as Freud must have seen him, was living the Moses legend in a much more literal manner than Freud was. Whereas Freud's Promised Land was only metaphoric, Herzl's had real soil. Not surprisingly, Freud's attitude toward Herzl was complex and ambiguous and concerned his own messianic identification. In *The Interpretation of Dreams*, Freud (1900) mentioned a play by Herzl in connection with a dream referring to Rome.

Bakan (1958) suggested that much of the specific content of psychoanalytic theory derived from Jewish mysticism. Kabbalistic ideas were deeply engrained in Eastern European Jewish culture, so that even if he had not read of them, Freud might still have been influenced by them. Specific similarities between psychoanalytic and Kabbalistic ideas apparently occur in relation to sexuality, socialization of children, word and number interpretation, free association, and the role of the healer. In the preface to a later edition of his book, Bakan (1975) described a conversation with an Orthodox Jew who had briefly visited Freud and had perused some of his bookshelves. He claimed to have seen copies of Kabbalistic books. It is of some incidental interest that he also considered stealing the manuscript of *Moses and Monotheism* in order to keep it from seeing the light of day. The thesis of this manuscript angered Orthodox Jews (see P. Gay, 1987).

Freud's account of superstition, reflecting as it must his personal experience of it, shows the extent to which Freud—despite his professed atheism—remained concerned with essentially religious phenomena. It also casts an interesting light on the relationship between the theory developed here and classical psychoanalysis. In *The Psychopathology of Everyday Life,* Freud (1901) treated superstition as the expectation of trouble, based on the fear of retribution for repressed hostile wishes. Fear of retribution, however, implies belief in a judging agent. In his later structural theory, Freud (1923a) named the agent that individuals seem to fear the *superego* and suggested that it was formed from models provided by punitive parents. I noted earlier that individuals may try to appease privately conceived beings somewhat akin to deities. Gamblers with the Monte Carlo fallacy, for instance, may try to appease agents they imagine are keeping records of their wins and losses. Such privately conceived beings result from social-analytical thinking; they differ from publicly worshipped deities in that they are nonconsensual. They are also, of course, much more vague in their histories and attributes than objects of public worship are. The case of Daniel Miller indicated how privately conceived deities may be modeled after the parents. All this suggests that many of what Freud would consider punitive superego manifestations might be seen as manifestations of private religious beliefs. Significantly, the German term *Ich,* rendered into *ego* by Freud's English translators, literally means the *I* (Bettelheim, 1982; Brandt, 1966; see, also, Eagle, 1984). Therefore, *uber-Ich,* rendered into *superego,* refers to an agent *above-the-I.* What better name could Freud have found for a person's private god?

In his thinking about compulsion neuroses, Freud seemingly verified that God and the superego differ mostly in the degree to which they are publicly worshipped. In a particularly well-known paper, for instance, Freud (1907) called compulsions "private religious system[s]" and religion a "universal obsessional neurosis." Compulsive rituals play in the private religion the same role liturgy plays in the public neurosis. He repeated this formulation twelve years later (Freud, 1919). Yet according to Freud's structural theory, which he developed in the 1920s, obsessional symptoms are aimed at appeasing the superego (Freud 1923a; see, also, Fenichel,

1945). Juxtaposing the two models of obsessional neurosis, we see how the superego plays a godlike role: Insofar as an obsessional neurosis is still to be considered a private religion, the superego must be the object of private worship—in other words, a private god. And insofar as religion is still to be considered a public obsessional neurosis, God must be a consensual superego!

Apparently, individuals who apply social-analytical schemata to their circumstances render unto their resulting deities that which they think is owed them. Worship may be public or private, fully conscious or unconscious. Public, fully conscious worship is in the domain of theology. Private, unconscious worship is in the domain of analysis.

Numerous observers of modern culture (see, for example, Rieff, 1966) have noted the extent to which psychoanalysts and psychotherapists have assumed what were previously priestly functions. This is especially so in the realm of defining guilt and sin and in defining just repentance. The viewpoint adopted here implies that insofar as he or she interprets the punitive superego, the psychotherapist is, in fact, a priest but is dealing with private religious beliefs.

I have alluded several times to the specific attributes assigned particular deities. The case of Daniel Miller, together with the relationship postulated here between the punitive superego and private deities, suggests that at least certain deities are assigned parental attributes. This, of course, is the Freudian view, especially with respect to the Oedipal father. Material in the preceding chapter suggests that deities are assigned attributes according to the functions they serve. Deities that subserve attachment strategies should have more prominent maternal qualities, for example, than a God like Luther's, who was preeminently a vehicle for the expression of Oedipal conflicts. Images of God are discussed in the following chapter.

Gods as Manifest Archetypes

Like Freud, Jung had a lifelong interest in religion, but in Jung's case, this interest was more sympathetic. Having come this far, it is possible to discuss Jung's ideas, as I promised in chapter 1. In doing so, I hope to answer some theoretical questions: How do Jungian archetypes fare in modern biology? How do they relate to the sociobiologic concepts described in chapter 2? Was Jung right in considering God an archetypal idea? If so, what is that archetype's place in the mental economy? Does it differ, as Jung thought, from the place of other archetypes?

Jung's ideas originated in mental health clinical settings, in which they are still applied. To understand these ideas in relation to more modern theories, it is important to remember that mental health practitioners have rather different concerns from those of ethologists and sociobiologists. Most significantly, ethologic and sociobiologic models take as their subject matter more or less complex behaviors. Mental health practitioners, in contrast, address not only behaviors, but also thoughts, affects, and fantasies. Their inquiries, in other words, are not only behavioral but also intrapsychic. Strict behaviorists, who are more or less a vanishing breed at the time this is being written, are, of course, an exception to this rule.

It is true, in a trivial sense, that insofar as a patient expresses thoughts, affects, or fantasies, those expressions constitute a class of overt behavior. Yet ethologists and sociobiologists, concerned as they are with inclusive fitness consequences, would for the most part accord this class very little importance. From the ethologic point of view, for instance, the magical fantasies accompanying an altruistic act are of little or no consequence in comparison with the act itself. From the clinical point of view, however, the fantasies may be everything. What the patient actually does may or may not be important and may depend on its subjective consequences.

It is this discrepancy between the subject matters of clinical psychology, on the one hand, and ethology and sociobiology, on the other, that no doubt led Greenberg and Mitchell (1983) to downplay the work of Bowlby in their scholarly review of psychodynamic theories—theories designed to account for fantasies, thoughts, and feelings encountered in clinical practice. Bowlby's (1969, 1973, 1980) trilogy on maternal–infant attachment is the foremost attempt to introduce ethologic ideas into clinical psychology and psychiatry. Yet Greenberg and Mitchell (1983) complained that for Bowlby, experiences and fantasies seem to be mere epiphenomena, and that Bowlby's theory, concerned as it is with behavior, ignores intrapsychic events. Greenberg and Mitchell devoted less than three pages to Bowlby's work, in spite of the fact that others (see Parkes & Stevenson-Hinde, 1982) consider his ideas essential to modern clinical theory.

Greenberg and Mitchell erred in discounting Bowlby. Bowlby's approach is far from merely behavioral. His three-volume work provides at least the outline for an ethologically based approach to intrapsychic material. His emphasis on objective, measurable behaviors should be understood within a historical context; it is a corrective to earlier psychodynamic theories that were entirely unrelated to objective behavioral studies. There is no indication that in stressing objective research, Bowlby meant to downgrade subjective mental experience. In a previous work (Wenegrat, 1984), I also attempted to show that commonly encountered affects and preoccupations can in fact be understood in terms of social strategies of the kind discussed in chapter 2.

However, though it may be in part chimerical and in other respects only relative, a gap still exists between the subject matters of ethology and sociobiology, on the one hand, and clinical practice, on the other. In an important work, Stevens (1983) suggested that this gap can be bridged by the Jungian theory of archetypes. Stevens corrected two misconceptions that obscure the relationship between Jung's ideas and sociobiology. First, casual readers of Jung are misled into thinking of archetypes as specific innate ideas. This error is made all the easier by conceptual confusion in Jung's earlier work. Yet, particularly in his later publications, Jung actually described archetypes as inherited dispositions toward species-typical subjective experiences. In response to certain events, these dispositions could produce experiences—not necessarily ideas at all—that are universal in their general form. The specific content of the experiences might be highly individual, but their formal structure—which Jung likened to the lattice determining growth of a crystal—would reflect human phylogeny. Events that activate these experiences would be those that had recurred and proved important in the course of human prehistory, and the form of the experiences would be such as to promote the survival of those who had them. "Just as his instincts," Jung (1919) wrote, "compel man to a specifically human mode of existence, so the archetypes force his ways of perception and apprehension into specifically human patterns." The affinity between this notion of the archetype and modern evolutionary ideas of proximate causation (see chapter 2) could hardly be more obvious.

The second misconception leads the casual reader of Jung to miss the importance of archetypes. The manifestations of archetypes described by Jung are for the most part in myths and works of art, and particularly in dreams. Although Jung described patients whose daytime preoccupations manifested archetypal patterns, the casual reader may miss the extent to which archetypal predispositions structure everyday normal, subjective life. Actually, Jung considered archetypal experiences the building blocks of all subjective events, the a priori structures from which all else is constructed. In this sense, Jungian archetypes are related to Kant's "pure concepts" (see Robinson, 1986). Personal histories—that is, events peculiar to the ontogeny of each individual—don't so much replace archetypal elements in subjective experience as particularize them, or at least their specific content. They fill out the flesh on the phylogenetic skeleton.

Insofar as mental life is dictated in form by archetypes, the apparent divergence between the interests of ethologists, who study species-typical behavior, and clinicians, who study apparently idiosyncratic subjective experience, is less a matter of substance and more a matter of viewpoint. That is, both ethologists and clinicians study the residua of previous selective pressures, but from differing angles. The ethologist sees these residua more or less anonymously; the clinician sees them in private matters, in the context of personal history.

An example or two might clarify the relationship proposed by Jung between archetypal experiences and species-typical behavior patterns. One particularly important archetype is that of the mother. Mythical and symbolic expressions of the maternal archetype are found in every culture. Erich Neumann's (1955) classic work described the maternal archetype's varied manifestations. Weigert-Vowinkel (1938) discussed some of these manifestations as they appear in religious life. Essentially, the great mother, worshipped in the form of Cybele, Isis, or Astarte—or, more recently, in the form of the Virgin Mary—has played a major role in virtually all religions. Rabbinic Judaism and Protestantism are exceptions to this rule, but the former at least was compensated by Kabbalistic and other traditions (see Patai, 1978). The reasons for the peculiar absence of a maternal figure in Protestantism were discussed in chapter 3. The maternal archetype, at least in its positive form, is a predisposition toward and a fascination with abundant and loving feminine figures.

In order to survive, the human infant must receive some modicum of motherlike care. Consequently, the fascination with creative maternal figures expressed in folklore, myths, and dreams, not to speak of everyday life, might seem to be a residue of early childhood experiences, not of human phylogeny. More sophisticated readers, and those who have read my earlier study (Wenegrat, 1984), will recognize that nature/nurture issues posed in this way are actually logically false. If an organism predictably develops something when exposed to its environment of adaptation, then that something is phylogenetically determined in the same way that lungs or the number of legs, for instance, are. Nothing can develop in any case without the environment of adaptation, so the need for it to be present hardly proves the absence of phylogenetic influence. In any event, it isn't at all clear that experience with the mother really antedates knowledge of what mothers are like. There is considerable scientific literature on this matter, both because of its intrinsic interest and because it has become the focus of debate between two theories in psychoanalysis—known, respectively, as *somatic drive* and *object relations* theories (see Greenberg & Mitchell, 1983). Freud, the somatic drive theorist par excellence, believed that infants don't know about concerned, loving mothers until they are taught by their mother's attentive care to their somatic needs. Stevens (1983) called this the "cupboard love" theory, since it would have the infant fall in love with his cupboard once he had learned what it held for him. Bowlby (1969, 1973, 1980), who in this matter, if in few others, represents the object relations position, argued that the infant is born with a behavioral repertoire that presupposes belief in such mothers, however unarticulated, and recognizes and falls in love with them according to criteria quite divorced from the provision of somatic rewards.

Though it cannot really be summarized here, the bulk of objective evidence favors Bowlby's position. First, a quarter-century ago, experiments with nonhuman primates showed that infants choose their attachment figures on grounds more complicated than provision of food or warmth (Harlow & Zimmerman, 1959). Studies of human orphans have likewise shown the relative unimportance of somatic gratifications (see Stevens, 1983). Second, infants appear to enter the world knowing approximately who their attachment figures will be and looking for certain responses from them. Before they could possibly learn of its importance, for example, human neonates pay special attention to the human face (Spitz, 1965). Infants seek responses in their parents' facial expressions, and although normal infants have had little or no chance to learn what blank stares mean, they are agitated by them (Brazelton et al., 1975; Trevarthen, 1979). Neonates are also responsive to the sound of the human voice, particularly that of the mother (DeCasper & Fifer, 1980). Within the first month of life, they are able to categorize speech sounds that may not even be used in their parents' own language (Eimas et al., 1971). These speech sounds form the building blocks of all human languages, so facility in their categorization is necessary to language acquisition (see Marler, 1979). Finally, human infants are well equipped to influence their attachment figures. Universally understood facial gestures (see Ekman, 1979) appear early in the neonatal period (Trevarthen, 1979) and develop without visual experience (Eibl-Eibesfeldt, 1973). Infantile gestures appear to be positive or negative reinforcers to attachment figures, who respond to them in a stereotypical and partially unconscious fashion (Papousek & Papousek, 1979; Trevarthen, 1979). The same remarks apply to infant vocalizations (see Donovan et al., 1978).

In many ways, therefore, human neonates act as if they were prepared to recognize and deal with mothers they haven't even met. Some readers might think that it is better—on purely logical grounds—not to speak of the neonate "knowing" anything. As Jung (1927/1931) pointed out, though, individuals who behave "as if" they were thinking something but are unable to give an account of it are said to have unconscious ideas (cf. Rubinstein, 1980, concerning unconscious wishes). Therefore, the "as if" behavior of the neonate may point toward implicit models on a logical par with adult unconscious ideas. The epistemological problems posed by the neonate's "knowledge," in any event, are no more serious than those posed by the adult unconscious (see Grünbaum, 1984), which have not led to its conceptual demise. Following Lumsden and Wilson (1981), we might refer to the infant as having a "knowledge structure"—in this case, a prototypical one manifest only through the infant's behavior. This might seem to avoid the problem of saying the infant "knows" anything. However, since Jung treated the archetype as the knowledge inherent in species-typical behavior, *knowledge structure,* as used in this context, and *archetype* are really equivalent terms.

A thought experiment will illustrate how much the infant knows, or, if the reader prefers, how much information is contained in its maternal knowledge structure or archetype or is implicit in its behavior. Imagine that we knew nothing of the human mother and could only piece her together from the newborn's observed actions. I assume that these actions are observed in a modern laboratory, so that physiologic as well as overt motor responses are available as evidence. First, since the infant cannot provide for its own needs, we could immediately deduce that the mother-caretaker must be present in the infant's environment of adaptation. From the newborn's stimulus preferences, we could guess that this mother-caretaker had a mouth, nose, and eyes, arranged in a particular configuration, and a relatively high-pitched voice. From the infant's autonomic responses, we could guess that she was warm-blooded, with a soft, pliant surface texture not unlike the newborn's own skin. We could further deduce that certain maternal facial configurations signify a positive disposition toward the newborn and others a negative or indifferent disposition. Similar deductions could be made concerning certain maternal vocalizations. From the infant's cries and gestures, studied in relation to their physiologic antecedents, we could guess at the mother's response patterns: that she is alerted to the newborn by crying, for instance, and that her behavior is somehow reinforced by other of the infant's actions. These deductions are just the most obvious ones. The information to be gained from the newborn and infant's behavior is in fact much more extensive than I can describe here. Depending on our experimental ingenuity and the subtlety of our recording devices, innumerable other things could be learned about the mother-caretaker without directly observing her.

Here I have discussed only the maternal archetype. Similar remarks might be made concerning several other knowledge structures that Jungian analysts consider archetypal, including the paternal archetype, the archetypes corresponding to one's own and the opposite gender, the so-called Trickster figure, and the Oedipal archetype (Jung, 1958). Stevens (1983) discussed the first four of these archetypes from an ethological viewpoint. In each case, information comprising the archetype is latent in universal response patterns, just as information concerning the mother is latent in the infant's attachment behavior. Jung (1925) noted, for example, that the psychological makeup of women could be deduced from the anima figures, or opposite-sex archetypes, of men without observing women directly. Jung's proposal directly parallels the thought experiment I just described for the mother figure. The universal response patterns with which these other archetypes are associated belong, like infantile proximity maintenance, to the innately probable strategies described in chapter 2. Because their behavioral and subjective manifestations develop later in life, though, the phylogenetic basis of the information they contain may seem, at first glance, less obvious than with the maternal archetype. The issue is too complex to treat completely here, but the reader should remember that the environment of adaptation, whether in utero, in the postpartum period, or during childhood and adolescence, will be essential for acquisition of any information, phylogenetic or not, and that the only criteria for phylogenetic fixation of particular response patterns should be universality with evolutionary stability (chapter 2).

As for the Oedipus complex, Jung (1958) considered it one among many archetypal experiences. Insofar as he criticized Freud, it was not because Freud discovered the Oedipus complex but because he ignored other archetypes. Freud, whose life's work was deeply affected by Darwin (Sulloway, 1979), also saw the Oedipus complex as rooted in human prehistory. This was why, according to Freud, even the kindest fathers became the objects of their sons' emnity. It was also the motive for *Totem and Taboo* (1913), one of Freud's most important books, which has been swept under the rug by many modern Freudians. In *Totem and Taboo,* Freud argued that the origin of exogamy laws, and consequently of the Oedipus complex, lay in a primal patricide followed by remorse. In retrospect, Freud's argument is clearly Lamarckian: A cultural response to the problem of patricide becomes somehow fixed in human biology. However, at the time Freud wrote *Totem and Taboo,* the conceptual difference between Darwinian and Lamarckian inheritance was less clear than it has become with the rise of neo-Darwinism. And in any event, in a footnote to *Totem and Taboo,* Freud noted that the primal patricide described in that book was one of countless similar events, thereby casting his argument back in Darwinian form. In a particularly interesting book, Fox (1980) framed Freud's argument in consistent Darwinian terms and found it biologically sensible. Had Freud written it that way to begin with, *Totem and Taboo* would have been the earliest study in sociobiology.

It should now be clear that Jung (1902, 1920/1948, 1928/1931, 1934, 1951, 1952, 1958) was correct in his basic approach to religious faith. If an archetype is an inherited disposition toward a species-typical subjective experience, then religious belief, as defined in chapter 1, must manifest an archetype. Religious beliefs are prototypical experiences to which all persons are predisposed by innate social-cognitive schemata. Like other archetypal dispositions, the social-cognitive schemata that produce religious beliefs are ubiquitous in their influence and imperfectly subject to conscious control. These points were made in the previous sections. On the other hand, to say that faith is archetypal is far from adequate. Many questions are left unanswered: How did the dispositions leading to faith come into being? Where do they fit in the structure of mind? With which advantageous behaviors have they been associated? These questions—none of which are satisfactorily answered by Jung—are precisely those illuminated by the sociobiologic concepts in this and previous chapters. Religious beliefs, according to the model presented here, manifest an evolved tendency to perceive events in social terms, whether or not those events are social. These beliefs are subjective results of previous social-selective pressures that have had the greatest efficacy in shaping cognitive structures, and they are used for social ends. Humans, in short, are social game players, and social game players are prone to invent gods who will then be used in social games.

However, gods differ in certain respects from other products of archetypes. Sociobiologic ideas can clarify these differences, which are mentioned here for the sake of completeness. First, other products of archetypes affect the perception of real persons. Individuals, according to Jung (see Stevens, 1983), tend to be stereotyped in terms of specific archetypes, such as paternal, maternal, masculine, or feminine archetypes. Stereotyping of this kind may structure normal relationships. Adequate mothers or fathers, for instance, may be those who active the appropriate archetypes, which then determine how their children perceive them. In sociobiologic terms, the adequate mother or father may be one who triggers certain of the child's attachment perceptions. Alternatively, individual patterns of stereotyping may reveal salient archetypes. An adult with a particularly active maternal archetype, for instance, will tend to see others as fitting the maternal mold. In sociobiologic terms, an adult who pursues an infantile proximity maintenance strategy (see chapter 2) will see others only as potential attachment figures. This stereotyping may do considerable violence to real people, who may not fit the archetypal pattern at all.

In psychotherapy, such stereotyping may lead to so-called transference. According to Freud, transference occurs when patients direct infantile instinctual aims toward the psychotherapist. In recent years, though, the term has been used in a wider sense, to denote the patient's tendency to misperceive the therapist according to earlier models. Insofar as they reflect archetypal stereotypes, transference distortions reveal the salient active archetypes, or the salient active strategies.

Religious beliefs have somewhat different perceptual effects. The sociobiologic model suggests that religious beliefs result from the misapplication of social-cognitive schemata to asocial events. Consequently, it should not be surprising that their primary perceptual effects concern apprehension of the asocial world. In light of religious beliefs, the asocial setting of human events seems to assume a social meaning. This is not to say that religious beliefs fail to affect perception of other people. However, they alter perception of others only secondarily, through their manifold social uses, described in chapter 3.

Second, manifestations of nonreligious archetypes are generally intrinsic to the specific social strategies that comprise their behavioral associations. Religious belief, by contrast, is far less specific in its strategic role. The specificity of nonreligious archetypal experience has been demonstrated only for the maternal archetype, which is associated with infantile proximity maintenance, but it is also true for the paternal and Oedipal archetypes, the animus and anima, and the Trickster. All of these archetypes, in fact, are plausibly intrinsic to sexual competitive strategies and to strategies related to group cohesion. On the other hand, in chapter 3, I showed how religious beliefs can serve various strategies and can serve particular strategies in highly individual ways. Rather than being intrinsic to any particular social game, such as attachment or mating, religious belief is a product of game-playing itself, of being a social animal.

Humans may or may not currently be playing a particular social game, but they are always playing some game. Furthermore, they are always in contact with the nonsocial world. Consequently, unlike other archetypal products, religious beliefs are liable to more or less constant excitation. Other products of archetypes may or may not be salient, depending on the person or circumstances, but religious beliefs are less contingent on specific social activities. The reader should note that I am discussing here not religious affiliation, church membership, or any other index of social religious behavior, but the product of an irrepressible cognitive style by which the world is personalized. The degree of surrender to religious ideas will, of course, be highly contingent on social circumstances and on the social uses to which these ideas are put (see chapter 3). The pervasiveness of religious thought, and its more or less constant excitation, may be why Jung (1958) considered the God archetype in a special relationship with the basic personality. Jung noted, for example, that symbols of the self, or of the whole personality, are consistently employed in religious contexts, as if faith and the core self are closely intertwined.

To pursue these ideas further would risk losing sight of our object of study, which is, after all, religious belief. More will be said concerning Jungian theory at the end of the following chapter. Suffice it to note here, as Stevens (1983) observed, that if Jungian psychologists updated their ideas with sociobiologic concepts, they would place their discipline back in the mainstream of behavioral science. Likewise, if modern Freudians paid closer attention to *Totem and Taboo,* their field, too, would benefit. Moreover, sociobiologists might be surprised to find their ideas presaged in the work of famous psychologists.

5
The Image of God

Divine Attributes as Transference-like Phenomena

Once they are led by their social-analytical schemata to postulate invisible beings, men and women quickly attribute to them features of real persons. In general, there seems to be a powerful tendency to attribute to unknown persons characteristics of those who are already known. It is hard to see how else social perceptions could proceed, if not by assuming that hitherto unknown persons are more or less like those that have come before. This conservative perceptual tendency is no doubt partly responsible for what psychotherapists call transference. In the preceding chapter, I noted that the term *transference* is now used to denote the patient's tendency to misperceive the therapist according to earlier models. Many psychotherapists keep the details of their own lives hidden from their patients in order to facilitate the emergence of transference, which provides clinically useful information.

Consensual deities are partially determined, of course, by shared religious beliefs. However, they remain sufficiently opaque to most people that something like transference can readily occur. That is, the worshipper can fill in the chinks between shared beliefs with mortar from past relationships. For that matter, even the shared beliefs represent accretions of transference-like material from previous generations and so are not radically different in kind. When it comes to private deities, restraints on personal attributions are entirely removed, and people are free to think of these deities as being like people they have known.

Insofar as individuals attribute to their deities characteristics of familiar persons, it is a matter of some interest to know who those persons might be. In *Totem and Taboo,* Freud (1913) argued that in every case, God takes his character from that of the child's father. From the child's point of view, the father seems to exercise nearly unlimited power. He therefore provides a model for a supernatural being. According to Freud, God is nothing more than an exalted father figure. The cases of Martin Luther and Daniel Miller, described in previous chapters, illustrate clearly how well Freud's theory accounts for the beliefs of certain persons. Also, according to Freud (1923a, 1924) the father forms the foundation for the superego. In the preceding chapter, I argued that manifestations of the punitive superego are really manifestations of private religious beliefs. Insofar as this formulation is correct, the Freudian hypothesis concerning the paternal origin of public gods would seem to apply to private gods as well. However, later psychoanalysts (see, for example, E. Jones, 1951; Vergote, 1988) have widened Freud's strictly paternal view to include the mother. Both parents, they argued, appear to the child as possessed of infinite power. Both potentially contribute to the final image of God. Ernest Jones (1951), for instance, described religion as "a dramatization on a cosmic plane of the emotions, fears and longings which arose in the child's relation to his parents." In the field of religion, Jones cast a wider net than Freud's. He seemed more aware of the maternal element in many religions, which is largely absent in rabbinic Judaism. He also seemed more aware of the need to study more than one religious system in order to draw generally valid conclusions.

Research has confirmed that images of God correlate with perceived parental characteristics. There is thus some quantitative corroboration of what Freud and other analysts observed qualitatively. In general, evidence has supported the wider view taken by Jones, rather than the narrowly paternal view taken by Freud. Beit-Hallahmi and Argyle (1975) reviewed a number of studies in this field. They concluded that the greatest similarities exist between the image of God and the preferred or, alternatively, opposite-sex parent. This would imply that for males, to whom Freudian theories are in general more readily applied, the Freudian theory of religious belief will most likely be wrong. For females, however, the same theory will more likely conform to the facts of belief.

I have already discussed men who construct their God image in the likeness of a hated father figure, for whom the Freudian formula seems strikingly apt. These cases indicate that factors other than sex and parental preference play determinate roles, at least in certain cases. At the very least, personal preoccupations and neurotic conflicts must be accorded some place in determining the likeness of God and parent. Furthermore, as psychoanalysts since Freud and Jones have increasingly recognized, specific aspects of parental images—so-called part objects—may be shuffled and recombined to form chimerical images that cannot be understood except as composites of both parents or of limited aspects of one or the other (see Greenberg & Mitchell, 1983). The important empirical finding, therefore, may be the resemblance of God and parental part objects. It may be that the question of parental dominance is no longer important, except when asked in regard to specific cases. In this section, I will briefly review evidence linking the image of God and partial images of one or both parents. In the following section, I will discuss how personal preoccupations and neurotic conflicts affect the image of God.

M.O. Nelson and Jones (1957) performed an early study showing the extent to which parental characteristics are ascribed to God. Sixteen Protestants, half of them male, were presented with a list of sixty statements. Each statement had to be sorted according to how well it agreed with their own feelings about God, Jesus, their fathers, and their mothers. For example, a subject might be presented with a card bearing the statement, "When I think about God, I have a feeling that I am understood." He or she could place that card into one of nine bins. The first bin would indicate strong agreement, the last bin strong disagreement, and the remaining bins intermediate degrees of concurrence. Later, the subject would have to sort other cards with the same statement, but relating to Jesus, to the father, or to the mother, rather than to God. Pearson product-moment correlations were calculated for sortings relating to God, Jesus, and father and mother and were used as a measure of construct similarity. Product-moment correlations vary from -1.0, in the case of completely opposite constructs, to 1.0, in the case of identical constructs. Correlations close to zero indicate that constructs are unrelated. Psychologists call this method of assessing construct similarity the *Q-sort technique*. Also, Nelson and Jones calculated an overall index of positive and negative feelings expressed toward each parent, in order to know which was viewed most favorably.

Correlations for the God and Jesus sortings varied from 0.34 to 0.95, indicating considerable variation in the extent to which subjects differentiated between the two figures. Correlations for the God and father sortings varied from −0.64 to 0.76, with a group mean of 0.188. This means that although some subjects had considerable similarities in their views of God and their fathers, others had rather opposite views—God and father were unlike for them. As a whole, the group showed rather little concordance of the God and father concepts. Correlations for the God and mother sortings varied from −0.29 to 0.89, with a group mean of 0.427. This means that some subjects had considerable similarities in their views of God and their mothers, whereas others had only mildly opposite views. The group as a whole showed a moderately strong resemblance of God and mother concepts. In general, male subjects saw God as more like their mothers and female subjects saw God as more like their fathers than would be expected on the basis of chance. Also, God was generally viewed as most like a favored parent, rather than like one who evoked negative feelings. Nelson and Jones's (1957) conclusions were among those reviewed by Beit-Hallahmi and Argyle (1975), whose conclusions reflect their findings concerning parental sex and favoritism.

Strunk (1959) studied twenty Protestant students in a church-based liberal arts college. Half the subjects were male. Subjects were administered the same sixty-statement Q-sort test used by Nelson and Jones (1957). Correlations for God and Jesus sortings ranged from 0.21 to 0.90, indicating the same range of differentiation found by Nelson and Jones. Correlations for God and father sortings ranged from −0.44 to 0.87, with a group mean of 0.45. Thus, Strunk found the same variability in the relationship of the God and father concepts, but with an overall greater degree of similarity than that found by Nelson and Jones (1957). Correlations for God and mother sortings ranged from −0.26 to 0.88, with a group mean of 0.50. These findings differ somewhat from those of Nelson and Jones, in that the group mean correlations of

the mother and father concepts with that of God are both significant and are approximately equal. Strunk found the same gender
and preference biases found by Nelson and Jones.

Siegman (1961) studied eighty-five Israeli undergraduate students, twenty-five of whom were male, and seventy-nine male medical students at the University of Maryland. Subjects completed a
three-part semantic differential test for their concepts of God and
father, and the similarity of these concepts was assessed using
product-moment correlations. This procedure is conceptually similar to the Q-sort test. Group mean correlations for both Israeli and
American subjects were low, although one of the correlations in
the American subsample reached statistical significance. However,
when the American subsample was divided into two subsets, according to their self-reported religiosity, an interesting finding
emerged. Among the highly religious, correlations of God and father concepts were all close to zero; in other words, the God and
father concepts were essentially unrelated. Among the irreligious
though, correlations of God and father concepts were all greater
than 0.30 and were all statistically significant. Siegman (1961) argued that the greater correlations among the irreligious contradict
the Freudian theory of religious motivation. The case of Daniel
Miller, discussed in the preceding chapter, should cause us to question whether the Freudian model really makes such a straightforward prediction. In any event, Siegman's findings are consistent
with a transference model of the God image: Insofar as their ideas
are relatively underdetermined by scripture, irreligious persons
should exhibit—in their image of God—more idiosyncratic impressions determined by experiences with parents. The generally low
correlations found by Siegman may be the result of the test he used,
which may fail to define the God and paternal concept sufficiently
for higher correlations to emerge clearly. Had he used the Q-sort
test, for instance, significant correlations might have emerged even
among religious subjects.

Larsen and Knapp (1964) studied forty subjects from a "com-
paratively orthodox" Protestant sect. Half of the subjects were male,
and ages ranged from fifteen to fifty-eight years. Subjects ranked
Rorschach blots according to how closely the blots resembled their
personal images of God. They then completed semantic differen-

tials tests for each blot they had rated. From these indirect measures, Larsen and Knapp concluded that their male subjects viewed God as more malevolent than their female subjects did. They interpreted this as evidence for the Freudian theory of God. For males, the father is more threatening and less benevolent than he is for females, so a god in his image would be more fearsome. Insofar as Larsen and Knapp's measures do reflect beliefs about God, their findings seem to contradict previously cited research concerning the effect of gender. According to this research, males should create their God image mostly along maternal lines, so God should seem benevolent. These findings also contradict studies of fear of God in other subject groups. Siegman (1961), for example, found that among her Israeli subjects, women seemed more fearful of God than men did. Larsen and Knapp's (1964) findings may reflect the theology to which their homogeneous sample was exposed. Ernest Jones (1951), for instance, argued that Protestant faiths have downgraded the maternal elements in religion in order to minimize Oedipal conflict. If so, denomination and gender must interact in determining the dominant parental model.

M.O. Nelson (1971) studied thirty-seven males and forty-seven females aged fifteen to forty-four years. Twenty-four were high school students and fifty-eight were college students. Three of the subjects were Jewish, and the remainder were approximately evenly divided between Catholic and Protestant faiths. Subjects completed the Q-sort test used by Nelson and Jones (1957) and were questioned about parental preferences. Subjects who expressed parental preferences showed higher correlations between the concept of God and that of the preferred parent. This replicates earlier findings. Most subjects preferred their mothers, but this tendency was much stronger among males than females. The opposite-gender effect on religious images may be wholly or partially reducible to a parental preference effect, with parental preferences differing among males and females. Subjects who denied having parental preferences showed approximately equal correlations between the God concept and that of the mother and father. In general, these correlations were higher than in subjects who reported preferences. Nelson suggested that absence of parental preference indicates a more harmonious family, with resulting concordance of God and parental images.

To further complicate the matter, findings by Vergote et al. (1969) raise the possibility that some of the apparently maternal aspects of the God image may derive from paternal models. Vergote and co-workers studied 180 Roman Catholic students in the United States. Sixty of them were high school students; the remainder were college undergraduates, evenly divided between liberal arts and science majors. Subjects were randomly presented with thirty-six traits and were asked to rate, using a seven-point scale, the degree to which each characterized his or her mother, father, and God. Ratings of parents and God were done separately, so as to minimize response artifacts. Eighteen of the traits presented had been chosen to represent qualities commonly deemed maternal. The remaining eighteen had been chosen to represent paternal qualities. Ratings of parents and God on maternal and paternal traits were statistically compiled and then compared using correlation coefficients.

Insofar as they relied on correlations, the Vergote et al. (1969) method is conceptually related to the Q-sort test. The researchers found that whereas images of the mother tended to be strongly associated with only maternal traits, images of the father were associated with both maternal and paternal traits. Images of God were more strongly associated with paternal traits, but maternal traits played an important role. Therefore, the maternal traits were important in all three images, but paternal traits were important only in the images of father and God. What Vergote and co-workers called maternal traits apparently included protective and nurturant qualities that actually characterize parents of both sexes. Considering only maternal traits, the mean correlation for ratings of God and father was 0.70, which was highly statistically significant. The corresponding correlation for ratings of God and mother was not statistically significant. Therefore, insofar as God was perceived as protective and nurturing, the pattern of divine attributes resembled that of the father, not that of the mother. On paternal traits, the correlations between ratings of God and father, or between those of God and mother, were both nonsignificant. Therefore, insofar as God was perceived as paternal, the pattern of divine attributes differed from that of either parent. Cultural and religious differences limit the generality of the Vergote et al. (1969) findings, which nonetheless indicate the difficulties encountered in tracing the origins of the God image.

In chapter 3, I referred to work by Spiro and D'Andrade (1958) and Lambert et al. (1959), who used ethnographic data to study the relationship between child-rearing methods and the form of religious beliefs. As I noted in chapter 3, parallels exist between culturally determined parental responses to childhood needs and expectations adults have of supernatural beings. As a cultural phenomenon, consistency of this kind requires explanatory concepts beyond those of individual psychology. As a personal phenomenon, however, reenactment of childhood expectations in adult religious experience is only to be expected from the transference-like quality of religious belief, as illustrated by studies of the kind being described.

Religions with more than one deity, or with ancillary supernatural figures, permit segregation of parental part objects, which can then be ascribed to separate supernatural beings. This is of particular psychological value when contradictory aspects of parental images are involved, because they may not lend themselves to easy integration in a single God image. The difficulty of integrating contradictory aspects of parental images is well known to students of transference as it occurs in psychotherapy. In psychotherapy, the inability of some patients to integrate contradictory part objects has been discussed under the rubric "splitting" (see, for example, Greenberg & Mitchell, 1983), which is an apt term for the same phenomenon as it occurs in the realm of religious transference. In Catholicism, for example, maternal attributes can be ascribed to the Virgin Mary and paternal attributes to God the Father. Problems of integrating maternal and paternal representations are thereby potentially circumvented, at least for the least sophisticated worshippers. Not surprisingly, attachment-related concerns will then be addressed to the Virgin and other concerns to God. There will be a division, so to speak, of psychological labour between the divine beings according to the transference-like attributes ascribed to them.

Differences in transference-like attributes might have contributed to the occasionally low correlations observed in Q-sort tests between the concepts of God and Jesus (M.O. Nelson & Jones, 1957; Strunk, 1959). For instance, at least some people might attribute parental characteristics to God, while they ascribe characteristics of an older sibling to Jesus.

Along the same lines, gender or parental preferences might affect emotional responses to supernatural beings with differing transference attributes. Given a choice of several supernatural beings that have variously assumed maternal and paternal characteristics, the worshipper's gender or parental preference might cause him or her to feel more strongly attached to one deity or another. Deconchy (1968) reported some preliminary data along these lines: Catholic boys from seven to sixteen years of age showed more free associations related to the Virgin Mary, while Catholic girls of the same age showed more related to the Divine Father. Insofar as associations reflect affective salience, Deconchy's results support a difference of the kind suggested here.

Religions that postulate good and evil beings allow worshippers to segregate good and bad parental impressions. In these cases, parental aspects are separated according to the degrees of hatred or love they manifest, rather than according to maternal or paternal roles. Freud (1923b) analyzed a case of possession described in a seventeenth-century manuscript. The possessed man, a painter by the name of Christoph Haitzmann, claimed that in a state of despair following his father's death, he had signed a pact with the devil. In exchange for Haitzmann's body and soul, the devil had obligated himself to perform certain unspecified services for Haitzmann. According to Freud, these services meant the devil had promised to act as a father substitute for the grieving painter. In his discussion of Haitzmann, Freud noted that ideas with opposed aspects tend to split into two contrasting ideas. In recent years, divisions of this kind have been thought to occur, first, with early ideas of the mother (see, for example, Fauteux, 1981). Freud hypothesized that God and the devil were once a single deity, but that with the passage of time, the benevolent and threatening aspects of the father had separated and had become assigned to distinct deities. The devil subsequently embodied feared and hated paternal characteristics, while God embodied paternal love. Hating only the devil, the worshipper was freed to love God unambivalently.

Vergote (1988) described Sister Jeanne de Ferry, a sixteenth-century nun who also claimed to have signed a pact with the devil. Her case is reminiscent of that of Christoph Haitzmann.

Following Freud, several other authors expanded on his theory of devil-like figures and noted the extent to which good and bad parental characteristics tend to be assigned to separate supernatural beings. Ernest Jones (1951), for example, claimed that the torments suffered in hell are simply the worshipper's own sadistic fantasies, originally directed toward the father figure but now administered in retaliation by the bad father, Satan.

Roheim (1946) described the so-called Tuesday Woman, a Rumanian folklore figure known under different names throughout Eastern Europe. In Western Europe, her equivalent was Saint Agatha, who was also known as the "cat saint." On Tuesday nights, washing, spinning, or sexual intercourse were avoided, for fear of provoking the Tuesday Woman's wrath. She would come as an old, deformed woman, or even in animal guise, and punish offenders with magical tricks. From tales told of her, Roheim deduced that the Tuesday Woman embodied hated and feared aspects of the maternal image. If so, she must have played the same role with regard to the Virgin Mary as Satan, according to Freud, played with regard to God. That is, by embodying the malicious and feared characteristics of real human mothers, the Tuesday Woman or her counterparts spared the Virgin Mary from less than desirable attributes.

Ernest Jones (1959) and Galvin and Ludwig (1961) made a similar point with respect to witches: The witch is to the mother figure what the devil is to the father figure. The bewitched Mexican-American family described by Galvin and Ludwig (1961) was discussed in a previous chapter. It is more than coincidental that a culture such as the Mexican-American, in which the Virgin Mary figures so prominently, would also support belief in evil witches. Psychologically, beliefs in good and bad supernatural mothers may reinforce each other. Spero (1982) also commented on the polarization of good and bad representations in religious heroes and villains. Perhaps because they are merely human, one-dimensional heroes and villains found in religious literature sometimes serve as identification figures for certain disturbed personality types.

Clear-cut separations between good and bad deities, and consequently between transference-like positive and negative attributes, are also encountered in the various Gnostic sects (see V. Weber, 1983). According to Gnostic doctrines, evil Demiurges control the material world and obscure mankind's view of the loving and perfect God beyond. This loving God can be seen only with mystical faith, not with the senses nor with reason. Early Christian Gnostics, for instance, considered Christ the true God and Jehovah an inferior Demiurge (see Shneidman & Levine-Schneidman, 1983). Although defeated by Trinitarianism, early Christian Gnosticism resurfaced in the Albigensian heresy, which played an important role in medieval Church history.

Gnostic elements are also to be found in certain modern cults. Not only does Gnostic theology separate good and bad parental representations, which are ascribed to opposing deities; it also embodies certain dynamic aspects of childhood ambivalence toward the parents. Just as the the child sees the bad, or frustrating, parent as an obstacle to his enjoyment of the good, or satisfying, parent, so the Gnostic worshipper sees the evil Demiurge as blocking his view of the loving God beyond. The very young child's perception isn't simply Oedipal: The "bad" mother, or the split-off frustrating aspect of the mother, may be seen as an obstacle to enjoyment of the "good" mother, or her split-off loving aspect. Likewise, the Gnostic belief that bad deities can block access to good ones may symbolize deeper themes than those of the Oedipus complex.

Along somewhat different lines, Jung (1952) discussed how the shadow archetype, which embodies disavowed aspects of the self, is segregated from the idealized self by projection onto satanic figures. God thereby remains the image of what we would like to be, while the devil represents what we deny being. This is splitting of the self, rather than of the parents. Clinicians have observed that persons who are unable to tolerate contradictory feelings about their parents are also frequently unable to tolerate contradictory feelings about themselves. Therefore, those who are prone to split parental characteristics among separate deities may also be prone to project the worst parts of themselves onto satanic figures. If so, devil or witch figures must be composed from hated aspects of parents and self. Projection of archetypes is discussed at the end of this chapter.

Divine Attributes as Sources of Personal Information

Psychotherapists believe that they can obtain useful information about their patients' past relationships by carefully observing how their patients respond to them. In particular, unrealistic, transferential perceptions of the psychotherapist show how patients perceived parents or other important figures from their past, and they illustrate how those perceptions affect current relationships. For example, a patient who complains that a normally considerate therapist is depriving and hostile may have had depriving and hostile parents, or he may have been hostile himself and expected retaliation. Details of the patient's history, together with details of the current transference, help to elucidate which of several historical possibilities are indicated by current distortions. Transference attributes ascribed to the psychotherapist are usually of widespread, if less obvious, significance in other relationships, too, so their clarification and elucidation of their origins may help to improve the patient's perception of reality.

To take another example: Every psychotherapist is inevitably flawed and imperfect; regardless of good intentions, he or she will sooner or later be late, inconsiderate, inattentive, or obtuse. If only in the matter of payment, the psychotherapist will have to insist that things be done for his or her convenience, rather than for that of the patient. Yet certain patients insist on viewing their psychotherapist as unequivocally perfect. These patients vehemently excuse or deny episodes of inconsideration, inattention, or obtuseness. They refuse to acknowledge that the psychotherapist is sometimes selfish. This type of transference, which consists less of attributions than of rigid refusal to view the psychotherapist as a complete human being, often recreates early relations to the parents. Unreliable or cruel parents, for example, can mobilize such powerful animosities from their children that the children respond by defensively denying their parents' faults completely. Alternatively, ill or depressed parents may seem fragile to their children, who then deny their criticism in order to protect their loved ones.

As in the previous example, specifics of the patient's history, together with details of the current transference, usually point toward specific historical possibilities, of which I have cited just two. Also as in the previous example, a transference distortion of this kind may be most evident in psychotherapy but will always be found to affect other important relationships. Many other transference attributions and distortions can become evident in psychotherapy, and all of them can be mined for information about the patient and about the nature of his or her relationships. As I noted earlier, many clinicians are so convinced of the value of information to be gained from transference that they take care not to obscure it by revealing information about their personal lives.

In the preceding section, I showed that attributes ascribed to divine beings are highly correlated with perceived parental characteristics—maternal, paternal, or both. Ideas of God, in other words, are at least in part tranference-like. Less religious persons, being relatively freed from theological constraint, are particularly likely to read parental characteristics into the image of God. There is, moreover, a correlation between the parental attributes ascribed to God and the strategic functions subserved by religious belief. Salient attachment functions, for example, are usually associated with a maternal image of God, or at least with an image of God based on the nurturant aspects of the father's behavior. These facts suggest that detailed investigations of religious beliefs—or in the case of the nonreligious, of the hypothetical image of God—may reveal information akin to that uncovered by psychotherapeutic transference and of the same general significance. I have already described individuals, such as Martin Luther and Daniel Miller, whose image of God more or less directly expressed their perceptions of an emotionally salient parental figure. Martin Luther, of course, never received psychotherapy. But if he had, it seems plausible that he would have perceived his psychotherapist as hostile and unsatisfied, just as he perceived God. The same remarks apply to Daniel Miller, who did receive psychotherapy but concerning whose transference Rizzuto (1979) provided no information. In other words, psychotherapeutic transferences and images of God likely provide much the same information, particularly in those who reject the theologies in which they were raised.

It has been known for a long time that religious ideas contain clinically useful information. Freud knew it, of course, as did Jung. And even fifty years ago, the mainstream psychologist Allport (1937) had suggested assessing religious beliefs for purposes of psychological diagnosis. Over twenty years ago, Draper et al. (1965) proved the potential value of religious information by studying fifty patients in psychiatric treatment. Psychiatrically untrained workers without knowledge of the patients' histories administered a semistructured interview concerning religious beliefs. Questions were asked concerning favorite biblical stories, concepts, and images. Verbatim material from religious interviews was reviewed by psychiatrists without other knowledge of the patients. Written diagnoses and psychodynamic formulations based on religious material were compared with diagnoses and formulations derived by the usual methods by the treating psychiatrists. Draper and co-workers found little difference between the two sets of diagnoses and formulations. Some patients were more willing to volunteer diagnostically and psychodynamically useful religious information than information of other kinds normally sought by clinicians. The authors concluded that religious ideation provides "another royal road" to unconscious material. The first "royal road," described by Freud (1900), is, of course, the dream.

More recent studies have extended these findings: Images of God correlate with clinically important psychological traits. Benson and Spilka (1973), for instance, showed that positive self-esteem correlates with images of a kindly, accepting God. Images of a vindictive, punitive God are generally expressed by persons with low self-regard. Flakoll (1974, cited in Spilka et al., 1985) found that loving God images are expressed by youngsters with fewer signs of emotional maladjustment. Extremely punitive and threatening God images, or images that are sexualized, are likely to indicate severe psychological disturbance (see Spilka et al. 1985), which may or may not be evident from other material the patient is willing to volunteer.

It is somewhat surprising, consequently, that those who now

wish to know more about people, such as today's psychologists and psychiatrists, seldom inquire very closely into religious beliefs (cf. Natale, 1985). At least initially, most psychotherapists currently in practice content themselves with obtaining the barest facts concerning denomination and attendance and perhaps a subjective estimate of the importance religion bears to the patient. Efforts to obtain detailed descriptions of God are seldom made, particularly when the individual being questioned denies belief in the first place. Yet even those who deny a belief in God are usually willing to describe the God they don't believe in—just as, for example, they might be willing to describe their fantasy of an alien being—and these are precisely the persons whose descriptions of God reveal the greatest amount of specifically personal information. These descriptions, when placed beside historical information and information later gathered from psychotherapeutic transference, round out the picture of the patient's psychological functioning: his or her perceptions of parents and other important persons, misreadings of current social relationships, strategic preoccupations, and expectations of reward or punishment.

Also, in light of arguments made in the preceding chapter, descriptions of the image of God are to some degree descriptions of the superego, the Freudian "above-I." Freudians, of course, would agree with this, since the deity is said by them to be partly projected superego. In the preceding chapter, however, I argued that what Freud called the superego is really a private god. His attributes may or may not coincide with those of the public deity, but extreme degrees of discordance between private and public deities might make official religion emotionally unconvincing. Although she couched her findings in somewhat different terms, research by Rizzuto (1979) showed that individuals are likely to view the public deity selectively in order to fit with their superego. Insofar as they reflect what Freudians call the superego, descriptions of the image of God are ipso facto worth obtaining for psychological purposes.

I will not discuss here the reasons that psychotherapists avoid close inquiries into religious ideas. These reasons are mostly adventitious—having to do with the training and background of psychotherapists, rather than with factors intrinsic to psychotherapy. Rizzuto (1979), for one, has shown how patient's ideas about God can be systematically surveyed and used to advance their psychological assessment. I strongly encourage readers who are psychotherapists to study Rizzuto's questionaire and her method of record keeping. Some of Rizzuto's most convincing material was displayed in tabular form. When statements about God and family members were placed side by side, extraordinary coincidences of wording and content could be clearly seen.

I have already discussed the case of Daniel Miller, a patient studied by Rizzuto (1979), whose representations of God and father were strikingly similar. Another of Rizzuto's cases, "Douglas O'Duffy," shows how psychologically important themes relating to the mother manifest themselves in the image of God. O'Duffy, a thirty-nine-year-old Pennsylvania State Police officer had taken to his bed with headaches, irritability, and depression following a motor vehicle accident in which he was knocked unconscious. He may have had postconcussive syndrome, which can cause mood changes for several months following a traumatic loss of consciousness (M.P. Alexander, 1982), or his depression may have been caused by psychological factors. While depressed, O'Duffy was preoccupied with attention and recognition and with his belief that he had not gotten the accolades he deserved. As Rizzuto pointed out, such preoccupations are thought to result from disturbances in the early consolidation of self-esteem, due to maternal unresponsiveness or disinterest. Winnicott (1971) and Kohut (1971, 1977) are the psychological theorists most closely associated with these ideas. In fact, O'Duffy did see his mother as lacking affection for him, and his image of God closely coincided with the image he held of his mother. According to O'Duffy, God was far too busy to bother helping him, or even to hear his prayers, and lacked compassion for him. O'Duffy thought that God just wanted him to behave and not to ask for anything. O'Duffy's image of God helped confirm the hypothesis that maternal representations of an uncaring type played an important role in his psychic life. It might have been used to promote insight or to predict later transference feelings if he received psychotherapy.

Insofar as negative images of God are transference-like, successful psychotherapy may lead to an increase in apparent religiosity. As transference distortions weaken, the patient–God relationship, so to speak, can improve in tandem with the patient–therapist relationship and with personal relationships in general (see Heinrichs, 1982; Hutch, 1983; Rossi, 1985; Vergote, 1988; Wack, 1968). Consequently, enhanced religious observance following psychotherapy is not necessarily a sign of unresolved conflict, as the Freudian view would seem to imply; it can also represent use of an adaptive pathway previously blocked by the neurotic process. Psychological adaptation via the religious pathway may or may not be suboptimal, but it is not in itself proof of poor health (see the Appendix).

The opposite process can also occur: Recrudescent childhood conflicts may shatter needed religious faith. Consider, for example, the following case, known to me: "George" was thirty-eight. He had suffered from posttraumatic stress disorder since his combat duty in Vietnam, some fifteen years previously. In Vietnam, George and a companion had triggered an enemy mine. His companion died on the spot. George suffered abdominal wounds, a punctured lung, and massive blood loss. His scalp, face, and eyes were peppered with shrapnel. During his slow recovery, he developed persistent nightmares, flashbacks, and panic attacks. He began to drink heavily and to use heroin, amphetamines, and cocaine. He attempted to kill himself by a half-dozen different means. For ten years following his discharge from the army, he was hospitalized nearly continuously for his suicidal thoughts. But even in the hospital, he could not be kept from drugs. On one occasion, he obtained a syringe and injected himself with wine. His prognosis was thought to be hopeless.

Unable to sleep at night, George eventually began watching a religious TV station featuring round-the-clock sermons by a fundamentalist preacher. The sermons, which reminded George of his childhood religious training, affected him deeply. They seemed to place the events in Vietnam, and his subsequent mental disorder, in a new light. He began to think that his troubles served some heavenly plan. If God allowed him to suffer, he reasoned, then God must have a purpose in mind. George resolved to live, and he promised God that he would give up drugs and alcohol. He kept his promise in spite of the fact that he still had flashbacks and night-mares. For the first time in years, he took passes outside the hos-pital. Eventually, George was discharged, still with his mental disorder but with an improved adaptation to life. George lived out of the hospital for three years. He watched the religious station and prayed several hours each day.

Studies described in the Appendix show that persons addicted to drugs or alcohol are often helped by religion to change their style of living. In fact, religious faith may be the most potent factor in changing addictive behaviors. In this respect, therefore, George was not unusual.

But in George's case, we see once again the coincidence of pa-rental—in this case, paternal—images and those of the deity. And the coincidence here proved fatal. George saw his father as prin-cipled and masculine: Although he cared about people, he expected a lot from them. He wasn't the type to help those who could not make it alone. George's God was much the same: Although he loved people, he was not the type to save someone who could not or would not be righteous. People had to obey the rules. George believed that God expected him to reform; it was entirely up to him whether or not he'd be damned.

Several years after his discharge from the hospital, George dis-covered that his brother—a homosexual who had been fired from a teaching job for sexual indiscretions—had falsified a job appli-cation in order to teach again. George expected his father to notify the authorities, but his father ignored the matter. George's father wanted to give his brother another chance in life. George had worked for his father's regard; he was furious that his father would forgive his brother who had not even tried to obey the rules. Child-hood feelings and conflicts concerning his efforts to please his fa-ther were suddenly reignited. His anger with his father spilled over onto God. God and his father were, after all, very much alike for George. He doubted the value of pleasing God. He wondered if God was predictable. Perhaps the sinners would be saved and the righteous damned. Since there was no way of knowing, he might as well do as he wished. Only suckers obeyed the rules. Angry with his father and with his paternal God, George began to drink. He died shortly afterward of a drug and alcohol overdose.

Divine Attributes as Sources of
Archetypal Information

The following discussion more or less continues with topics raised at the end of chapter 4. As I noted in chapter 4 it is possible to take a somewhat different view of transference from the classical Freudian view. Transferential distortions may be based not only on parental models but on archetypal models as well. Archetypal perceptions of others are part and parcel of following social strategies. Therefore, when they are evident, they provide a clue to the salient social strategies. An example was given in chapter 4 of an adult who continued to manifest salient infant attachment strategies. Such an adult would see in other persons potential or failed attachment figures. He or she would see everywhere only maternal archetypes, in their positive and negative forms. Likewise, young men pursuing sexual competitive strategies see older men as the potentially hostile father, an aspect of the paternal archetype related to the Oedipus complex. Other, more complex examples are somewhat beside the point here.

Insofar as the image of God forms from something like transference, then perceptions of God might betray some archetypal material, too. That is, deities in general might be seen not only as like the parents, but as like prototypical beings associated with archetypes. In the preceding chapter, I mentioned how the archetypal mother appears in most religions. Neumann (1955) and Weigert-Vowinkel (1938) described her various forms. In chapter 3, I described how religious beliefs may serve proximity maintenance strategies. These are the strategies in which the mother archetype might play a prominent role. The archetypal father appears in religion, too. His manifestations form the basis for the Freudian theory of religious belief (see earlier discussion). In chapter 3, I showed how religion may serve male competitive strategies. These are the strategies in which the father archetype might play a prominent role. Particular case histories illustrated how sexual competitive preoccupations sometimes coincide with a negative paternal image of God. Preoccupations, so to speak, with the Oedipal archetype also affect perceptions of God. Earlier in this Chapter, I also mentioned Jung's notion of the projection of the shadow, or the disa-

vowed parts of the self. Once again the pattern is clear: A deity—
in this case, an inferior God—becomes the vehicle for an archetypal personification.

Jung believed that personified archetypes are at the root of
religious faith. Jung's theory, however, was based less on the archetype's role in structuring social perceptions than on the strong
emotional valence of an archetypal portrait. Consider, for example,
the archetypal mother, viewed in the light of modern attachment
theory (see Stevens, 1983). Given an environment resembling that
of adaptation, a great deal of phylogenetically acquired information concerning the typical mother should be available to the human infant. This information, which is presumably retained
throughout life, is summarized in a personification—that of the
positive mother. That is, archetypal information about the prototypical mother is contained in a portrait of the "great mother's"
attributes. She is loving, abundant, generous and wise, forgiving,
omnipresent, and responsive to need. Her huge breasts are always
full, and everything living came from her womb. Her symbols fill
entire books (see Neumann, 1955)! She is also, like other personified portraits of archetypal experience, uncanny, wierd, and seemingly numinous. In her seeming holiness, she stands apart from the
merely profane world inhabited by real persons. According to Jung
(1919, 1920/1948, 1928, 1951, 1958), the uncanny feelings evoked
by archetypal portraits lead to their being perceived as gods. If they
cannot be seen as gods, then their seemingly alien nature will be
expressed in secular myths, such as in modern fantasies of extraterrestrial beings on Earth (Jung, 1958).

If, either because of their role in structuring previously unstructured social perceptions or because of the emotional valence of
their associated personifications, archetypes do determine the image of God, then their role in this regard might seem to contradict
the previous emphasis placed on early parental impressions. Phylogenetic influence, in effect, might seem to undermine the importance of personal history in determining the culturally indeterminate
attributes ascribed to unseen beings. Actually, though, the various
possibilities are not at odds with each other. All three are variants
of a single basic position. As I noted in the preceding chapter, for
example, a father's or mother's adequacy may reside in his or her

being able to trigger archetypal experiences. Once triggered, archetypal experiences determine how the child will perceive the parent. For instance, the mother who is just warm and nurturant enough to trigger her child's maternal archetype will be seen as warm and loving, in spite of the fact that her real behavior might be much more complex. Insofar as the parents are perceived in archetypal terms, no conflict should exist between archetypal and parental models in determining the image of God. As a result of either their role in structuring social perceptions or their emotional valence, archetypes will directly shape the image of God; because of their influence on the perception of parents, archetypes will shape the image of God indirectly.

Second, insofar as personal history determines the salient social strategies, it will also determine which archetypes play the important perceptual roles. This is because archetypes—with the exception of religious faith itself—are subjective correlates of particular social strategies. Characteristics of the parents—such as their tendency to trigger negative parental archetypes—may consequently leave their children in the grips of particular archetypes even after they've grown. Insofar as these archetypes later determine the image of God, parental characteristics will have had an indirect influence.

Third, archetypal and personal information differ in kind from each other. Archetypal information is on the order of an organizational scheme. Personal information provides the material on which this scheme is brought to bear. In the preceding chapter, I noted that personal histories do not so much replace archetypal elements in subjective experience as particularize them. Developmental events fill out the flesh on the phylogenetic skeleton. Insofar as conflict may exist between archetypal and personal information, it lies not in frank contradiction but in the way phylogenetic biases may force real perceptions into a Procrustean bed. Particularly salient archetypes may organize social perceptions in a way that does violence to the real complexity of particular persons. Therefore, insofar as archetypes monopolize the God image, they will not so much replace the parents in this regard as, at most, preclude manifestation of their contradictory features in the religious realm.

Finally, emotional responses to archetypal personifications are intrinsic to their role in the organization of social perception. After all, affective responses evolved because they increase fitness (see Marks, 1987). Presumably, affective responses to archetypal personifications reinforce (see chapter 2) the advantageous social strategies to which they are related. Insofar as the emotional valence of archetypal personifications subserves their social-perceptual role, then the contradiction between the transference model of their role in formation of the God image and the classical Jungian treatment of the same phenomenon also disappears. That is, saying that archetypes organize previously unstructured social situations, including those with deities, is really not so different from saying that their emotional salience leads to their projection.

Insofar as archetypal and personal sources of the God image are not only intertwined but more or less equivalent, we have found for religious images precisely what we discovered when we studied overt behaviors (see chapter 2). This discovery is the real answer to the nature/nurture issue. The archetypal and personal sources of the God image lead to a kind of chicken-and-egg conundrum: Prototypical experiences structure developmental events, which have as their main significance activation of archetypes. Both prototypical and acquired dispositions can be said to determine the image of God without either loss of accuracy or substantive change in meaning. In the case of overt behaviors, innately probable social strategies pattern behavior in particular environments that resemble those of adaptation. These environments, however, activate components of particular social strategies. Either social strategies or the environment, or both, can be said to determine overt behaviors, again without loss of accuracy. In each case, attempts to clearly distinguish nature from nurture prove to be sterile exercises. No component of experience or behavior is ever purely phylogenetic, and none are purely epigenetic. Whether we choose to emphasize one or the other is determined only by their relative heuristic values (see, for example, Wenegrat, 1984).

6
Afterword: An Illusion of the Future

Freud opposed religious beliefs, which he considered forms of infantilism. The solaces of religion, according to Freud, are obtained at the cost of remaining a child, which is too high a price to pay for whatever religion offers. Freud (1927) envisioned a "race of men who have renounced all illusions," foremost among them religious beliefs. Instead of relying on God, these men of the future would rely on science. Though science provides only partial solutions to the problems of life, they are more than can be expected from believing in illusions. Also, since they do not require the sacrifice of reason, they ultimately cost less than those obtained from religious beliefs.

Psychology and religion are no longer as opposed as Freud would have liked to see them. First, theorists who have followed Freud have generally been able to see some good in religious faith. Even some psychoanalysts have argued for rapprochement with the religious-minded (see, for example, Fromm, 1950; P. Gay, 1987; Meissner, 1984; Ostow, 1980; Sullivan, 1947; Zilboorg, 1962; cf. Bonaparte, 1958). Some have treated religion as creative adaptation, a form of regression in the service of the ego (see, for example, Allison, 1968; Fingarette, 1958). In other words, though the process is admitted to be infantile, the aim of religion is nonetheless viewed as mature. Other accounts of religious faith based on the so-called transitional realm (see chapter 4) have had the same implication: that adaptive ends can be served by strictly irrational means. Those who aim to reconcile religion and psychoanalysis have treated Freud's militant atheism as a purely personal matter, unrelated to the science he founded. As described in chapter 3, such arguments are easily sustained by the facts now known of Freud's life. No one can doubt that Freud was biased with regard to religious faith.

Jung has also exerted a melioristic influence. Working from a different theoretical framework from Freud's, Jung (1916/1957, 1922) argued that a life without myth is impossible. Myths, including religious beliefs, are not mere cultural artefacts but arise from within individuals and reflect prototypical thought forms. Insofar as Jung was correct, to renounce illusions is to renounce human nature. Freud's race of men without illusions would be something other than human.

Throughout his life, and particularly in his work on religion, Jung tried to take seriously every type of human experience. For example, with the support of Eugen Bleuler, the great Swiss psychiatrist who did pioneering work in the phenomenology of schizophrenia, Jung wrote his doctoral thesis on occult phenomena. From his study of the occult, Jung developed many of the ideas that would later become important in psychological theory. Jung's basic premise was that no matter how absurd its ordinary interpretation, every experience signifies something, if only about the person who has the experience. Insofar as the experience is valued, that which it signifies is likely to be the more important to learn about. This is, of course, the position adopted here toward religious beliefs.

Jung's attitude has influenced modern-day investigators, who have been freed by it to study topics that might seem unworthy of great effort from a more rationalistic viewpoint. For example, in recent years, reputable investigators have shown an interest in studying so-called near-death experiences reported by persons who have been gravely ill or injured (see, for example, Greyson, 1983; Greyson & Stevenson, 1980; Heaney, 1983; Noyes, 1980; Sabom, 1980; Siegel, 1980; Stevenson & Greyson, 1979); trances and mystical states (see, for example, Allison, 1970; Dean, 1970, 1973; Gallemore et al., 1969; Gellhorn & Kiely, 1972; Glenn, 1970; Horton, 1973; Ludwig, 1966; Robbins, 1969; Shimano & Douglas, 1975; Spilka et al., 1985, chap. 8; R.K. Wallace, 1970; R.K. Wallace et al., 1971; Wenger & Bagchi, 1961; Wenger et al., 1961);

and visions and cosmic perceptions (see, for example, Comer et al., 1967; Tart, 1975; A.F.C. Wallace, 1959).

Finally, cultural changes have played a role in the reconciliation of psychology and religion. The years since Freud have been marked by increasing secularization. At the beginning of this century, the authority of religious institutions, and the educational and civil power they exerted, made the debate between science and religion a highly practical issue. Scientists under attack by religious authorities had to defend themselves, by counterattacks if necessary. The waning of religious authority has somewhat blunted the debate with science. Theologians no longer fight the newest scientific theories, and even top-notch scientists go to church these days. Exceptions to this reconciliation, such as continued attempts by "creationists" to block the teaching of Darwinism, have for the most part been localized in the least cosmopolitan regions. Most theologians and scientists seem content to live in peace.

As a measure of how far things have come, today there are even pastoral psychologists. One's attitude toward these counselors depends on whether one feels that religious belief is compatible with the highest level of mental health. If it is, then pastoral psychology is a perfectly sensible calling. If it is not, as Freud believed, then the term *pastoral psychology* is oxymoronic. If it made sense at all, it would be equivalent to such terms as *industrial psychology* or *advertising psychology,* in which it is understood that the "psychology" is put to work for industrial or advertising purposes. In fact, psychologists and psychiatrists have taken every possible position toward the mixing of clinical and religious models (see, for example, Carbine, 1980; Franzblau, 1960; Griffith, 1983; W.S. Hill, 1955; Kemp, 1985; Levy-Suhl, 1946; Mollica et al., 1986; Moore, 1944; Nelson & Torrey, 1973; Ostow, 1980; Pattison, 1966; Rayburn, 1985; Spero, 1985, 1987). The most striking feature is the lack of a philosophical or scientific consensus half a century following Freud's attack on religion. By default, the debate over pastoral psychology has shifted in recent years from philosophical and scientific issues to those more easily addressed: standards of practice, malpractice insurance, and channels of reimbursement.

However, the religious implications of psychological theories are still of practical importance, especially for clinicians. These implications are not merely theoretical, and they cannot simply be shelved in the interests of public relations. First, I show in the Appendix how religious beliefs may be important factors in psychological adaptation, the topic of most interest to those who work with patients. Understanding the psychology of religion is essential to understanding factors in adaptation. Second, the treatment of religious patients or the handling of religious material is more or less directly determined by how the psychological clinician views religion. If he or she sees religious material as infantile, for example, that outlook will dictate very different reactions than if he or she sees it as a mature response to existential problems. If he or she believes that people can function without religion, that belief will dictate very different reactions than if he or she sees religion as a real necessity.

In previous chapters, I have used sociobiologic concepts developed in recent years to analyze various facets of belief in God. Here I would like to apply the ideas developed thus far to the valuative issues discussed by Freud, by Jung, and by latter-day analysts that still confront us today. Do the ideas developed here place a particular value on belief in God? Do they promote a particular stance with regard to religion? What do they say of Freud's vision—a race without religion? Would such a race be better than ours, as Freud explicitly argued, or would it be something inhuman, as Jung would have certainly countered?

First, in chapter 3, I used sociobiologic concepts to categorize psychologically the functions of religious faith. In the process, the costs of faith were also partially categorized. For example, it was evident in chapter 3 that religious faith can provide otherwise absent group affiliations, the lack of which produces alienation and loneliness. At the same time, it was evident that individual believers might pay for these affiliations with their life or liberty, or at the cost of family or social ties antedating their conversion. The reader might think that benefits and costs catalogued as they were in chapter 3 can provide some guide to the overall value of religious faith. But the matter is much more complicated.

To begin with, most of the potential costs and benefits catalogued in chapter 3 go unrealized for any particular believer. There are two main reasons for this. First, not all faiths are the same. As was evident in chapter 3, some faiths serve certain functions better than others or exact different costs. Traditional Protestantism, for example, provides a particularly poor vehicle for attachment concerns but an excellent means for decreasing Oedipal anxiety. Along the same line, one is much more likely to forfeit life and liberty by joining a far-out cult than by attending the local reform synagogue. Second, the great religions are all sufficiently rich that individual believers can pick and choose, at least to some extent, from traditional themes that best serve their personal needs. In the process, of course, individuals also choose to pay different costs. A Roman Catholic monk, for example, can solve his sexual problems at the cost of social withdrawal. Another Roman Catholic might worship the Virgin Mary, thereby reducing separation fear at a cost that is rather minimal compared to that borne by the monk. The fact that religions differ, and that the same religion can serve wholly different functions and exact different costs, means that costs and benefits as they are actually realized are an individual matter. Potential costs and benefits can only serve as guidelines to individual cases. They provide no guide to valuation of religious faith in general.

Second, the uses and costs of religious faith cannot be assessed except in relation to what might take its place. Whether or not faith is a good way to ameliorate attachment anxiety, for instance, depends on what alternative methods exist for doing the same thing. There is some evidence, for example, that some adults with attachment anxiety are prone to addictive behaviors. Only the most doctrinaire opponent of religious faith would find it inferior to drug abuse. Likewise, religious faith is certainly superior to the phobic, hypochondriacal, or dependent adaptations that the same individuals are prone to develop. Psychotherapeutic resolution of attachment anxiety might be preferable to its religious amelioration. But in the world of real, as opposed to theoretical, options, psychotherapy isn't viable. Most people can't afford it; if they could, there wouldn't be enough psychotherapists to go around; and if even if there were, psychotherapy is a very weak treatment in the face of most attachment disorders. Its use to relieve attachment anxiety is questionable to begin with. Psychotherapists, in any event, are in no position to cast stones at priests when it comes to improving the quality of life for those with attachment problems.

To take another example, the use of faith to obtain affiliation must be assessed in relation to alternatives. Certainly, participation in a democratic community would be superior to membership in a religious cult as a means of gaining friends. Interdependent, democratic communities seldom squash individual character as religious cults do, and they rarely require surrendering family ties. On the other hand, another alternative to religious cult membership is membership in hate groups. There have recently been reports of paramilitary hate groups active in the United States. Younger persons—of the same age group that joins cults—are apparently joining such groups as the Ku Klux Klan. It seems highly probable that the young persons who are joining hate groups are seeking the same group membership that motivates those in religious cults. Once again, only the most doctrinaire opponent of religious faith would prefer to see people joining hate groups than participating in religious cults.

It is true, of course, that religious beliefs frequently seem to promote acts of group violence. In this century alone, religious wars have claimed millions of victims and have squandered priceless resources. However, in the absence of religious motives, secular motives are apparently adequate to inspire the worst type of slaughter. Recent secular bloodbaths clearly indicate that human group violence will survive the demise of religion, if that should ever occur as Freud predicted. Abolition of violence requires control of human groups, not of religious faith per se. In the same vein, book burnings and thought control are as likely occasioned by secular as by religious motives.

The state worship of Nazism and the cynical use of Marxist ideology to control the Soviet people have likewise shown that religion is inessential to the ruling class. This is in contrast to the way it seemed during the last century (see Harrington, 1983). If a religious opiate isn't available, in the narrow sense in which I have employed the term *religious,* the class in power will indoctrinate those who serve them with secular ideologies (see, also, Gruter, 1983).

Although the functions and costs categorized in chapter 3 provide no basis for a general valuation of religion, the material in chapter 4—concerning the origins of religious belief—turns out to be more relevant to Freud's attack on faith. In particular, the origins of belief are highly germane to Freud's future vision: a "race of men who have renounced all illusions." The thesis of chapter 4 was that Jung was correct in treating faith as an archetype. Specifically, I argued that social-cognitive schemata inherent in human thinking cause people to postulate unseen beings. These schemata reflect previously dominant pressures in human evolution, which lay in the social arena. Individuals, of course, can disbelieve in unseen beings, especially those postulated by others. Intelligent and educated persons with self-critical dispositions may be more likely to disbelieve in any particular unseen being. But the social schemata in question exert a ubiquitous influence, so that generalized disbelief may be more rare than is evident from superficial inquiries. For instance, individuals who disavow belief in publicly worshipped unseen beings may nonetheless act as if to please private unseen beings. I have claimed that the superego is, in essence, a private deity. And disavowal itself may be a social act aimed at an unseen being or may be motivated by social goals unrelated to faith, such as the wish to annoy one's parents. Case histories illustrating these points were cited in previous chapters.

Insofar as religious faith reflects prototypical experience, Freud's race without religious illusions is unlikely to be born from any existing society. If it were born, it would shortly die. This is consistent with Jung's position on the life devoid of myth as well as with observations by religious anthropologists (Eliade, 1969). For human beings, the absence of religious belief of the type I have considered is not a passive but an effortful state. Individuals in Freud's race would have to actively resist believing in the unseen beings they would still continue to postulate as the result of their social-cognitive schemata. Superegos would have to be banned from the public domain! Such resistance to belief would require training and social force. From among the impaired, the insane, or the uneducated, and from among those resistant to training and social pressure, prophets would arise. These prophets would create new faiths to replace those of their ancestors. Precisely because of the lack of religious institutions, faith would spread all the more rapidly in an irreligious world. Just as Islam exploded into the religious vacuum of seventh-century Arabia (see chapter 3), so new forms of worship would explode to fill the vacuum at the heart of Freud's utopia. The race without illusions would sooner or later become a race of newborn zealots.

But theory aside, Freud's vision might seem on the verge of realization, at least in specific societies. Since World War I, Communist bloc governments have tried to suppress religious faith. At the same time, in industrialized Western nations, sociological and economic factors have weakened religious commitments. Neo-Darwinism, psychoanalysis, existentialism, and even modern physics have severely undermined religion's credibility. Among Western educated classes in particular, many people consider religion an antediluvian oddity. Yet progress toward Freud's vision may be more apparent than real. Insofar as it has been real, it may have already run its course, leaving the world far short of what Freud actually hoped for. In both Communist and Western nations, religion retains an active grasp on the people's imagination.

In Poland, for example, the Catholic Church has recently shown the power it still commands after forty years of Communist rule. In the Soviet Union, religious belief has survived three generations of Communist rule. There is no way to know how many Russian Orthodox there are in the Soviet Union, but the number is undoubtedly greater than just those who go to church. Although many Jews wish to leave the Soviet Union to escape educational and job discrimination, others desire to leave in order to practice their religion. Groups of Pentecostalists have also tried to emigrate. In the southern Soviet Union, Islam remains a potentially powerful force. In the West, recent studies have shown a swing back to religious faith. In Muncie, Indiana, for example, there has been a significant rise in church attendance and other indicators of religiosity since the original "Middletown" surveys in the 1920s and 1930s (Caplow et al., 1983). It is hard to assess the meaning of this change, since ritual may be retained—or even flourish—after faith has departed (see, for example, Allport et al., 1948; MacIntyre, 1978). At the very least, though, evidence of increased religiosity challenges the assumption that secularization is always irreversible (Roof, 1984). Recent surveys cited by Spilka et al. (1985) indicated that the vast majority of Americans today claim to believe in God, admit to private prayer, and express confidence in religious institutions. Insofar as belief has eroded, it has likely been at the expense of liberal churches, while fundamentalist churches have thrived (see Spilka et al., 1985).

Successful new cults also belie the notion that religious belief is declining. It seems especially significant that most of the new cult recruits are young people raised in a nonreligious climate (see chapter 3).

Actually, even if formal religion waned, belief in unseen beings might nonetheless be retained among the apparently secularized. For example, Jung (1958) pointed out that modern popular myths, such as those concerning flying saucers, might serve the same functions as religious beliefs but in a technological idiom more suitable to the age. In fact, popular books and movies credit visiting aliens with powers and moral sensibilities resembling those of deities. Like gods, aliens have been credited with historical interventions as well as with interventions in the lives of private persons. One extremely popular type of science fiction is difficult to describe except in religious, messianic terms. Its popularity among the young betrays religious tendencies that, no longer channeled by formal religion, are freely expressed in pseudotechnical metaphors. L. Ron Hubbard, who understood quite well the connection between religion and science fiction, wrote best-selling science fiction after founding the Church of Scientology. And certain "flying saucer" cults are virtually indistinguishable from millenial religious cults of a more traditional type (see, for example, Festinger et al., 1956).

"Pop psychology," too, has its religious overtones. People who are unable to accept formal religion can sometimes accept religion dressed up as psychology. For example, *A Course in Miracles,* an expensive three-volume mixture of pop psychology and Gnostic religious ideas, has sold more than 150,000 copies in the last decade. Adherents study the *Course* in the same way Christians study the Bible. Some claim the *Course* can be used as a basis for therapy (see Wapnick, 1985).

Therefore, neither theoretical arguments derived from modern ideas on human nature nor recent events seem to offer support for Freud's hope for the future—that men and women will one day live without religious illusions. Consequently, we should now abandon Freud's vision and aim for something more modest and capable of attainment. For example, religious beliefs might be reshaped to promote improved adaptations. The functions of religion summarized in chapter 3 could conceivably be accomplished at less personal cost to religious believers.

Modern ideas on human nature, together with empirical studies, allow us to forecast potential ill effects caused by religious systems. We know for example, that dependent individuals are likely to become enthralled by religious leaders posing as loving parents. Enthrallment may lead to abuse and to loss of personal liberty. We know that excessively strict suppression of sexual drive is likely to produce neurotic sexuality. The same can be said for excessively strict suppression of aggressive behavior. We know that dogmatic emphasis on group cohesion is likely to encourage violence against outsiders. The material in chapter 3 points toward many other examples of predictable untoward effects. Insofar as issues of dogma were decided with such data in mind, religious beliefs of the future might prove, on the whole, less costly than those that have evolved without psychological input.

This is not to say, of course, that in the name of improved adaptive functioning psychologists should start writing fairy tales. Theologians and prophets will have to fashion the illusions of the future, just as they once fashioned today's illusions. The process will be influenced by many diverse factors, most of them unrelated to the ones discussed here. Psychologists and psychiatrists, though, can at least try to affect honest and humane religious thinkers by disseminating among them information gained from the study of adaptation.

At least in North America and Europe, information from modern psychology has already greatly influenced many religious leaders. This has occurred in spite of Freud's position, which discourages the psychological education of clergy by denying them a valid place in the conduct of human affairs. It is not surprising, perhaps, that Jung, who judged religion by its psychological meaning and not by the question of truthfulness, has had an especially great impact on religious thinkers seeking psychological guidance. The pastoral psychology movement reflects the clergy's interest in psychological matters. It deserves at least qualified support from mental health professionals who believe that religion is here to stay. Their major concern should be to improve the education of pastoral psychologists, both for clinical reasons and as a means of communicating with the religious world.

Rejection of Freud's vision—or, what is the same thing, acceptance of religion as a permanent fixture in human society—also has an effect in clinical practice. The psychotherapist has no business encouraging illusions, of course, but insofar as illusions reflect human nature, it makes no sense to discourage them indiscriminately as a sign of impaired functioning. There will always be people who, for one reason or another, are able to "do what comes naturally" without reservation or lingering doubt; they will wholeheartedly see the world in terms of social schemata. On the other hand, there will also always be people who deny being religious but are secretly in the grip of the very same cognitive process. Atheism is as likely to be neurotic as religiosity is to be infantile. If the clinician really wants to help people, rather than to impose upon them a set of extrinsic values, therapy should aim at elucidating the uses and costs of religious beliefs, not at giving them up. If the patient is an atheist, therapy should aim at elucidating *why*. Some individuals, of course, will give up their religious beliefs once their uses have been elaborated. As seen in previous chapters, though, others might become religious once their disavowed beliefs have been subjected to scrutiny. The therapeutic outcome, in any case, should not be judged on the degree of the patient's atheism when therapy has ended.

The sociobiologic model described in chapter 2 implies that for human beings, meaning must be social. If our raison d'être is to play social games, an asocial world will seem a mere stage—a mechanical, lifeless platform on which we lead our lives. Many people, of course, profess to find meaning in contemplating a purely mechanical cosmos. In light of chapters 4 and 5, in which I tried to show that religious beliefs are frequently hidden from view, it seems possible that many of those who claim to find meaning in an asocial universe actually find meaning by imagining its creator. But if an asocial universe is necessarily meaningless, then Freud's desire to see religion wither is also a wish that people give up meaning, at least on the suprahuman scale. This follows from the notion developed in chapter 4—that religious beliefs socialize that which is really nonsocial. There is, in fact, an entire literature, not coincidentally new to this century, that purports to show the moral and intellectual superiority of life in a basically meaningless world. But no matter how philosophically preferable it may be, people dislike life devoid of higher meaning. Too many needs go unsatisfied when the once living and social world becomes a dead mechanism. Many of these needs are described in chapter 3. Nor is it reasonable for psychologists to ask that people forgo their satisfactions when, in reality, we have nothing better to offer them than their own hopes and fantasies.

This line of argument will be uncongenial to rationalists, who condemn religious beliefs because they believe that they are untrue. Freud, of course, was the quintessential rationalist. Whatever Freud's biases were, his rejection of religion was ultimately based on a rationalist ideal—that people should not deceive themselves with untrue beliefs. This very same ideal is still deeply ingrained in modern psychoanalytic practice (for example, see Eagle, 1984; Schafer, 1976, 1978). However, the sociobiologic model employed in this study suggests that Jung was right: Human beings can strive after reason but will never be perfectly reasonable. They are not tabulae rasae. The sources of unreason are found within, and even in the most rational society, they will exert pressure in favor of recidivism.

To put the matter most strongly, if there is ultimately room in the human psyche for only one or the other, a future race without science remains psychologically more probable than one without religion. Even the highest civilization is susceptible to erosion down to psychological bedrock. If this happens, sophisticated citizens will be left perplexed and astonished precisely to the degree that they thought human nature had been definitely tamed. In light of the two- or three-million-year history of intelligent hominids, science is a new and possibly fragile bloom, religion a great Hydra. Rationalists who fail to note this ominous fact are suffering the most dangerous illusion of all.

Appendix: Faith, Psychopathology, and Adaptation

The model developed in this study is as follows: Humans normally adhere to certain innately probable social strategies. Among other factors that promote adherence to these strategies, feelings triggered by common social events play an important role. For example, separation anxiety triggered by transient loss reinforces the proximity maintenance requisite to survival. Unpleasant feelings, if they cannot be relieved by social acts directed toward other people, are potentially relieved by belief in an unseen being. For example, when there are no people around to serve as trusted attachment figures, belief in a nurturing god may relieve separation fear. Obedience to a paternal god may relieve anxiety related to sexual strategies. Conversely, pleasant feelings that cannot be achieved in real social relationships might be achieved in a relationship with an unseen being. Feelings of security, for example, may result from belief in an omnipresent god who is watching out for one's welfare. Feelings of belonging may be achieved through shared patterns of worship. Many other examples are given in chapter 3.

Because of the primacy of social-selective forces in molding human intelligence, social-cognitive schemata play a prominent, or perhaps predominant, role in human thought. When applied to nonsocial events, social-cognitive schemata produce an impression that unseen beings are working to make things happen as they are. Individuals differ greatly in the extent to which they acknowledge this impression, in the degree to which they accept it without doubt, and in the conformity they achieve in adjusting their own impression to consensual religious beliefs. An important factor affecting overt belief is the usefulness of the unseen being for relieving unpleasant feelings and producing pleasant feelings. These issues are discussed in chapters 4 and 5.

Belief in unseen beings might harm mental health in several ways. First, religious beliefs may affect the fate of entire societies or social classes. Their economic and political effects have sometimes proved disastrous to personal and public health, including mental health. Second, instinctual repression in the name of religion can produce intrapsychic conflict. Conflicts of this type, and consequent neurotic symptoms, were the major focus for early psychoanalysis. Third, affective satisfactions achieved in relationships with unseen beings could conceivably attenuate motivation for real social relationships or for resolution of problems attendant to real relationships. Consequent deterioration of real social life could harm mental health in obvious ways. Finally, habits of magical thinking condoned by belief in unseen beings might conceivably weaken reality testing in persons who are at risk for major mental disorders. In fact, persons with major mental disorders are often preoccupied with apparent religious ideas (see later discussion). Belief in unseen beings, in other words, might be mentally unhygienic for vulnerable individuals.

Advocates of religion can defend it against each charge. First, because they occur for economic, historic, and sociological reasons, foolish wars, economic and political oppression, and instinctual repression can and will occur without religion, which has played an instrumental, not an etiologic, role. Also, religions have promoted positive social causes that improve general welfare, not just war and oppression. Many humane institutions and laws are partly due to religion. Second, no evidence exists that large numbers of people have neglected real relationships as a result of their beliefs in unseen beings. For most people, religious affiliations enhance their social connections. People who neglect human relationships for ostensibly religious reasons are probably incapable of satisfactory relationships for reasons unrelated to their beliefs. Finally, in spite of the religious preoccupations of the insane, normally religious persons are fully in touch with reality. If anything, shared religious beliefs limit flights of individual fantasy and prevent idiosyncrasy.

Such claims and counterclaims are somewhat beyond the scope of this study. But the model developed here does, on the whole, imply an optimistic view regarding religion and mental health. To begin with, the social-cognitive schemata that produce beliefs in unseen beings are active factors in mental life regardless of whether their products are subject to critical scrutiny. Insofar as overt religiosity reflects a failure of critical thinking about the products of social-cognitive schemata, the causes for that failure lie outside religion per se. In any event, overt belief is an unreliable guide to the real power of social-cognitive schemata, which may be especially dominant in certain types of atheists. Moreover, the uses of belief described by this model are mostly ameliorative: to relieve unpleasant feelings and produce pleasant feelings when real social channels are blocked. If anything, the model implies that unhappy individuals with limited social opportunities or capacities might be helped to feel better by belief in unseen beings if they can believe in beings who are more or less benign.

In this Appendix, I will show that studies of mental health are generally consistent with the melioristic view implied by the model developed in this book: Although the insane are prone to religious preoccupations, and although some religious innovators may have been insane, no evidence exists that religious beliefs are mentally pathogenic. There are several ways in which religious preoccupations could develop out of insanity, rather than the reverse. Also, unhappy people with various failures of social adaptation seem to do better if they develop belief in an unseen being. Although we cannot rule out the possibility that religious beliefs sometimes impair social functioning, they are more commonly seen relieving distress consequent to existing social problems.

Religion as a Symptom

In 1621, Robert Burton, a clergyman, wrote about melancholia, emphasizing the frequency of religious signs and symptoms. Subsequent experience has justified Burton's emphasis; it is now common knowledge that mental disorders of several types may be manifested through abnormal religious concerns. Of course, because these concerns are responsive to the religious environment of the day, they have diminished in frequency as daily life has been secularized since Burton's time.

Records from France illustrate how rapidly the mentally ill can respond to changing social circumstance: Before the Revolution, Pinel—then chief physician at the largest asylum in France—noted that nearly one-quarter of his patients had prominent religious preoccupations. Such preoccupations were rare by the 1820s (S. Stone, 1934). Social life had been secularized in the intervening years (see chapter 4). Walters (1964) argued that, as a result of continuing secularization, religious preoccupations among the insane have declined in this century, too.

But if secularization can decrease religious preoccupations among the insane, religious revivals can stir them up again. During the first half of the nineteenth century, for example, a revival of religious interest swept the United States. The Mormons and other new sects were formed during this period, which has been called "the great awakening" (Garvey, 1983). A particularly important figure in this movement was a farmer named William Miller, who predicted the second coming for 1843. Fifty thousand people eventually believed him. In 1843, while Miller and his followers were eagerly waiting for Christ, a great comet appeared. Thinking that the Millenium was at hand, many Millerites left their work and gave away their possessions. The first state mental hospitals opened their doors at about the time the Millerite frenzy reached its peak. Their case records illustrate the effect Miller had on the mentally ill. For example, of 100 patients admitted in the first nine months to the New Hampshire State Hospital, 24 patients were psychotically preoccupied with the Millerite prophecies. (S. Stone, 1934). Significantly, many of the patients who had had earlier psychotic episodes had not previously expressed religious delusions; they emerged only during the religious ferment of the early 1840s.

At the turn of this century, a similar religious revival in Wales resulted in a sixfold increase in religious symptoms in those admitted to mental hospitals. At the same time, admissions for alcoholism fell by the same number of cases (Beit-Hallahmi & Argyle, 1977).

Studies performed before 1950 (Farr & Howe, 1932; Oates, 1949) indicated that between 10 and 50 percent of patients admitted to state mental hospitals had prominent religious preoccupations. This figure may be different today and may vary from state to state, but religious symptoms are still commonly seen in every part of this country.

Boisen (1936, 1960), who founded the pastoral psychology movement, argued that some psychoses are really religious crises. Religious preoccupations, according to Boisen, are not just morbid symptoms; they show the true psychotic concerns, which are existential in nature. Boisen himself suffered five psychotic episodes. Those who have been impressed by the seemingly mystical aspect of psychotic illness (see, for example, Wasserman, 1982), and who consequently have emphasized religious symptomatology, have elaborated further on Boisen's ideas.

Psychotic religious concerns differ qualitatively from the religious concerns of normal persons (Lowe, 1955; Rutledge, 1951; Stark, 1971). In some religious delusions, certain elements of normal religiosity—especially ideas of sin, redemption, and personal mission—achieve grotesque proportions. For instance, insane persons with religious delusions occasionally commit idiosyncratic violent crimes to achieve their "religious" goals. These crimes differ from communal acts of violence by the sane religious. One husband and wife team recently described in a San Francisco newspaper called themselves "Moslem warriors." They apparently suffered a folie à deux. In response to mental orders from God and in keeping with their idiosyncratic interpretation of the Koran, they traveled throughout Northern California killing young women they thought might be witches. In Michigan recently, a twelve-year-old boy was beaten to death by his mother. She claimed that God had ordered the child killed. In France, a man instructed by God to kill those around him murdered and ate a number of victims before he was apprehended (Benezech et al., 1981). In New Guinea, an elderly, psychotic cargo cultist ritually decapitated his young grandnephew. The sacrifice, he believed, would usher in a new age, in which food and consumer goods would arrive for the natives on ships and planes (Burton-Bradley, 1972). In the same area, a thirty-year-old cargo cultist influenced by the story of Abraham and Isaac ritually murdered his own infant son. Believing that by doing so he could induce God to send food and money, he cooked and ate slices from his son's heart (Burton-Bradley, 1976).

Insane persons often believe that they themselves are important religious figures. Patients of any faith may develop these delusions, though atheists may be relatively immune to them (R.A. Clark, 1980). One famous study described what happened when three men—each believing that he was Christ—were treated together on the same psychiatric ward in Michigan (Rokeach, 1981). Levinson (1973) reviewed the records of eight patients admitted to a general psychiatry service with the delusion of being Christ, the Messiah, or the Son of God. He found that delusions of being able to control others' thoughts, read others' minds, and teach cosmic truths were prominent in all these cases. One patient had written a 1,700-page treatise that he considered a new bible. Levinson's patients were grandiose and aggressive.

Ernest Jones (1951) argued that fantasies of being God, Jesus, or the Virgin Mary are not rare and that they antedate the psychotic disturbances in which they are manifested as delusions. Once again, character types prone to these fantasies are remarkable for narcissistic, grandiose traits. Aloofness and haughty inaccessibility are hidden beneath a thin veneer of modesty and self-effacement. Fantasies of omnipotence, omniscience, wealth, and immortality are frequently also present.

Fodor (1958) also discussed identification with Christ. One woman mentioned by Fodor believed that she had been Christ in a previous life. In her present life, she thought of herself as Vanzetti, who, like Christ, was put to death by the state. Ideas of punishment were clearly prominent in this case. Another patient believed that, like Christ, he had been sent on a mission by God. Something had gone wrong, though, and he and God had lost touch. Not surprisingly, he felt estranged from his real father. A third patient identified with the crucified Christ. He expressed in this way his own sense of victimization.

Auditory hallucinations, which are common in patients with several types of psychosis, may be important in producing religious delusions. Hallucinated voices are sometimes those of identifiable persons familiar to the patient; in other cases, they may be unfamiliar and associated with feelings of dread and awe. In our society, children of an impressionable age are exposed to stories in which men and women hear the voice of God, the Virgin Mary, the devil, or other religious figures. As far as children can tell, such stories —told to them by serious adults—are as plausible as any other worldly facts. It is not surprising, therefore, if many years later they invoke religious theories to account for otherwise incomprehensible, emotionally charged auditory hallucinations.

Grandiose religious delusions occur mostly in manics and paranoids (Beit-Hallahmi & Argyle, 1977), whereas delusions of sin and damnation occur in patients with depressive psychoses. Patients with affective disorders may be especially susceptible to environmental factors that promote religious delusions. Eighteen of the twenty-four patients hospitalized in the New Hampshire State Hospital with delusions related to the Millerite movement were manic (Stone, 1934). Of the remainder, three were psychotically depressed and two were catatonic. Catatonia can occur in affective illness as well as in schizophrenia. Recently completed studies of psychiatric disorders among Old Order Amish in Lancaster County, Pennsylvania (Egeland & Hostetter, 1983; Egeland et al., 1983; Hostetter et al., 1983), revealed that 78 percent of the Amish patients with mania developed grandiose religious delusions.

In mental patients, voices, visions, and belief in a grandiose mission chosen for them by God are taken as evidence of psychological disturbance. But some past religious leaders, of the type M. Weber (1963) called "emissary prophets," have made claims similar to those heard from patients today. Could they have been insane? Consider the prophet Ezekiel. The son of a priest, Ezekiel was deported to Babylon in 597 B.C. In Babylon, he experienced visions and ecstasies akin to those described by the mentally ill. He believed that God had appointed him his messenger to Israel. Arlow (1951) argued that Ezekiel's "appointment" was a primitive sexual fantasy of a type often heard from psychotics. Ezekiel was given to strange symbolic acts: He cut, burned, and dispersed his hair to show the fate of Israel; and he ate cakes baked from dung. Such symbolic acts are also encountered in present-day patients. Though Jung (1952) defended his sanity, no one with a knowledge of madness can feel completely confident that Ezekiel was sound of mind.

Shabbetai Zevi, about whom more is known, was born in Smyrna, in what is now Turkey, in 1626. His family were Marranos—descendants of Spanish Jews expelled in 1492. A brilliant student, he became a rabbi at eighteen. By age twenty, he had developed alternating periods of depression and euphoria, consistent with manic-depressive disorder. When he was depressed, Zevi lived as a recluse and believed himself worthless. When he was euphoric, he impulsively committed forbidden religious and sexual acts. He called himself the Messiah and uttered the mystical name of God as only the Messiah would dare. Driven from Smyrna, he traveled to Jerusalem. In Jerusalem, he felt possessed by demons. He married a prostitute, Sarah, who claimed to be the Messiah's bride. In 1665, he met Nathan of Gaza, a young rabbi who, having had a vision of his own, became his prophet. Together, the two men canvassed the Holy Land, gathered followers, appointed apostles, and rewrote Jewish law.

Though he was banished from Jerusalem, word of Shabbetai Zevi spread to Jews in Europe. The recent Chmielnicki massacres had demoralized and disorganized Eastern European Jews, who were therefore especially susceptible to fantastic claims of every kind. Scholars were sent to interrogate the would-be Messiah and to bring back word of his teaching. In spite of his megalomania, profanity, and sexual licentiousness, Shabbetai Zevi still had lucid moments, and he managed to impress many of the Talmudists sent to him. Hearing positive reports, European Jews carried his portrait in the streets. Riots broke out in many cities. According to contemporary chronicles, at least some Christians were so impressed by the Jewish fervor that they began to doubt Christ. Alarmed by his following, Turkish authorities imprisoned Shabbetai Zevi in Constantinople. From prison, he signed his letters with the name of God. He threatened rabbis who were allowed to visit him.

In time, though, Zevi again became depressed. He lost faith in himself and converted to Islam. The sultan appointed him chamberlain. Shabbetai Zevi, now called Mehmet Effendi, died in 1676. Nathan of Gaza, who had never doubted his master, died three years later. Although small groups of his followers persisted in Europe for nearly a century, disillusionment in the messianic ideal created by Shabbetai Zevi may have hastened the secularization of

European Jewry and may have led indirectly to modern-day liberal movements.

What might have happened had Shabbetai Zevi not become melancholic and lost faith in himself? Would the sultan then have martyred him, founding a new religion? Certainly, there seems to be no perfect correlation between the durability of a religious movement and the sanity of its orinator. George Fox, whom William James (1902) treated as a prototypical pathological religious character, founded a religion (the Quakers) that has long outlived him. This is regardless of the fact that he heard voices, had visions, and behaved no less oddly, if perhaps more chastely, than the Shabbetai Zevi.

Questions concerning the mental health of religious leaders are currently out of fashion. For one thing, the doctrine of cultural relativism—which states that behavior can be assessed only by the standards of the culture in which it occurs—has been taken rather too literally. Insofar as they have followers, religious leaders must live in societies that are not purely rationalistic. The doctrine of cultural relativism, therefore, can be misconstrued to imply that religious leaders cannot be judged by rationalistic standards. In fact, it is well known that cultural and especially religious expectations can produce behaviors in normal persons that mimic signs of mental illness in our own society. For example, otherwise normal persons may hallucinate in response to social and religious expectations (see Al-Issa, 1977; Andrade et al., 1988; Schwab, 1977; Young et al., 1987).

Yet, taken too literally, cultural relativism inhibits certain studies of religious psychology that can be framed in valid cultural terms. In the sixteenth and seventeenth centuries, for instance, witch-hunting crazes erupted in Europe. The coerced confessions of at least some accused persons suggest that they suffered from mental illness, which may have been on the rise at the time (Zilboorg, 1935, 1941). For social psychologists, deviance theorists, and psychiatrists, it would certainly be interesting if witch hunts, among their other functions, served to rid society of the mentally ill. In that case, it would also be interesting to know who wanted the mentally ill eliminated, and why.

A number of interesting questions would follow if it were determined that a significant proportion of accused witches were, in fact, mentally ill. This might be ascertainable from collateral evidence, such as available life histories, behavioral oddities prior to accusations of witchery, and later-life stories of those who were spared. Actually, some inquiries of these kinds have already been made, with rather equivocal results. Yet cultural relativists have denounced psychopathological inquiries on the grounds that accused witches came from a different culture. According to Schoeneman (1982), for instance, past behaviors cannot be held accountable to present-day standards of normalcy: If sixteenth-century Europeans interpreted hallucinations and grandiose ideas in spiritual terms, then we have no valid basis for assessing them diagnostically.

Here is another example: Around the turn of this century, several authors used material in the New Testament to argue that Jesus suffered a paranoid psychosis. Basically, the diagnosis depended on Jesus having had referential delusions: He believed that Old Testament passages and the widespread belief in the coming Messiah referred to himself. In 1913, as the thesis submitted for his doctorate in medicine at Strassburg University, Albert Schweitzer (1948) undertook to refute these authors. Schweitzer made several points, the most telling of which concerned the lack of valid data concerning the historical Jesus; he also claimed that Jesus' acts and utterances can be judged only in the conceptual world of first-century Judea. This, of course, is a cultural relativist position. Although the first of Schweitzer's points can hardly be refuted, his point concerning cultural relativity seems overstated. Belief in the coming Messiah may have been widespread, but was it statistically normal in first-century Judea for a man to believe that he himself was the object of messianic references? Certainly, there is an empirical question that can be asked here, regardless of the fact that Jesus lived in a world alien to us. Belief in the Messiah was also widespread among seventeenth-century Jews, but does that mean that Shabbatai Zevi was sane? A blanket relativist position inhibits such questions before they can even be posed in culturally appropriate terms.

Anthropologists in particular sometimes assume that would-be religious leaders who are truly insane will be recognized as such by prospective followers from their own culture. Therefore, successful religious leaders able to gather followers must be sane. This assumption, insofar as it depends on members of a common culture automatically recognizing what is and is not deviant, is closely related to the doctrine of cultural relativism. Certainly, virtually every culture seems to label mental illness and to distinguish between various of its types (J.M. Murphy, 1976; Warner, 1983; Westermeyer & Wintrob, 1979a, 1979b). Although considerable "diagnostic" differences exist between traditional and modern labeling systems, the disorders recognized by differing cultures more or less correspond to the disorders recognized by modern medicine. Odd ideas and correspondingly odd behavior are particularly important to traditional diagnoses, whereas hallucinations as such tend to be viewed less seriously than they are by Western psychiatrists (A.F.C. Wallace, 1959). Hallucinations, in fact, are frequently welcomed as sources of information—a fact that is especially important for the cross-cultural evaluation of religious leaders. There is also evidence that invidious distinctions are drawn in religious groups between mentally normal and abnormal persons. Littlewood and Lipsedge (1978) recounted an amusing example of this. One of the authors was asked to examine a West Indian nurse who was working in a London hospital. Earlier in the day, she had attended her usual Pentecostal prayer meeting, during which glossolalia was practiced. After coming on duty, she had begun to speak in a pressured, incoherent manner. She was emotionally labile and easily excited. The author decided that she was speaking in tongues, and he urged her to rest before going home. At that moment, fellow members of her Pentecostal congregation arrived. They assured the author that the nurse was now mentally ill. What sounded like glossolalia to him was gibberish to them. He changed his diagnosis to hypomania and treated her successfully with lithium.

Boyer et al. (1964) provided more systematic evidence concerning the tendency of a cultural group to discriminate against abnormal would-be religious leaders. During the years 1959 to 1961, they obtained 72 Rorschach protocols from Apache males living on the Mescalero Indian Reservation. Fifty-two of these were from individuals who had never claimed to be shamans (controls), twelve were from recognized shamans, and seven were from individuals who claimed to be shamans but were not accorded this status by their fellow Apaches (pseudoshamans). Both the shamans and the pseudoshamans differed from the controls, but in opposite ways. In general, the shamans appeared to be well-integrated personalities with intact reality testing but with a high potential for phenomena that, in our society, would be called hysterical. They seemed to the researchers to be healthier and more creative than typical Apache males. Pseudoshamans, on the other hand, lacked creative potential and seemed to the researchers to be generally impoverished personalities: The pseudoshamans were deficient in initiative and flexibility, and they lacked charismatic appeal.

Nevertheless, the assumption that religious leaders who are able to gather followers are necessarily sane in the context of their own culture has been empirically disproved. Several exceptions have been described. Jim Jones, for example, was highly successful in spite of what, in retrospect, was an obvious, culturally deviant, paranoid psychosis (C. Goldberg, 1983). Jones's father was an unemployed member of the Ku Klux Klan. Jones's mother, who was given to visions and believed herself to be the reincarnation of Mark Twain, considered her son the Messiah. She shared this belief with the young Jones, who later incorporated it into his own delusions. After leaving Indianapolis, which he thought would be destroyed by an atomic bomb, Jones settled in San Francisco, where he founded a large congregation. Though many of Jones's followers were poor and were attracted by the emphasis he placed on social equality, a substantial proportion were highly educated and upper middle class in origin. Civic and political leaders curried his favor. His grandiose and persecutory delusions, though evident from early on, were somehow overlooked in the general approbation. Eventually, though, complaints about Jones began to leak out, and stories of mistreatment appeared from a few disillusioned members of the so-called People's Temple. Anticipating that he and his followers would be persecuted, Jones fled San Francisco. In Guyana, he imposed a virtual police state on his followers. He separated families and dictated sexual activities. He denounced the New Testament, claiming that his own authority exceeded that of scripture. He imposed physical and emotional torments in order to test his followers' loyalty. Believing that he was finally cornered, he murdered congressional investigators and ordered his flock to die with him. Virtually all of them did.

Deutsch (1975, 1980, 1983) provided a fascinating account of how a psychotic religious leader can gain a loyal following. "Baba," the religious leader studied by Deutsch, established himself on a public bench near Central Park in New York City. From September 1972 until January 1973, he spent fifteen hours a day on this bench, eventually collecting a following of fifty to seventy-five persons. Baba's closest followers spent most of the day with him. Food, flowers, and vegetarian meals cooked in a nearby apartment house were brought to the group, who were protected from the elements only by plastic sheets. A follower's apartment was used as a "crash pad"; Baba slept on the roof. Baba never spoke, but he communicated in a private sign language developed with his first follower.

In January 1973, Baba and thirty of his followers decamped in an old school bus. After much traveling, they eventually formed an agricultural commune, where the total number of followers eventually reached one hundred. Baba, however, grew increasingly more bizarre. He struck people, made senseless purchases, and sexually abused some of his female followers. He grimaced strangely, and no one could follow his sign language. To determine whether he was still alive, he asked that a tape recording be made of his voice. On hearing a Christian radio program, he decided that the Indian guru he had worshipped was the devil. He led his followers in a frenzied exorcism and baptized them as fundamentalist Christians before stepping down as their leader.

Later interviews with Baba established beyond any reasonable doubt that he had been psychotic from very early on. As a teenager, he had had a period of mutism. Years before coming to Central Park, he had required psychiatric hospitalization. During the period described by Deutsch, he heard voices, which he thought were evil spirits. He believed that these spirits flung him against walls, made him walk jerkily, and would have caused him to have motor vehicle accidents had he not foiled them by giving up driving. He thought he was absorbing evil shed by others, and he experienced what he thought were sexual visions from hell. After leaving his commune, he roamed aimlessly and eventually became a Hassidic Jew.

The most instructive aspects of Baba's case were his followers' responses. As his behavior deteriorated, they gradually admitted that he was insane. However, this was taken as evidence of his spiritual struggle and as a sign of divine energy fluxes. His rages were manifestations of Shiva. Cruelty and sexual abuse were intended as spiritual lessons. "He is teaching us to surrender," his followers thought. One follower, whom Baba had struck twenty times, prostrated himself naked in the snow to show Baba his gratitude. At the end, many of Baba's followers willingly became Christians. To many of them, Baba still seemed an inspired leader who had gone too far in his cosmic quest and, as a result, had lost his spiritual way.

Cases of mentally ill cargo cultists described by Burton-Bradley (1970, 1972, 1976, 1978) illustrated that deranged persons may also obtain followers in contemporary cultures other than our own. Although their behavior and thought patterns were abnormal in the context of their own native culture, some of these individuals were nonetheless credible preachers. One such man, who claimed to be Christ-like and to have supernatural powers, stated that the president of the United States had promised to reward him and his followers. Although his claims were thoroughly deviant in the context of his own group, and although medical examination indicated that he had general paresis, other natives still took him seriously.

An excited, hypomanic man suffering from hyperthyroidism also had his followers. This twenty-two-year-old man, with a family history of hypomania, was hyperactive and had pressured speech. His thought patterns were classically manic. He claimed that he was Jesus Christ and that his skin would soon turn white. He was somewhat improved by antipsychotic medication but then went untreated for four years. Throughout this time, he retained a large and enthusiastic local following. They continued to believe his claims, which, for his social group, were indeed extraordinary.

Another man dressed in flamboyant Kung Fu robes and gestured strangely at intersections. He believed that he had magical control over passing cars. Though most Melanesians considered him insane, he was able to find an assistant who considered him his master.

Religion and Mental Disorder

Although the mentally ill often have religious preoccupations, numerous studies contradict the notion that religion is strongly pathogenic. It may not be pathogenic at all. Therefore, religious preoccupations of the insane are most likely secondary: They reflect an enhancement of religious interest resulting from abnormal experiences, feelings, or thought patterns. In this section, I review the numerous studies that have failed to show a strong pathogenic effect.

To begin with, there have been a few studies of mentally disordered patients with religious symptoms. For example, Farr and Howe (1932), whose work I mentioned in the preceding section, reviewed 500 consecutive psychiatric admissions to the Pennsylvania Hospital in Philadelphia. Sixty-eight of these patients expressed distinctly religious ideas. Case histories were used to classify these sixty-eight patients into one of three groups: (1) those in whom religious ideas seemed to play an etiologic role; (2) those in whom conflict over the moral and social aspects of religion were prominent; and (3) those in whom religious ideas seemed purely symptomatic of mental disorder. Twelve patients were categorized in group 1, twenty-three patients in group 2, and thirty-three patients in group 3. Therefore, if these categorizations are accurate, religion seemed to play an inciting role in only 2.4 percent of the total patient sample. Ethical and social conflict only secondarily related to religious beliefs contributed to another 4.6 percent of the admissions. In 93 percent of the admissions, and in nearly 50 percent of those patients with religious preoccupations, there was no evidence that religion had played an etiologic role directly or indirectly.

To illustrate how they classified patients, Farr and Howe provided some case histories. On the whole, the classifications based on these histories are reasonable and convincing. Case number 10971, for example, is that of a forty-eight-year-old Episcopalian female. As a young woman, she had had a love affair, but her lover had left her to become an Episcopal priest. Her intense interest in church work dated from that period. Over the years, her missionary activities took more and more of her time, and eventually she entered an Episcopal convent. Friends and family disapproved strongly. A year later, she developed delusions of sin and worthlessness and made several suicide attempts. She recovered from her depression after one year in the hospital and did not return to her sisterhood. She was said to have developed a more moderate attitude toward her religion. Farr and Howe noted the potential part played by sexual conflict in this patient's problems. However, in light of the long-term role played by religion, they categorized her in group 1, those in whom religious ideas might have played an etiologic role.

Patient number 10965 was a twenty-six-year-old Russian Jewish woman. Years before, she had seen two of her brothers murdered by cossacks during a pogrom. She herself had been assaulted. At about the same time, both her parents had died. After coming to the United States, she had married and had been mentally well except for mild depression. Nine days before her hospital admission, she had received a letter from a maternal aunt still living in Russia. It was winter in Russia, and people were desperate for heat. The wooden tablet marking the grave of her mother and brothers had been stolen for firewood. The patient became depressed but three days later developed a manic reaction. She claimed to be extremely happy. She tried to call her dead mother on the telephone. She had hallucinations and was religiously preoccupied. After nine months, she recovered spontaneously. Farr and Howe categorized her in group 2, those for whom the moral or social aspects of religion had played an etiologic role. In this case, the social factor was religious persecution.

Case number 11110 was a sixty-seven-year-old woman who developed a toxic delirium associated with a viral infection. During her delirium, the patient believed she was being tested by God. She saw religious visions and dreamed that the devil had visited her. She had always been a religious person, but only conventionally so. Farr and Howe categorized her in group 3, those for whom religious preoccupations were only symptomatic—in this case, of her delirium.

In another frequently cited study, Oates (1949) obtained material on sixty-eight psychiatric patients hospitalized in the Kentucky State Hospital. He found that thirty-two of these patients had significant religious preoccupations. The large percentage of religiously preoccupied patients undoubtedly reflects the extremely religious, rural Kentucky areas in which most of these patients lived. Like Farr and Howe, Oates attempted to categorize the religiously preoccupied patients according to the role religious factors actually seemed to play in their mental illnesses. In eleven cases (16.2 percent of the total sample), he considered long-term religious conflict an etiologic factor in the patient's mental illness. In nearly all of these cases, the patient had rebelled against the family religion. By renouncing their parents' faith, these patients had tried unsuccessfully to achieve some autonomy. Several patients were the children of Protestant ministers. In another seven cases (10.3 percent of the total sample), Oates considered religious factors active in precipitating the patient's illness. In many of these cases, the patient's religious involvement was a last ditch effort to maintain sanity in spite of other major losses. In the remaining fourteen religiously preoccupied patients (20.5 percent of the total sample), Oates believed that religious factors played no etiologic role. Instead, religion had supplied the ideational content for psychoses that would have developed in any event.

Oates considered religion to have played an etiologic or precipitating role in 27 percent of the sixty-eight cases he studied. Superficially, this would appear to indicate a more powerful causal role for religious factors than that suggested by Farr and Howe. Oates's figure, though, is overinflated by several factors. When corrections are made for these factors, Oates's findings are probably consistent with those of Farr and Howe and, like theirs, indicate that religion per se is a relatively weak pathogenic factor. First, Oates's subjects came from religious families. This factor is undoubtedly responsible for the large number of religiously preoccupied patients he found. It would also cause patients to express psychological problems unrelated to religion in religious-sounding terms. The real role played by religion in these patients' lives would consequently be easily overemphasized. Oates's informants, moreover, were student chaplains assigned to hospital wards. As opposed to medical personnel, who wrote the case histories studied by Farr and Howe, student chaplains are likely to see life conflicts in religious terms and to elicit religious conflicts from the patients with whom they have contact. They are correspondingly inexpert at eliciting information about conflicts of other kinds.

But even when judged by the data at hand, Oates's categorizations seem to overinflate the religious factor. Ten of the eleven patients for whom long-term religious conflicts were thought to play etiologic roles had had severe family conflicts over denominational and belief issues. As described in chapter 3 and 5 of this book, family conflicts are often expressed in regard to religious denomination and belief. There is no basis for putting the religious cart before the family horse—that is, for considering what are probably family issues as fundamentally religious conflicts. The eleventh patient for whom religious conflict was thought to be etiologically significant had been normally religious until he became senile. There is no reason to think that he would have become religiously preoccupied in the absence of brain disease.

Among the patients for whom Oates considered religion a precipitating factor, the role of other losses seems evident. One patient entered the ministry following his wife's death and became mentally ill at the time of his ordination. In such cases, religious activities are plausibly just defensive, not contributing causes at all. Salzman (1953) reported that emotionally disturbed persons frequently attempt to stave off their problems with religious involvement. If this fails, psychopathology becomes overt. Salzman cited, for example, a Navy study that showed a high frequency of religious conversions immediately prior to suicide attempts. Numerous subsequent observations support Salzman's argument (see, for example, Cavenar & Spaulding, 1977; C. W. Christensen, 1963; Kildahl, 1965; Roberts, 1965; Spellman et al., 1971).

Lowe (1953, 1954, 1955) studied eleven psychotic patients at the Colorado State Hospital. The six female and five male patients all had religious delusions, including psychotic identifications with Jesus, the Holy Ghost, and the biblical Ruth. Other patients believed that they could communicate with God or had a special relationship with him. One patient believed that she was Jesus' sister and bride. All patients were given approximately twenty one-hour interviews and Rorschach, Thematic Apperception, and Religious Projection tests. The Religious Projection test is similar to the Thematic Apperception test, but it incorporates various symbols intended to provoke religious ideas. Some of the patients also provided written biographies and dream reports. In his original account of these patients, Lowe noted that their grandiose religious delusions protected them against anxiety and against awareness of their own failures in life. In all cases, religious preoccupation appeared to be secondary to psychosis, not a cause of it. Insofar as etiologic factors could be identified, they appeared to be severe personality problems. In his second report, Lowe noted that most of these patients had suffered from more or less lifelong poverty and from overwhelming social and family stresses. Their religious preoccupations were elaborations of culturally approved ideas. With their delusions, the patients attempted to express themselves in culturally understood terms. In his final report, Lowe emphasized the importance of early childhood religious training. Besieged by adult life, the patients sought to understand their problems using the religious symbols recalled from their childhood years. These symbols, however, played little or no pathogenic role.

Lowe's observations concerning secondary gains from religious delusions, which include their defensive, intellectual, and communicative functions, are consistent with ideas expressed by several other authors. Allport (1950), for example, noted that when fantasies and emotions run wild, religious symbols alone may be adequate for their expression. Rationalization of these fantasies and emotions may require religious ideas, which nonetheless play no part in originating them. More recently, Vergote (1988) expressed very similar views. R.A. Clark (1944) described five psychiatric patients who had joined theosophical cults. According to Clark, these patients were attracted to the occult because occult symbols provided means of expressing their own irrational thoughts. There was no evidence that these symbols played a pathogenic role (see, also, Casey, 1945).

Finally, Proudfoot and Shaver (1975) were able to treat normal religious experience in terms of *attribution theory,* a branch of cognitive psychology (Kelley & Michela, 1980). According to Proudfoot and Shaver, anomalous arousal experiences accompanied by physiologic activation may, if attributed to a divine cause, create the subjective certainty of an encounter with God, the Holy Ghost, or other religious figures. This type of attribution is particularly likely to be made if the individual has previously been indoctrinated with religious ideas or following vivid prayer meetings. For example, Stephen Bradley, whose encounter with the Holy Spirit and subsequent conversion was described at length by William James (1902), had cardiac palpitations on returning home following a late-night revival meeting. He soon became convinced that his palpitations and emotional excitement were the effects of the Holy Spirit. According to Proudfoot and Shaver (1975), Bradley ascribed his palpitations and excitement to the presence of the Holy Spirit because the Holy Spirit was already on his mind. Once made, the attribution transformed an anomalous emotional and physiologic arousal into a religious "certainty."

Although Proudfoot and Shaver applied their attribution theory to normal religious experience, it may be even more readily applicable to the religious experiences of the mentally ill. This is because anomalous emotional and physiologic excitements are part and parcel of major mental disorders. Experiencing frequent, inexplicable emotional and physiologic upheavals, the mentally ill person may be particularly prone to seize on religious explanations. These explanations would be more salient if religious symbols were available from childhood or if the social environment encouraged religion. In spite of the fact that they are motivated by the desire to fit anomalous experiences into a socially shared framework, religious attributions by the mentally ill might end in full-blown delusions.

Attribution theory might also account for data on temporal lobe epileptics, who may experience intense and inexplicable emotional states because of their disease. Several authors have noted that temporal lobe epileptics are prone to sudden religious experiences, often leading to lasting religious conversions, when their disease is uncontrolled (Dewhurst & Beard, 1970; Landsborough, 1987; Tucker et al., 1987; cf. Sensky et al., 1984). Landsborough (1987) argued that St. Paul's conversion on the road to Damascus may have been due to a temporal lobe seizure, which he interpreted in terms of the new sect he was in the process of persecuting. I have encountered patients with full-blown religious delusions that emerged abruptly from powerful affective states associated with temporal lobe activation (Wenegrat, 1988).

The studies considered thus far are mostly impressionistic. Religious researchers have criticized such studies for methodological reasons (see, for example, Larson et al., 1986). However, there are other studies, of a more statistical type, that compare the religious affiliations of mentally ill persons with those of normal subjects.

Alternatively, they compare rates of mental illness in different religious groups. When allowances are made for socioeconomic, cultural, and other confounding factors, these studies, too, fail to show that religion is pathogenic or affects mental disorder. I will briefly review these studies.

Buckalew (1980) studied the religious affiliations of mentally ill patients. He reviewed 2,659 first-admission adult psychiatric patients at the Georgia Central State Hospital, 1,323 of whom had *functional* mental illnesses—that is mental disorders without a (currently) demonstrable neurologic, endocrinologic, or physiologic cause. Most of these patients were schizophrenics. The majority of the remaining patients had diseases affecting the brain that produce behavioral changes. Of the 2,659 patients, 1,807 were Baptists and 562 were Methodist. The Pentecostal, Presbyterian, Church of Christ, Catholic, and Episcopal faiths each accounted for fewer than 100 patients. Buckalew found that each of the seven denominations he studied had the same proportion of patients with functional mental illness. Therefore, there was no evidence that the specific religions he studied predisposed believers to functional illness per se. Among the functionally disturbed patients, there were significant denominational differences in diagnoses. Catholics had a slightly higher chance of being diagnosed as schizophrenic than Protestants; and among Protestants, Episcopalians and Presbyterians had a slightly higher chance than Methodists and Baptists. The Methodists and Baptists were more likely to be diagnosed as neurotic. In all cases, though, differences were small and might have been caused by significant economic and cultural discrepancies among the various religious groups.

MacDonald and Luckett (1983) performed a study similar to Buckalew's. Their subjects were 7,050 psychiatric patients terminated from treatment in a midwestern community mental health center during a four-year period. Except for 124 mentally retarded patients, all of MacDonald and Luckett's subjects had functional mental disorders. Of the 7,050 patients, 3,012 stated no religious preference, 1,831 were "non-mainline" Protestants, 1,118 were "mainline" Protestants, 564 were Catholics, and 61 were members of "sects." Mainline Protestant denominations included the Church of Christ and the Presbyterian, Lutheran, Methodist, and Episcopal churches. Non-mainline Protestant denominations included Mennonite, Amish, Missionary, and Baptist churches. Sects included the Christian Science, Jehovah's Witness, Latter Day Saints, and Seventh-Day Adventist churches. Obviously, not everyone would agree with these classifications. Because 274 patients simply called themselves Protestants, they could not be further categorized, and 190 patients claimed religious affiliations that were not classified.

Several significant diagnostic differences emerged among the various religious groups. The sect members tended to be psychotic. The patients who did not have any religious preference or whose preference could not be classified frequently abused drugs. The non-mainline Protestants commonly had adjustment reactions, and the mainline Protestants had marital problems. The patients who had no religious preference also tended toward paranoid schizophrenia. Unfortunately, MacDonald and Luckett's conclusions are vitiated by their disregard of coinciding factors. They provided no information on age or socioeconomic status nor on alternative sources of treatment or counseling available to members of different religious groups. Nor did they consider group differences in behavioral norms. Sect members, for example, may consider neurotic or marital problems spiritual; they may consult psychiatrists only in cases of flagrant insanity.

Kleiner et al. (1959) studied 2,496 Protestant and Catholic first-admission state mental hospital patients from Philadelphia. The Catholics included a higher proportion of paranoid and schizophrenic patients, whereas the Protestants included a higher proportion of patients with behavioral disturbances secondary to brain disease. Consistent with their diagnoses, the Catholic patients tended to be younger and the Protestant patients older at the date of their first admission. The authors attributed these differences to discrepancies in social status between Catholics and Protestants. In a later study, Kleiner et al. (1962) studied 269 white Protestants who had been consecutively admitted to a psychiatric evaluation facility in Philadelphia. The 131 Presbyterian and Episcopalian patients were compared to the 138 Methodist and Baptist patients. The Methodists and Baptists tended to be diagnosed as paranoid or schizophrenic, whereas the Presbyterians and Episcopalians tended to have organic brain disease. Consistent with their diagnoses, the Methodist and Baptist patients were younger and the Presbyterian and Episcopalian patients older at the time of their admission. Once again, the authors attributed diagnostic differences to discrepancies in social status—in this case, between Protestant denominations.

Murphy and Vega (1982) studied first admissions to psychiatric hospitals in Northern Ireland. Like Kleiner et al. in Philadelphia, they found that Catholics were overrepresented among the patients diagnosed as schizophrenic. Although social class per se could not account for this excess, sexual and marital conflicts and a relative sense of social deprivation among Catholics in Northern Ireland were cited as potential contributing causes. A study by Spencer (1975), which showed a higher hospital admission rate for schizophrenia and paranoid psychosis among Jehovah's Witnesses in Western Australia, failed to note social class or other confounding factors.

Durkheim (1897) found that in Europe, suicide rates among Protestants were higher than those among Catholics or Jews. Halbwachs (1930, cited in Beit-Hallahmi, 1975) corroborated Durkheim's findings, which were extended to the United States by Dublin (1933). Argyle (1959) suggested that the apparently greater suicidal propensities of Protestants could be explained by the "intropunitive" styles of handling aggression encouraged by Protestant faiths. Catholicism, on the other hand, was said to encourage "extrapunitive" aggressive styles.

L.B. Brown (1965) administered the Rosenzweig Picture Frustration Study to 258 first-year psychology students at the University of Adelaide. He was able to confirm Argyle's hypothesis concerning extrapunitive styles only when Roman Catholics were compared to Methodists. There was no significant differences between Catholics and members of other Protestant denominations. Argyle's hypothesis concerning intropunitive styles was confirmed only for females. There was no control for socioeconomic class, and Brown argued that religious beliefs were unlikely to play a direct role in the few differences that were found.

Denominational differences also exist in attitudes toward suicide (Domino et al. 1981), but these may or may not affect actual suicidal behavior. In light of denominational differences in suicide risk, suicidologists have attempted to account for discrepancies in national suicide rates in terms of the predominant religious faith. However, these efforts have proved statistically unsupportable, indicating that religion—even if it does affect suicide risk—is only one among other more important factors (Beit-Hallahmi, 1975). In fact, the effect of religious beliefs on suicide risk might have been much overrated. Morphew (1968), for instance, studied fifty patients who had been admitted to the Birmingham, England, General Hospital with self-inflicted poisonings. Each patient was questioned concerning, among other things, his or her religious affiliation, frequency of religious participation, and degree of belief in God. No clear pattern of religious beliefs or history emerged from these would-be suicides, and Morphew concluded that religious factors seemed to play a minor role in originating or preventing what were, for the most part, impulsive acts.

In Los Angeles, Kranitz et al. (1968) compared twenty psychiatric patients with suicidal histories with twenty controls matched for race, age, marital status, and religion. Each group included twelve Protestants, seven Catholics, and one Jew. The patients and controls were questioned concerning their religious beliefs, including faith in God and belief in an afterlife. No statistically significant differences were found between suicidal patients and their controls on any religious variable. Hole (1971) studied thirty depressed patients at the University of Basel. Interviews and questionnaires were administered in order to judge the effect of religious belief on suicide risk. Hole concluded that religious beliefs had little impact on suicidal behavior. Only the strongest religious convictions seemed to offer any protection against either suicidal impulses or chronic suicidal motives.

In summary, neither case material nor demographic and epidemiologic studies have thus far proved that religion is pathogenic with respect to mental illness. To the contrary, these studies give the impression that religious factors, if they are active at all, are of negligible importance compared with personal and social problems. Therefore, the religious preoccupations of mentally ill persons are probably secondary: When affect and thought are disordered, religious ideas become more salient.

Religion and Psychological Adaptation

Not only is there little or no evidence that religion is pathogenic, but there is actually evidence that unhappy people with failures of adaptation to life can benefit from religious beliefs. In chapter 3, I described the many functions that religious beliefs can serve. Here I will review some systematic surveys relating to adaptation.

Galanter and Buckley (1978) administered questionnaires to 119 members of the Divine Light Mission. The Divine Light Mission originated in India and spread to the United States in 1971, following a visit by its then thirteen-year-old leader, Guru Maharaj Ji. Converts to the Divine Light Mission report unusual visual, auditory, and somesthetic experiences, depersonalization, and time distortion (Buckley & Galanter, 1979). Subjects were asked to rate the extent to which they had experienced a variety of psychological symptoms before they had joined the Mission, immediately after they had joined, and in the most recent two-month period. Subjects reported that all psychological symptoms except auditory hallucinations had diminished precipitously after joining. Use of marijuana, alcohol, heroin, and other drugs had likewise greatly declined. Numerous studies have confirmed that religious activities decrease drug use (see, for example, Goodwin et al., 1969; Hochman & Brill, 1973; Janus & Bess, 1973; Larson & Wilson, 1980; Linden & Currie, 1977; McIntosh et al., 1981; Rohrbaugh & Jessor, 1975; Steffenhagen et al., 1972; Vaillant, 1983; Westermeyer & Walzer, 1975). In many cases, conversion to the Divine Light Mission appeared to be an alternative to psychosocial maladjustment. Galanter and Buckley's data seem to confirm the findings of Starbuck (1897), a classic author on religious psychology. Starbuck considered conversion experiences generally restorative.

Galanter et al. (1980) analyzed questionnaires from 237 members of the Unification ("Moonie") Church, along with questionnaires from 104 nonmembers who were participating in residential workshops preparatory to joining the Unification Church. Of the latter group, 9 subjects eventually became members. The questionnaires required subjects to rate their use of various drugs before they had joined the Unification Church, immediately after they had joined, and in the most recent two-month period. Like members of the Divine Light Mission, members of the Unification Church reported precipitous declines in their level of drug use following their conversion. Levels of drug use among nonmember workshop participants were comparable to those retrospectively reported by long-standing members, suggesting that retrospective bias was probably not responsible for the reported diminution in drug use. Unification Church members were also administered a questionnaire intended to judge their psychological well-being during the same time periods (Galanter et al., 1979). Unification Church membership, like membership in the Divine Light Mission, afforded members considerable relief from previously high levels of psychological distress. In another study, Galanter (1980) showed that individuals about to join the Unification Church had more psychological distress than those already in the group. As in the case of drug use, apparent symptomatic relief as the result of membership is unlikely to result from retrospective exaggeration of earlier symptoms.

Subjective relief of psychological distress seems to be independent of particular religious creeds. Levine and Salter (1976) interviewed 106 members of nine religious cults, including the Hare Krishna society, the Divine Light Mission, the Unification Church, the Church of Scientology, and others. Subjects were asked why they had joined their cults and why they stayed in them. The most common reasons offered for joining were psychological: feeling sad, rejected, lonely, or aimless. Sixty-four subjects reported that, since joining, they felt calmer, happier, and more self-actualized than in their previous lives. Fifty-one subjects reported that they had a sense of belonging that previously was lacking. Spiritual benefits of continued membership were cited less frequently than psychological benefits. According to Levine and Salter's subjects, psychological and psychosomatic symptoms were dramatically reduced and feelings of security enhanced as the result of their religious conversion.

W.P. Wilson (1972) administered a questionnaire to sixty-three Christian subjects who had had salvation experiences. Seventy percent of these subjects reported psychological distress prior to being "saved." After salvation, the great majority of subjects reported diminished psychological symptoms. Nearly half the subjects had used alcohol prior to being saved, and all of them later stopped.

Subjects reported that their family and work lives were improved, and one subject reported that his salvation experience cured him of homosexuality.

Pattison and Pattison (1980) described eleven men who claimed to have been cured of homosexuality by involvement in Pentecostalism. It seems likely that their homosexuality was a source of psychological distress to them prior to their religious activity. All of them had experienced homosexual impulses before the age of fifteen, and all had considered themselves exclusively homosexual. After conversion, eight of these subjects reported that they were both behaviorally and psychologically heterosexual. Three subjects, though functionally heterosexual, admitted continued conflict over their sexual orientation. Six of the subjects were married.

Along the same line, Galanter (1986) described a thirty-six-year-old male homosexual who joined the Unification Church. After joining, he still had homoerotic fantasies, but he no longer felt despair over being homosexual. Eventually, he volunteered for a mass engagement ceremony, in which members of the church were engaged to be married to partners chosen for them by Reverend Moon. His homosexual fantasies stopped with his engagement, and he later had satisfactory sexual relations with his new wife.

Nicholi (1974) reported on extensive interviews with seventeen Harvard and Radcliffe students who had experienced religious conversions. None had joined a cult. Nicholi's subjects reported dramatically decreased use of drugs, alcohol, and cigarettes; improved school performance; and lessening of depressed feelings following their conversions. Feelings of meaninglessness and death anxiety were particularly diminished. They felt closer to other persons and, in contrast to many cult members, reported improved relationships with their parents.

Obviously, the most downtrodden elements of society may need more relief from distress than those who are more fortunate. For this reason, religion may perform a particularly important psychological function for minority or poor individuals (see Griffith et al., 1980).

Comparisons of religious and nonreligious subjects on measures of psychological distress have produced ambiguous findings. This is not surprising. Because it appears to bring psychological relief, religion may be especially attractive to troubled individuals. In the preceding section, I cited evidence supporting Salzman's (1953) claim that emotionally disturbed individuals try to stave off their problems with religious involvement. The tendency of religious believers to be more distressed may or may not be offset by whatever relief religion offers them. Self-selection for psychological problems might even introduce a temporal factor, as relief of distress by religious beliefs may take time to develop. Barton and Vaughan (1976), for instance, administered a personality questionnaire to 593 New Zealand high school seniors. The same questionnaire was readministered five years later. Fifty-three subjects who denied a religious affiliation during the five-year period were compared with 108 subjects who reported a continuous and active affiliation throughout the five years. Actively religious subjects showed elevated initial anxiety levels, which disappeared on retesting five years later. Barton and Vaughan speculated that churches selectively attract more anxious young persons, who gradually become less anxious as the result of religious activity. Thus, over time, religious persons become more like nonreligious ones.

Insofar as subjective certainty and fervor are required to obtain benefits from religion, religiosity and distress might also be related by an inverse U-shaped curve. The religiously disinterested, most of whom feel less need for relief, and the very religious, who obtain the relief they need, should be better off than the moderately religious, who need relief but cannot believe wholeheartedly. Studies have been performed that seem to support this model. Williams and Cole (1968), for example, studied 161 undergraduates from a southern state university. Subjects were classified according to their degree of religiosity and were administered scales intended to measure generalized insecurity and death anxiety. Galvanic skin response was measured following random tachistoscopic presentations of death-related and emotionally neutral words. Galvanic skin responses to neutral stimuli were assumed to be physiologic measures of baseline anxiety levels. Highly and moderately religious students showed less generalized insecurity than those who were least religious, but moderately religious students showed the most baseline anxiety and the most apparent death-related anxiety.

Shaver et al. (1980) examined ninety-seven-item questionnaires from 2,500 readers of a popular women's magazine. When degrees of religiosity were compared to measures of unhappiness, the relationship that emerged resembled an inverted U. Moderately religious subjects were more unhappy than very religious ones, but irreligious subjects were also better off. When degrees of religiosity were compared to measures of psychosomatic symptoms, the same relationship appeared. Slightly and moderately religious subjects had more symptoms than either the very religious or the irreligious.

The importance of religious beliefs to individual adaptation and their role in relieving psychological distress undoubtedly account for the extraordinary commitment displayed by some religious believers. Religious beliefs that are fully integrated in the believer's adaptive pattern are difficult to dislodge; many believers will sacrifice nearly everything in their service. Worldly goods, family ties, and personal safety may all be tossed overboard should religious consistency require it. Secular values, cherished ideals, and knowledge of the real world may all be renounced should they come into conflict with the religious world view. Extremes of religious commitment are described in every history book; there is no need to review them here. However, since I previously noted the relief of psychological distress evident among Unification Church members, it seems apropos to mention a modest example involving them.

In 1979, the leader of the Unification Church, Reverend Sun Myung Moon, held an engagement ceremony for 1,400 of his followers. Reverend Moon had personally acted as a matchmaker, pairing off members of his church without regard to their feelings. In fact, most members engaged by Moon had never even met their proposed marriage partners. Nearly half of the engaged members lived more than 500 miles from their proposed partner, and many of them lived on different continents. Some of the couples Moon created shared no common language. Since the great majority of engaged members were college-educated Americans or Western Europeans, their engagement to persons they either did not know or had not chosen themselves was a major test of their faith. In effect, Reverend Moon was asking them to show their commitment to the church by renouncing what for most of them was a culturally sanctioned value in which they had received lifelong instruction: freedom of marital choice.

Galanter (1983) administered questionnaires to 321 of the participants in this unusual engagement ceremony. Four percent of these subjects reported that Reverend Moon had engaged them to the partners of their choice. Another 7 percent had successfully requested that they be engaged to someone other than the persons chosen for them by Reverend Moon. Although 9 percent found themselves engaged to someone they did not want to marry, and the great majority had expressed no desire to marry anyone, only 3 percent of the entire sample (nine subjects) seriously considered breaking off their arranged engagements. A three-year follow-up showed remarkable compliance (Galanter, 1986): Only 5 percent of the entire sample had left the church during the follow-up period. Only one of the nine subjects who had considered breaking off their engagements actually left the church. Many of the engaged had consummated their marriages, and most were reasonably satisfied. Both initially and at follow-up, whatever distress there was as the result of the engagements seemed to be ameliorated by feelings of group solidarity. Galanter observed that for many of his subjects, affiliation with the Unification Church relieved psychological suffering and that acceptance of Reverend Moon's right to betroth them was an implied condition of continued membership. In the case of religion, it seems, incremental commitments can be refused only by forfeiting the adaptive benefits on which the believer has come to depend.

Bibliography

Adorno, T.W., Frenkel-Brunswik, E., Levinson, D.J., & Sanford, R.N. (1950). *The authoritarian personality*. New York: Harper.

Alexander, M.P. (1982). Traumatic brain injury. In D.F. Benson & D. Blumer (Eds.), *Psychiatric aspects of neurologic disease, Vol. II*. New York: Grune & Stratton.

Alexander, R.D. (1979). *Darwinism and human affairs*. Seattle: University of Washington Press.

Alexander, R.D. (1987). *The biology of moral systems*. Hawthorne, NY: Aldine de Gruyter.

Alexander, R.D., Hoogland, J.L., Howard, R.D., Noonan, K.M., & Sherman, P.W. (1979). Sexual dimorphisms and breeding systems in pinnipeds, ungulates, primates, and humans. In N.A. Chagnon & W. Irons (Eds.), *Evolutionary biology and human social behavior: An anthropological perspective*. North Scituate, MA: Duxbury Press.

Al-Issa, I. (1977). Social and cultural aspects of hallucinations. *Psychological Bulletin* 84:570.

Alland, A. (1962). "Possession" in a revivalistic Negro church. *Journal for the Scientific Study of Religion* 1:204.

Allen, R.O., & Spilka, B. (1967). Committed and consensual religion: A specification of religion-prejudice relationships. *Journal for the Scientific Study of Religion* 6:191.

Allison, J. (1968). Adaptive regression and intense religious experiences. *Journal of Nervous and Mental Disease* 145:452.

Allison, J. (1970). Respiratory changes during Transcendental Meditation. *Lancet* 1:833.

Allport, G.W. (1937). *Personality: A psychological interpretation*. New York: Holt.

Allport, G.W. (1950). *The individual and his religion*. New York: Macmillan.

Allport, G.W. (1954). *The nature of prejudice*. Cambridge, MA: Addison-Wesley.

Allport, G.W. (1966). The religious context of prejudice. *Journal for the Scientific Study of Religion* 5:447.

Allport, G.W., Gillespie, J.M., & Young, J. (1948). The religion of the post-war college student. *Journal of Psychology* 25:3.

Allport, G.W., & Ross, J.M. (1967). Personal religious orientation and prejudice. *Journal of Personality and Social Psychology 5*:432.

Andrade, C., Srinath, S., & Andrade, A.C. (1988). True hallucinations as a culturally sanctioned experience. *British Journal of Psychiatry 152*:838.

Anthony, S. (1972). *The discovery of death in childhood and after.* New York: Basic Books.

Argyle, M. (1959). *Religious behavior.* London: Routledge & Kegan Paul.

Arlow, J.A. (1951). The consecration of the prophet. *Psychoanalytic Quarterly 201*:374.

Axelrod, R. (1984). *The evolution of cooperation.* New York: Basic Books.

Badcock, C.R. (1986). *The problem of altruism: Freudian-Darwinian solutions.* New York: Blackwell.

Bakan, D. (1958). *Sigmund Freud and the Jewish mystical tradition.* New York: Schocken.

Bakan, D. (1975). *Sigmund Freud and the Jewish mystical tradition.* Boston: Beacon Press.

Baldwin, J.M. (1896). A new factor in evolution. *American Naturalist 30*:441.

Barchas, J.D., Berger, P.A., Ciaranello, R.D., & Elliott, G.R. (1977). *Psychopharmacology: From theory to practice.* New York: Oxford University Press.

Barton, K., & Vaughan, G.M. (1976). Church membership and personality: A longitudinal study. *Social Behavior and Personality 4*:11.

Bassuk, E.L. (1984). The homelessness problem. *Scientific American 251*(1):40.

Batson, C.D. (1976). Religion as prosocial agent or double agent. *Journal for the Scientific Study of Religion 15*:29.

Batson, C.D. (1983). Sociobiology and the role of religion in promoting prosocial behavior: An alternative view. *Journal of Personality and Social Psychology 45*:1380.

Batson, C.D., & Gray, R.A. (1981). Religious orientation and helping behavior: Responding to one's own or the victim's needs? *Journal for the Scientific Study of Religion 40*:511.

Bear, D., Freeman, R., Schiff, D., & Greenberg, M. (1985). Interictal behavioral changes in patients with temporal lobe epilepsy. In R.E. Hales & A.J. Frances (Eds.), *American Psychiatric Association annual review* (Vol. 4). Washington, DC: American Psychiatric Press.

Beit-Hallahmi, B. (1975). Religion and suicidal behavior. *Psychological Reports 37*:1303.

Beit-Hallahmi, B., & Argyle, M. (1975). God as a father-projection: The theory and the evidence. *British Journal of Medical Psychology 48*:71.

Beit-Hallahmi, B., & Argyle, M. (1977). Religious ideas and psychiatric disorders. *International Journal of Social Psychiatry 23*:26.

Bellah, R.N. (1964). Religious evolution. *American Sociological Review 29*:358.

Bellah, R.N., Madsen, R., Sullivan, W.M., Swidler, A., & Tipton, S.M. (1985). *Habits of the heart: Individualism and commitment in American life.* Berkeley: University of California Press.

Benezech, M., Bourgeois, M., Boukhabza, D., & Yesavage, J. (1981). Cannibalism and vampirism in paranoid schizophrenia. *Journal of Clinical Psychiatry* 42:290.

Benson, P.L., Dehorty, J., Garman, L., Hanson, E., Hochswender, M., Lebold, C., Rohr, R., & Sullivan, J. (1980). Intrapersonal correlates of nonspontaneous helping behavior. *Journal of Social Psychology* 110:87.

Benson, P.L., & Spilka, B. (1973). God image as a function of self-esteem and locus of control. *Journal for the Scientific Study of Religion* 13:297.

Berger, P.L., & Luckmann, T. (1966). *The social construction of reality: A treatise in the sociology of knowledge.* Garden City, NY: Doubleday.

Bergson, H. (1935). *The two sources of morality and religion.* New York: Holt.

Bertram, B.C.R. (1982). Problems with altruism. In King's College Sociobiology Group (Eds.), *Current problems in sociobiology.* Cambridge: Cambridge University Press.

Bettelheim, B. (1982). *Freud and man's soul.* New York: Knopf.

Betzig, L.L. (1982). Despotism and differential reproduction: A cross-cultural correlation of conflict asymmetry, hierarchy, and degree of polygyny. *Ethology and Sociobiology* 3:209.

Betzig, L.L. (1986). *Despotism and differential reproduction: A Darwinian view of history.* Hawthorne, NY: Aldine de Gruyter.

Black, M.S. & London, P. (1966). The dimension of guilt, religion, and personal ethics. *Journal of Social Psychology* 69:39.

Blanck, G., & Blanck, R. (1974). *Ego psychology: Theory and practice.* New York: Columbia University Press.

Blanck, G., & Blanck, R. (1979). *Ego psychology II.* New York: Columbia University Press.

Blood, R.O. (1969). *Marriage.* New York: Free Press.

Blumer, D., & Benson, D.F. (1975). Personality changes with frontal and temporal lobe lesions. In D.F. Benson & D. Blumer (Eds.), *Psychiatric aspects of neurologic disease.* New York: Grune Stratton.

Blumer, D., & Benson, D.F. (1982). Psychiatric manifestations of epilepsy. In D.F. Benson & D. Blumer (Eds.), *Psychiatric aspects of neurologic disease* (Vol.II). New York: Grune & Stratton.

Boisen, A.T. (1936). *The exploration of the inner world.* New York: Harper.

Boisen, A.T. (1939). Economic distress and religious experience: A study of the Holy Rollers. *Psychiatry* 2:185.

Boisen, A.T. (1960). *Out of the depths.* New York: Harper.

Bokenkotter, T. (1979). *A concise history of the Catholic Church* (rev. ed.). Garden City, NY: Doubleday.

Bonaparte, M. (1958). Psycho-analysis in relation to social, religious and natural forces. *International Journal of Psycho-analysis* 39:513.

Bowlby, J. (1969). *Attachment and loss: Vol. I. Attachment.* New York: Basic Books.

Bowlby, J. (1973). *Attachment and loss: Vol. II. Separation.* New York: Basic Books.

Bowlby, J. (1980). *Attachment and loss: Vol. III. Loss.* New York: Basic Books.

Boyd, R., & Richerson, P.J. (1985). *Culture and the evolutionary process.* Chicago: University of Chicago Press.

Boyer, L.B., Klopfer, B., Brawer, F.B., & Kawai, H. (1964). Comparisons of the shamans and pseudoshamans of the Apaches of the Mescalero indian reservation: A Rorschach study. *Journal of Projective Techniques 28*:173.

Brandon, R.N., & Burian, R.M. (Eds.). (1984). *Genes, organisms populations: Controversies over the units of selection.* Cambridge, MA: MIT Press.

Brandt, L.W. (1966). Process or structure? *Psychoanalytic Review 53*:50.

Brazelton, T., Tronick, E., Adamson, L., Als, H., & Wise, S. (1975). Early mother–infant reciprocity. *CIBA Foundation Symposium 33*:137.

Brenner, C. (1939). On the genesis of a case of paranoid dementia precox. *Journal of Nervous and Mental Disease 90*:483.

Breuer, G. (1982). *Sociobiology and the human dimension.* Cambridge: Cambridge University Press.

Brooks, A. (1986). "Cults" and the aged: A new family issue. *New York Times,* April 26:52.

Brown, D.G., & Lowe, W.L. (1951). Religious beliefs and personality characteristics of college students. *Journal of Social Psychology 33*:103.

Brown, L.B. (1962). A study of religious belief. *British Journal of Psychology 53*:259.

Brown, L.B. (1965). Aggression and denominational membership. *British Journal of Social and Clinical Psychology 4*:175.

Brown, L.B. (1966). Egocentric thought in petitionary prayer: A cross-cultural study. *Journal of Social Psychology 68*:197.

Brown, L.B. (1968). Some attitudes underlying petitionary prayer. In A. Godin (Ed.), *From cry to word: Contributions towards a psychology of prayer.* Brussels: Lumen Vitae.

Bruch, H. (1973). *Eating disorders: Obesity, anorexia nervosa, and the person within.* New York: Basic Books.

Buckalew, L.W. (1980). A descriptive study of denominational concomitants in psychiatric diagnosis. *Social Behavior and Personality 6*:239.

Buckley, P., & Galanter, M. (1979). Mystical experience, spiritual knowledge, and a contemporary ecstatic religion. *British Journal of Medical Psychology 52*:281.

Burton-Bradley, B.G. (1970). The New Guinea prophet: Is the cultist always normal? *Medical Journal of Australia 1*:124.

Burton-Bradley, B.G. (1972). Human sacrifice for cargo. *Medical Journal of Australia 2*:668.

Burton-Bradley, B.G. (1976). Cannibalism for cargo. *Journal of nervous and Mental Disease 163*:428.

Burton-Bradley, B.G. (1978). Kung Fu for cargo. *Journal of Nervous and Mental Disease 166*:885.

Campbell, D.T. (1960). Blind variation and selective retention in creative thought as in other knowledge processes. *Psychological Review 67*:380.

Campbell, D.T. (1979). Comments on the sociobiology of ethics and moralizing. *Behavioral Science* 24:37.

Caplovitz, D., & Sherrow, F. (1977). *The religious dropouts*. Beverly Hills, CA: Sage.

Caplow, T., Bahr, H.M., Chadwick, B.A., et al. (1983). *All faithful people: Change and continuity in Middletown's religion*. Minneapolis: University of Minnesota Press.

Carbine, M.E. (1980). Religion, psychology, and mental health: The problems of partnership. *Journal of Religion and Health* 19:40.

Casey, R.P. (1945). Religion and personal adjustment. *Psychiatry* 8:13.

Cavenar, J.O., & Spaulding, J.G. (1977). Depressive disorders and religious conversions. *Journal of Nervous and Mental Disease* 165:200.

Chagnon, N.A. (1974). *Studying the Yanomamo*. New York: Holt, Rinehart & Winston.

Chagnon, N.A. (1977). Yanomamo: The fierce people (2nd ed.). New York: Holt, Rinehart & Winston.

Chagnon, N.A. (1979a). Mate competition, favoring close kin, and village fissioning among the Yanomamo Indians. In N.A. Chagnon & W. Irons (Eds.), *Evolutionary biology and human social behavior: An anthropological perspective*. North Scituate, MA: Duxbury Press.

Chagnon, N.A. (1979b). Is reproductive success equal in egalitarian societies? In N.A. Chagnon & W. Irons (Eds.), *Evolutionary biology and human social behavior: An anthropological perspective*. North Scituate, MA: Duxbury Press.

Chagnon, N.A. (1980). Kin-selection theory, kinship, marriage and fitness among the Yanomamo Indians. In G.W. Barlow & J. Silverberg (Eds.) *Sociobiology: Beyond nature/nurture*. Washington, DC: American Association for the Advancement of Science.

Chagnon, N.A. & Bugos, P.E. (1979). Kin selection and conflict: An analysis of a Yanomamo ax fight. In N.A. Chagnon & W. Irons (Eds.), *Evolutionary biology and human social behavior: An anthropological perspective*. North Scituate, MA: Duxbury Press.

Chagnon, N.A., Flinn, M.V., & Melancon, T.F. (1979). Sex-ratio variation among the Yanomamo Indians. In N.A. Chagnon & W. Irons (Eds.), *Evolutionary biology and human social behavior: An anthropological perspective*. North Scituate, MA: Duxbury Press.

Chance, M.R.A. (1962). Social behavior and primate evolution. In A. Montagu (Ed.), *Culture and the evolution of man*. New York: Oxford University Press.

Chandrashekar, C.R. (1981). A victim of an epidemic of possession syndrome. *Indian Journal of Psychiatry* 23:370.

Chepko-Sade, B.D. (1979). Monkey group splits up. *New Scientist* 82:348.

Christensen, C.W. (1963). Religious conversion. *Archives of General Psychiatry* 9:207.

Christensen, H.T. (1953). Studies in child spacing: Premarital pregnancy as measured by the spacing of the first birth with marriage. *American Sociological Review* 18:53.

Christensen, H.T. (1960). Cultural relativism and premarital sex norms. *American Sociological Review* 25:31.

Clark, H.H., & Clark, E.V. (1977). *Psychology and language: An introduction to psycholinguistics.* New York: Harcourt Brace Jovanovich.

Clark, J.G. (1983). On the further study of destructive cultism. In D.A. Halperin (Ed.), *Psychodynamic perspectives on religion sect and cult.* Boston: John Wright Press.

Clark, R.A. (1944). Theosophical occultism and mental hygiene. *Psychiatry* 7:237.

Clark, R.A. (1980). Religious delusions among Jews. *American Journal of Psychotherapy* 34:62.

Clutton-Brock, T.H., & Harvey, P.H. (1976). Evolutionary rules and primate societies. In P.P.G. Bateson & R.A. Hinde (Eds.), *Growing points in ethology.* New York: Cambridge University Press.

Clutton-Brock, T.H., & Harvey, P.H. (Eds.). (1978). *Readings in sociobiology.* San Francisco: W.H. Freeman.

Cole, M., Hood, L., & McDermott, R. (1982). Ecological niche picking. In U. Neisser (Ed.), *Memory observed: Remembering in natural contexts.* San Francisco: W.H. Freeman.

Comer, N.L., Madow, L., & Dixon, J.J. (1967). Observations of sensory deprivation in a life-threatening situation. *American Journal of Psychiatry* 124:164.

Coomaraswamy, A.K. (1945). Spiritual paternity and the puppet-complex. *Psychiatry* 8:287.

Cooper, W.S. (1987). Decision theory as a branch of evolutionary theory: A biological derivation of the Savage axioms. *Psychological Review* 94:395.

Corning, P.A. (1983). *The synergism hypothesis: A theory of progressive evolution.* New York: McGraw-Hill.

Cosmides, L. (1989). The logic of social exchange: Has natural selection shaped how humans reason? Studies with the Wason selection task. *Cognition* 31.

Cosmides, L., & Tooby, J. (1987). From evolution to behavior: Evolutionary psychology as the missing link. In J. Dupre (Ed.), *The latest on the best: Essays on evolution and optimality.* Cambridge, MA: MIT Press.

Cosmides, L., & Tooby, J. (1989). Evolutionary psychology and the generation of culture, part II. Case study: A computational theory of social exchange. *Ethology and Sociobiology* 10:51.

Creese, I. (1985). Dopamine and antipsychotic medications. In R.E. Hales & A.J. Frances (Eds.), *American Psychiatric Association Annual Review* (Vol. 4). Washington, DC: American Psychiatric Press.

Crisp, A.H. (1984). The psychopathology of anorexia nervosa: Getting the "heat" out of the system. In A.J. Stunkard & E. Stellar (Eds.), *Eating and its disorders.* New York: Raven Press.

Darley, J.M., & Batson, C.D. (1973). From Jerusalem to Jericho: A study of situational and dispositional variables in helping behavior. *Journal of Personality and Social Psychology* 27:100.

Darwin, C. (1859). *The origin of species by means of natural selection.* London: Murray.

David-Neel, A. (1979). *Buddhism: Its doctrines and its methods.* New York: Avon.

Davies, N.B. (1982). Behaviour and competition for scarce resources. In King's College Sociobiology Group (Eds.), *Current problems in sociobiology.* Cambridge: Cambridge University Press.

Davis, M., & Wallbridge, D. (1981). *Boundary and space: An introduction to the work of W.W. Winnicott.* New York: Brunner/Mazel.

Davis, W. (1985). The serpent and the rainbow. New York: Warner Books.

Dawkins, R. (1982). *The extended phenotype: The gene as the unit of selection.* New York: Oxford University Press.

Dean, S.R. (1970). Is there an ultraconscious beyond the unconscious? *Canadian Psychiatric Association Journal 15:57.*

Dean, S.R. (1973). Metapsychiatry: The interface between psychiatry and mysticism. *American Journal of Psychiatry 130:1037.*

DeCasper, A.J., & Fifer, W.P. (1980). Of human bonding: Newborns prefer their mothers' voices. *Science 208:1174.*

Deconchy, J. (1968). God and the parental images: The masculine and feminine in religious free associations. In A. Godin (Ed.), *From cry to word: Contributions towards a psychology of prayer.* Brussels: Lumen Vitae.

Deutsch, A. (1975). Observations on a sidewalk ashram. *American Journal of Psychiatry 32:166.*

Deutsch, A. (1980). Tenacity of attachment to a cult leader: A psychiatric perspective. *American Journal of Psychiatry 137:1569.*

Deutsch, A. (1983). Psychiatric perspectives on an eastern-style cult. In D.A. Halperin (Ed.), *Psychodynamic perspectives on religion sect and cult.* Boston: John Wright Press.

Deutsch, A., & Miller, M.J. (1983). A clinical study of four Unification Church members. *American Journal of Psychiatry 140:767.*

Dewhurst, K., & Beard, A.W. (1970). Sudden religious conversions in temporal lobe epilepsy. *British Journal of Psychiatry 117:497.*

Dixon, R.D., & Kinlaw, B.J.R. (1982). Belief in the existence and nature of life after death: A research note. *Omega 13:287.*

Domino, G., Cohen, A., & Gonzalez, R. (1981). Jewish and Christian attitudes on suicide. *Journal of Religion and Health 20:201.*

Donovan, W.L., Leavitt, L.A., & Balling, J.D. (1978). Maternal physiological responses to infant signals. *Psychophysiology 15:68.*

Douglas, M. (1975). *Implicit meanings.* London: Routledge & Kegan Paul.

Draper, E., Meyer, G.G., Parzen, Z., & Samuelson, G. (1965). On the diagnostic value of religious ideation. *Archives of General Psychiatry 13:202.*

Dreger, R.M. (1952). Some personality correlates of religious attitudes. *Psychological Monographs 66(3).*

Drinka, G.F. (1984). *The birth of neurosis: Myth, malady and the Victorians.* New York: Simon & Schuster.

Dublin, L.I. (1933). *To be or not to be.* New York: Smith & Hass.

Dudley, R.L. (1978). Alienation from religion in adolescents from fundamentalist religious homes. *Journal for the Scientific Study of Religion 17*:389.

Dudycha, G.L. (1933). The religious beliefs of college students. *Journal of Applied Psychology 17*:585.

Durham, W.H. (1978). Toward a coevolutionary theory of human biology and culture. In A.L. Caplan (Ed.), *The sociobiology debate*. New York: Harper & Row.

Durkheim, E. (1897). *Suicide*. London: Routledge & Kegan Paul.

Durkheim, E. (1912). The elementary forms of the religious life. London: Allen & Unwin.

Eagle, M.N. (1984). *Recent developments in psychoanalysis: A critical evaluation*. New York: McGraw-Hill.

Ebaugh, H.R.F. (1977). *Out of the cloister: A study of organizational dilemmas*. Austin: University of Texas Press.

Egeland, J.A., & Hostetter, A.M (1983). Amish study I: Affective disorders among the Amish. *American Journal of Psychiatry 140*:56.

Egeland, J.A., Hostetter, A.M., & Eshleman, S.K. (1983). Amish study III: The impact of cultural factors on diagnosis of bipolar illness. *American Journal of Psychiatry 140*:67.

Ehrhardt, A.A., & Meyer-Bahlburg, H.F.L. (1981). Effects of prenatal sex hormones on gender-related behavior. *Science 211*:1312.

Eibl-Eibesfeldt, I. (1973). The expressive behavior of the deaf-and-blind born. In M. von Cranach & I. Vine (Eds.), *Social communication and movement*. New York: Academic Press.

Eigen, M. (1981). The area of faith in Winnicott, Lacan, and Bion. *International Journal of Psychoanalysis 62*:413.

Eimas, P.D., Siqueland, E.R., Jusczyk, P., & Vigorito, J. (1971). Speech perception in infants. *Science 171*:303.

Ekman, P. (1979). About brows: Emotional and conversational signals. In M. von Cranach, K. Foppa, W. Lepenies, & D. Ploog (Eds.), *Human ethology: Claims and limits of a new discipline*. Cambridge: Cambridge University Press.

Eliade, M. (1958). *Patterns in comparative religion* (R. Sheed, Trans.). New York: New American Library.

Eliade, M. (1969). *The quest: History and meaning in religion*. Chicago: University of Chicago Press.

Enna, S.J. (1985). Gamma-aminobutyric acid, pharmacology and neuropsychiatric illness. In R.E. Hales & A.J. Frances (Eds.), *American Psychiatric Association annual review* (Vol. 4). Washington, DC: American Psychiatric Press.

Erikson, E.H. (1962). *Young man Luther: A study in psychoanalysis and history*. New York: W.W. Norton.

Erikson, E.H. (1969). *Gandhi's truth: On the origins of militant nonviolence*. New York: W.W. Norton.

Etemad, B. (1978). Extrication from cultism. *Current Psychiatric Therapies. 18*:217.

Evans-Pritchard, E.E. (1937). *Witchcraft, Oracles and Magic among the Azande*. Oxford: Oxford University Press.

Ewing, K.P. (1983). The messengers of the 1890 Ghost Dance. In D.A. Halperin (Ed.), *Psychodynamic perspectives on religion sect and cult.* Boston: John Wright Press.

Fabian, J. (1983). Anthropological approaches to religious movements. In D.A. Halperin (Ed.), *Psychodynamic perspectives on religion sect and cult.* Boston: John Wright Press

Farr, C.B., & Howe, R.L. (1932). The influence of religious ideas on the etiology, symptomatology and prognosis of the psychoses. *American Journal of Psychiatry* 11:845.

Fauteux, K. (1981). Good/bad splitting in the religious experience. *American Journal of Psychoanalysis* 41:261.

Fenichel, O. (1945). *The psychoanalytic theory of neurosis.* New York: W.W. Norton.

Festinger, L., Riecken, H.W., & Schachter, S. (1956). *When prophecy fails: A social and psychological study of a modern group that predicted the destruction of the world.* Minneapolis: University of Minnesota Press.

Feuerbach, L. (1957). *The essence of Christianity.* New York: Harper.

Fingarette, H. (1958). The ego and mystic selflessness. *Psychoanalysis and the Psychoanalytic Review* 45:5.

Fisher, S. (1964). Acquiescence and religiosity. *Psychological Reports* 15:784.

Fodor, N. (1958). People who are Christ. *Psychoanalysis and the Psychoanalytic Review* 45:100.

Fox, R. (1980). *The red lamp of incest.* New York: E.P. Dutton.

Franzblau, A.N. (1960). Distinctive functions of psychotherapy and pastoral counseling. *Archives of General Psychiatry* 3:583.

Frazer, J.G. (1976). *The golden bough.* London: Macmillan.

Freud, S. (1900). The interpretation of dreams. In J. Strachey (Ed. and Trans.), *The standard edition of the complete psychological works of Sigmund Freud* [hereafter, *standard ed.*] (Vols. 4, 5). London: Hogarth Press.

Freud, S. (1901). The psychopathology of everyday life. In *Standard ed.* (Vol. 6). London: Hogarth Press.

Freud, S. (1907). Obsessive actions and religious practices. In *Standard ed.* (Vol. 9). London: Hogarth Press.

Freud, S. (1911). Psychoanalytic notes upon an autobiographical account of a case of paranoia. In *Standard ed.* (Vol. 12). London: Hogarth Press.

Freud, S. (1913). Totem and taboo. In *Standard ed.* (Vol. 13). London: Hogarth Press.

Freud, S. (1914). The Moses of Michelangelo. In *Standard ed.* (Vol. 13). London: Hogarth Press.

Freud, S. (1919). Preface to Reik's *Ritual: Psycho-analytic studies.* In *Standard ed.* (Vol. 17). London: Hogarth Press.

Freud, S. (1923a). The ego and the id. In *Standard ed.* (Vol. 19). London: Hogarth Press.

Freud, S. (1923b). A neurosis of demoniacal possession in the seventeenth century. In *Standard ed.* (Vol. 19). London: Hogarth Press.

Freud, S. (1924). The dissolution of the Oedipal complex. In *Standard ed.* (Vol. 19). London: Hogarth Press.

Freud, S. (1926). Inhibitions, symptoms, and anxiety. In *Standard ed.* (Vol. 20). London: Hogarth Press.

Freud, S. (1927). The future of an illusion. In *Standard ed.* (Vol. 21). London: Hogarth Press.

Freud, S. (1928). A religious experience. In *Standard ed.* (Vol. 21). London: Hogarth Press.

Freud, S. (1939). Moses and monotheism. In *Standard ed.* (Vol. 23). London: Hogarth Press.

Fromm, E. (1950). *Psychoanalysis and religion.* New Haven, CT: Yale University Press.

Furman, E. (1974). *A child's parent dies.* New Haven, CT: Yale University Press.

Galanter, M. (1978). The "relief effect": A sociobiological model for neurotic distress and large-group therapy. *American Journal of Psychiatry 135:*588.

Galanter, M. (1980). Psychological induction into the large group: Findings from a modern religious sect. *American Journal of Psychiatry 137:*1574.

Galanter, M. (1982). Charismatic religious sects and psychiatry: An overview. *American Journal of Psychiatry 139:*1539.

Galanter, M. (1983). Engaged members of the Unification Church: Impact of a charismatic large group on adaptation and behavior. *American Journal of Psychiatry 40:*1197.

Galanter, M. (1986). "Moonies" get married: A psychiatric follow-up study of a charismatic religious sect. *American Journal of Psychiatry 143:*1245.

Galanter, M., & Buckley, P. (1978). Evangelical religion and meditation: Psychotherapeutic effects. *Journal of Nervous and Mental Disease 166:*685.

Galanter, M., Buckley, P., Deutsch, A., Rabkin, R., & Rabkin, J. (1980). Large group influence for decreased drug use: Findings from two contemporary religious sects. *American Journal of Drug and Alcohol Abuse 7:*291.

Galanter, M., Rabkin, R., Rabkin, J., & Deutsch, A. (1979). The "Moonies": A psychological study of conversion and membership in a contemporary religious sect. *American Journal of Psychiatry 136:*165.

Galanter, M., & Westermeyer, J. (1980). Charismatic religious experience and large-group psychology. *American Journal of Psychiatry 137:*1550.

Gallemore, J.L., Wilson, W.P., & Rhoads, J.M. (1969). The religious life of patients with affective disorders. *Diseases of the Nervous System 30:*483.

Galper, M.F. (1983). The atypical dissociative disorder: Some etiological, diagnostic, and treatment issues. In D.A. Halperin (Ed.), *Psychodynamic perspectives on religion sect and cult.* Boston: John Wright Press.

Galvin, J.A.V., & Ludwig, A.M. (1961). A case of witchcraft. *Journal of Nervous and Mental Disease 133:*161.

Garvey, K. (1983). The prophet from Palmyra: Joseph Smith and the rise of Mormonism. In D.A. Halperin (Ed.), *Psychodynamic perspectives on religion sect and cult.* Boston: John Wright Press.

Gay, P. (1987). *A godless Jew: Freud, atheism, and the making of psychoanalysis.* New Haven, CT: Yale University Press.

Gay, V.P. (1975). Psychopathology and ritual: Freud's essay "Obsessive Actions and Religious Practices." *Psychoanalytic Review 62*:493.

Gay, V.P. (1980). Individual needs and charismatic promises. *Journal of religion and Health 19*:24.

Gay, V.P. (1982). Repression and sublimation in religious personalities. *Journal of Religion and Health 21*:152.

Gellhorn, E., & Kiely, W. (1972). Mystical states of consciousness: Neurophysiological and clinical aspects. *Journal of Nervous and Mental Disease 154*:399.

Geshwind, N. (1979). Specializations of the human brain. *Scientific American 241*:180.

Glenn, M.L. (1970). Religious conversion and the mystical experience. *Psychiatric Quarterly 44*:636.

Glick, I.O., Weiss, R.S., & Parkes, C.M. (1974). *The first year of bereavement.* New York: Wiley.

Gluckman, M. (1963). *Order and rebellion in tribal Africa.* London: Cohen & West.

Godelier, M. (1977). *Perspectives in Marxist anthropology.* Cambridge: Cambridge University Press.

Goldberg, B.Z. (1958). *The sacred fire: A history of sex in ritual, religion and human behavior.* Secaucus, NJ: Citadel Press.

Goldberg, C. (1983). Courage and fanaticism: The charismatic leader and modern religious cults. In D.A. Halperin (Ed.), *Psychodynamic perspectives on religion sect and cult.* Boston: John Wright Press.

Goldsen, R.K., Rosenberg, M., Williams, R.M., & Suchman, E.A. (1960). *What college students think.* Princeton, NJ: Van Nostrand.

Goodall, J. (1979). Life and death at Gombe. *National Geographic 155*:591.

Goodwin, D.W., Johnson, J., Maher, C., Rappaport, A., & Guze, S.B. (1969). Why people do not drink: A study of teetotalers. *Comprehensive Psychiatry 10*:209.

Gordon, J.S. (1987). *The golden guru: The strange journey of the Bhagwan Shree Rajneesh.* Lexington, MA: Stephen Greene Press.

Gouldner, A. (1960). The norm of reciprocity: A preliminary statement. *American Sociological Review 47*:73.

Goy, R.W., & McEwan, B.S. (1980). *Sexual differentiation in the brain.* Cambridge, MA: MIT Press.

Graff, R.W., & Ladd, C.E. 1971. POI correlates of a religious commitment inventory. *Journal of Clinical Psychology 27*:502.

Greenberg, J.R., & Mitchell, S.A. (1983). *Object relations in psychoanalytic theory.* Cambridge, MA: Harvard University Press.

Greyson, B. (1983). Near-death experiences and personal values. *American Journal of Psychiatry 140*:618.

Greyson, B., & Stevenson, I. (1980). The phenomenology of near-death experiences. *American Journal of Psychiatry 137*:1193.

Griffin, D.R. (1981). *The question of animal awareness: Evolutionary continuity of mental experience* (rev. ed.). Los Altos, CA: Kaufmann.

Griffith, E.E.H. (1983). The significance of ritual in a church-based healing model. *American Journal of Psychiatry 140:568.*

Griffith, E.E.H., English, T., & Mayfield, V. (1980). Possession, prayer, and testimony: Therapeutic aspects of the Wednesday night meeting in a black church. *Psychiatry 43:120.*

Grünbaum, A. (1984). *The foundations of psychoanalysis: A philosophical critique.* Berkeley: University of Calif. Press.

Gruter, M. (1983). Biologically based behavioral research and the facts of law. In, M. Gruter and P. Bohannon (Eds.), *Law, biology and culture: The evolution of law.* Santa Barbara, CA: Ross-Erikson.

Halperin, D.A. (1983a). Self-help groups for parents of cult members: Agenda, issues, and the role of the group leader. In D.A. Halperin (Ed.), *Psychodynamic perspectives on religion sect and cult.* Boston: John Wright Press.

Halperin, D.A. (1983b). Psychiatric consultation and supervision in the treatment of cult members. In D.A. Halperin (Ed.), *Psychodynamic perspectives on religion sect and cult.* Boston: John Wright Press.

Halperin, D.A. (1983c). Group processes in cult affiliation and recruitment. In D.A. Halperin (Ed.), *Psychodynamic perspectives on religion sect and cult.* Boston: John Wright Press.

Hamilton, W.D. (1964). The genetical evolution of social behavior. *Journal of Theoretical Biology 7:1.*

Harlow, H.F., & Zimmerman, R.R. (1959). Affectional responses in the infant monkey. *Science 130:421.*

Harrington, M. (1983). *The politics at God's funeral: The spiritual crisis of Western civilization.* New York: Penguin.

Hartog, J. (1980). The anlage and ontogeny of loneliness. In J. Hartog, J.R. Audy, & Y.A. Cohen (Eds.), *The anatomy of loneliness.* New York: International Universities Press.

Hassett, J. (1981). "But that would be wrong": *Psychology Today*'s report on cheating, lying, and bending the rules in everyday life. *Psychology Today,* November, p. 34

Haun, D.L. (1977). Perception of the bereaved, clergy, and funeral directors concerning bereavement. *Dissertation Abstracts International A37:6791.*

Heaney, J.J. (1983). Recent studies of near-death experiences. *Journal of Religion and Health 22:116.*

Heinrichs, D.J. (1982). Our Father which art in heaven: Parataxic distortions in the image of God. *Journal of Psychology and Theology 10:120.*

Herold, E.S., & Goodwin, M.S. (1981). Adamant virgins, potential nonvirgins, and nonvirgins. *Journal of Sex Research 17:97.*

Hill, J. (1984). Prestige and reproductive success in man. *Ethology and Sociobiology 5:77.*

Hill, W.S. (1955). The psychology of conversion. *Pastoral Psychology 6:48.*

Hine, V.H. (1969). Pentecostal glossolalia: Toward a functional interpretation. *Journal for the Scientific Study of Religion 8*:211.

Hochman, J.S., & Brill, N.Q. (1973). Chronic marijuana use and psychosocial adaptation. *American Journal of Psychiatry 130*:132.

Hoelter, J.W., & Epley, R.J. (1979). Religious correlates of fear of death. *Journal for the Scientific Study of Religion 18*:404.

Hole, G. (1971). Some comparisons among guilt feelings, religion, and suicidal tendencies in depressed patients. *Life-Threatening Behavior 1*:138.

Hood, R.W., Jr. (1972). Normative and motivational determinants of reported religious experience in two Baptist samples. *Review of Religious Research 13*:192.

Hood, R.W., Jr. (1973). Forms of religious commitment and intense religious experience. *Review of Religious Research 15*:29.

Hood, R.W., Jr. (1978). The usefulness of the indiscriminately pro and anti categories of religious orientation. *Journal for the Scientific Study of Religion 17*:419.

Hood, R.W., Jr., & Morris, R. (1981). Sensory isolation and the differential elicitation of religious imagery in intrinsic and extrinsic persons. *Journal for the Scientific Study of Religion 20*:261.

Horton, P.C. (1973). The mystical experience as a suicide preventive. *American Journal of Psychiatry 130*:294.

Hostetter, A.M., Egeland, J.A., & Endicott, J. (1983). Amish study II: Consensus diagnoses and reliability results. *American Journal of Psychiatry 140*:62.

Humphrey, N.K. (1976). The social function of intellect. In P.P.G. Bateson & R.A. Hinde (Eds.), *Growing points in ethology.* New York: Cambridge University Press.

Hunsberger, B. (1980). Problems and promise in the psychology of religion: An emerging social psychology of religion. *Canadian Journal of Behavioral Science 12*:64.

Hunt, R.A., & King, M.B. (1971). The intrinsic-extrinsic concept: A review and evaluation. *Journal for the Scientific Study of Religion 10*:339.

Hutch, R.A. (1983). An essay on psychotherapy and religion. *Journal of Religion and Health 22*:7.

Irons, W. (1979). Investment and primary social dyads. In N.A. Chagnon & W. Irons (Eds.), *Evolutionary biology and human social behavior: An anthropological perspective.* North Scituate, MA: Duxbury Press.

Irons, W. (1980). Is Yomut social behavior adaptive? In G.W. Barlow & J. Silverberg (Eds.), *Sociobiology: Beyond nature/nurture.* Washington, DC: American Association for the Advancement of Science.

Irons, W. (1983). Human female reproductive strategies. In S.K. Wasser (Ed.), *Social behavior of female vertebrates.* New York: Academic Press.

James, W. (1902). *The varieties of religious experience: A study in human nature.* Boston: Longmans, Green.

Janus, S., & Bess, B. (1973). Drug abuse, sexual attitudes, political radicalization, and religious practices of college seniors and public school teachers. *American Journal of Psychiatry 130:*187.

Jenner, F.A. (1978). Psychiatry, biology and morals. In G.S. Stent (Ed.), *Morality as a biological phenomenon.* Berlin: Dahlem Konferenzen.

Johnson, B. (1963). On church and sect. *American Sociological Review 28:*539.

Jones, E. (1951). *Essays in applied psychoanalysis* (Vol. II). London: Hogarth Press.

Jones, E. (1957). *The life and work of Sigmund Freud* (Vol. III). New York: Basic Books.

Jones, E. (1958). The birth and death of Moses. *International Journal of Psychoanalysis. 39:*1.

Jones, E. (1959). *On the nightmare.* New York: Grove Press.

Jones, E.S. (1926). The opinions of college students. *Journal of Applied Psychology 10:*427.

Joyce, V. (1985). The play of illusion as an opening to the future of the self: Reflections of a religious clinician occasioned by rereading *The future of an illusion.* In E.M. Stern (Ed.), *Psychotherapy and the religiously committed patient.* New York: Haworth Press.

Jung, C.G. (1902). On the psychology and pathology of so-called occult phenomena. In The collected works of Carl G. Jung (R.F.C. Hull, Trans.) [hereafter, *Collected works*] (Vol. 1). Princeton, NJ: Princeton University Press.

Jung, C.G. (1916/1957). The transcendent function. In *Collected works* (Vol. 8). Princeton, NJ: Princeton University Press.

Jung, C.G. (1919). Instinct and the unconscious. In *Collected works* (Vol. 8). Princeton, NJ: Princeton University Press.

Jung, C.G. (1920/1948). The psychological foundations of belief in spirits. In *Collected works* (Vol. 8). Princeton, NJ: Princeton University Press.

Jung, C.G. (1922). On the relation of analytical psychology to poetry. In *Collected works* (Vol. 15). Princeton, NJ: Princeton University Press.

Jung, C.G. (1925). Marriage as a psychological relationship. In *Collected works* (Vol. 17). Princeton, NJ: Princeton University Press.

Jung, C.G. (1927/1931). The structure of the psyche. In *Collected works* (Vol. 8). Princeton, NJ: Princeton University Press.

Jung, C.G. (1928). The relations between the ego and the unconscious. In *Collected works* (Vol. 7). Princeton, NJ: Princeton University Press.

Jung, C.G. (1928/1931). The spiritual problem of modern man. In *Collected works* (Vol. 10). Princeton, NJ: Princeton University Press.

Jung, C.G. (1934). The soul and death. In *Collected works* (Vol. 8). Princeton, NJ: Princeton University Press.

Jung, C.G. (1939/1954). Psychological commentaries on "The Tibetan Book of the Great Liberation." In *Collected works* (Vol. 11). Princeton, NJ: Princeton University Press.

Jung, C.G. (1951). Aion: Researches into the phenomenology of the self. In *Collected works* (Vol. 9, Pt. II). Princeton, NJ: Princeton University Press.

Jung, C.G. (1952). Answer to Job. In *Collected works* (Vol. 11). Princeton, NJ: Princeton University Press.

Jung, C.G. (1958). Flying saucers: A modern myth. In *Collected works* (Vol. 10). Princeton, NJ: Princeton University Press.

Kahoe, R.D., & Dunn, R.F. (1975). The fear of death and religious attitudes and behavior. *Journal for the Scientific Study of Religion 14:379.*

Kaufman, M.R. (1939). Religious delusions in schizophrenia. *International Journal of Psychoanalysis 20:363.*

Kelley, H.H., & Michela, J.L. (1980). Attribution theory and research. *Annual Review of Psychology 31:457.*

Kemp, H.V. (1985). Psychotherapy as a religious process: A historical heritage. In E.M. Stern (Ed.), *Psychotherapy and the religiously committed patient.* New York: Haworth Press.

Kiev, A. (1964). Psychotherapeutic aspects of pentecostal sects among West Indian immigrants to England. *British Journal of Sociology 15:129.*

Kildahl, J.P. (1965). The personalities of sudden religious converts. *Pastoral Psychology 16:37.*

Kinsey, A.C., Pomeroy, W.B., & Martin, C.E. (1948). *Sexual behavior in the human male.* Philadelphia: Saunders.

Kinsey, A.C., Pomeroy, W.B., Martin, C.E., & Gebhard, P.H. (1953). *Sexual behavior in the human female.* Philadelphia: Saunders.

Kleiner, R.J., Tuckman, J., & Lavell, M. (1959). Mental disorder and status based on religious affiliation. *Human Relations 12:273.*

Kleiner, R.J., Tuckman, J., & Lavell, M. (1962). Mental disorder and status based on Protestant subgroup membership. *Journal of Social Psychology 58:345.*

Koegel, P., Burnam, M.A., & Farr, R.K. (1988). The prevalence of specific psychiatric disorders among homeless individuals in the inner city of Los Angeles. *Archives of General Psychiatry 45:1085.*

Kohut, H. (1971). *The analysis of the self.* New York: International Universities Press.

Kohut, H. (1977). *The restoration of the self.* New York: International Universities Press.

Konner, M. (1982). *The tangled wing: Biological constraints on the human spirit.* New York: Harper & Row.

Kranitz, L., Abrahams, J., Spiegel, D., & Keith-Spiegel, P. (1968). Religious beliefs of suicidal patients. *Psychological Reports 22:936.*

Kris, E. (1952). *Psychoanalytic explorations in art.* New York: International Universities Press.

Kumasaka, Y. (1966). Soka Gakkai: Group psychologic study of a new religio-political organization. *American Journal of Psychotherapy 20:462.*

Kummer, H. (1978). Analogs of morality among nonhuman primates. In G.S. Stent (Ed.), *Morality as a biological phenomenon.* Berlin: Dahlem Konferenzen.

Kurland, J.A. (1979). Paternity, mother's brother, and human sociality. In N.A. Chagnon, & W. Irons (Eds.), *Evolutionary biology and human social behavior: An anthropological perspective.* North Scituate, (MA:) Duxbury Press.

Kushner, A.W. (1967). Two cases of auto-castration due to religious delusions. *British Journal of Medical Psychology 40:*293.

Kutty, I.N., Froese, A.P., & Rae-Grant, Q.A.F. (1979). Hare Krishna movement: What attracts the Western adolescent? *Canadian Journal of Psychiatry 24:*604.

Lambert, W.W., Triandis, L.M., & Wolf, M. (1959). Some correlates of belief in the malevolence and benevolence of supernatural beings: A cross-cultural study. *Journal of Abnormal and Social Psychology 58:*162.

Landsborough, D. (1987). St. Paul and temporal lobe epilepsy. *Journal of Neurology, Neurosurgery, and Psychiatry 50:*659.

Langton, J. (1979). Darwinism and the behavioral theory of sociocultural evolution: An analysis. *American Journal of Sociology 85:*288.

Larsen, L., & Knapp, R.H. (1964). Sex differences in symbolic conceptions of the deity. *Journal of Projective Techniques 28:*303.

Larson, D.B., Pattison, E.M., Blazer, D.G., Omran, A.R., & Kaplan, B.H. (1986). Systematic analysis of research on religious variables in four major psychiatric journals, 1978–1982. *American Journal of Psychiatry 143:*329.

Larson, D.B., & Wilson, W.P. (1980). Religious life of alcoholics. *Southern Medical Journal 73:*723.

Leacock, E. (1978). Women's status in egalitarian society: Implications for social evolution. *Current Anthropology 19:*247.

Leacock, E. (1980). Social behavior, biology and the double standard. In G.W. Barlow & J. Silverberg (Eds.), *Sociobiology: Beyond nature/nurture.* Washington, DC: American Association for the Advancement of Science.

Levin, T.M., & Zegans, L.S. (1974). Adolescent identity crisis and religious conversion: Implications for psychotherapy. *British Journal of Medical Psychology 47:*73.

Levine, R.A., & Campbell, D.T. (1972). *Ethnocentrism: Theories of conflict, ethnic attitudes, and group behavior.* New York: Wiley.

Levine, S.V. (1979). Role of psychiatry in the phenomenon of cults. *Canadian Journal of Psychiatry 24:*593.

Levine, S.V. (1983). Alienated Jewish youth and religious seminaries: An alternative to cults? In D.A. Halperin (Ed.), *Psychodynamic perspectives on religion sect and cult.* Boston: John Wright Press.

Levine, S.V., & Salter, N.E. (1976). Youth and contemporary religious movements: Psychosocial findings. *Canadian Psychiatric Association Journal 21:*411.

Levinson, P. (1973). Religious delusions in counter-culture patients. *American Journal of Psychiatry 130:*1265.

Levy-Bruhl, L. (1926). *How natives think.* London: Allen & Unwin.

Levy-Suhl, M. (1946). The role of ethics and religion in psycho-analytic theory and therapy. *International Journal of Psychoanalysis 27:*110.

Lifton, R.J. (1979). *The broken connection: On death and the continuity of life.* New York: Simon & Schuster.

Linden, R., & Currie, R. (1977). Religiosity and drug use: A test of social control theory. *Canadian Journal of Criminology and Corrections 19:*346.

Lippman, T.W. (1982). *Understanding Islam: An introduction to the Moslem world.* New York: New American Library.

Littlewood, R., & Lipsedge, M. (1978). Migration, ethnicity and diagnosis. *Psychiatria Clinica 11:15.*

Lofland, J., & Stark, R. (1965). Becoming a world-saver: A theory of conversion to a deviant perspective. *American Sociological Review 30:862.*

Long, T.E., & Hadden, J.K. (1983). Religious conversion and the concept of socialization: Integrating the brainwashing and drift models. *Journal for the Scientific Study of Religion 22:1.*

Lopreato, J. (1984). *Human nature and biocultural evolution.* Boston: Allen & Unwin.

Lorand, S. (1962). Psycho-analytic therapy of religious devotees (A theoretical and technical contribution). *International Journal of Psychoanalysis 43:50.*

Loveland, G.G. (1968). The effects of bereavement on certain religious attitudes. *Sociological Symposium 1:17.*

Lowe, W.L. (1953). Psychodynamics in religious delusions and hallucinations. *American Journal of Psychotherapy 7:454.*

Lowe, W.L. (1954). Group beliefs and socio-cultural factors in religious delusions. *Journal of Social Psychology 40:267.*

Lowe, W.L. (1955). Religious beliefs and religious delusions. *American Journal of Psychotherapy 9:54.*

Lubin, A.J. (1958). A feminine Moses: A bridge between childhood identifications and adult identity. *International Journal of Psychoanalysis 39:535.*

Luckmann, T. (1979). Personal identity as an evolutionary and historical problem. In M. von Cranach, K. Foppa, W. Lepenies, & D. Ploog (Eds.), *Human ethology: Claims and limits of a new discipline.* Cambridge: Cambridge University Press.

Ludwig, A.M. (1966). Altered states of consciousness. *Archives of General Psychiatry 15:225.*

Lumsden, C.J., & Wilson, E.O. (1981). *Genes, mind, and culture: The coevolutionary process.* Cambridge, MA: Harvard University Press.

Lumsden, C.J., & Wilson, E.O. (1983). *Promethean Fire: Reflections on the origin of mind.* Cambridge, MA: Harvard University Press.

Luyster, R. (1980). King Ego and the double-sex dancer. *Journal of Religion and Health 19:121.*

Maccoby, E.E., & Jacklin, C.N. (1974). *The psychology of sex differences.* Palo Alto, CA: Stanford University Press.

MacDonald, C.B., & Luckett, J.B. (1983). Religious affiliation and psychiatric diagnoses. *Journal for the Scientific Study of Religion 22:15.*

MacIntyre, A. (1978). *Against the self image of the age.* Notre Dame, IN: University of Notre Dame Press.

Maleson, F.G. (1981). Dilemmas in the evaluation and management of religious cultists. *American Journal of Psychiatry 138:925.*

Malinowski, B. (1974). *Magic, science and religion, and other essays.* London: Souvenir Press.

Markl, H.S. (1978). Evolution of morals? Morals of evolution? Group report. In G.S. Stent (Ed.), *Morality as a biological phenomenon*. Berlin: Dahlem Konferenzen.

Marks, I.M. (1987). *Fears, phobias, and rituals: Panic, anxiety, and their disorders*. New York: Oxford University Press.

Marler, P. (1979). Development of auditory perception in relation to vocal behavior. In M. von Cranach, K. Foppa, W. Lepenies, D. Ploog (Eds.), *Human ethology: Claims and limits of a new discipline*. Cambridge: Cambridge University Press.

Martin, C., & Nichols, R.C. (1962). Personality and religious belief. *Journal of Social Psychology 56*:3.

Mauss, M. (1954). *The gift* (I. Cummison, Trans.). London: Cohen & West.

Maxwell, M. (1984). *Human evolution: A philosophical anthropology*. New York: Columbia University Press.

Maynard Smith, J. (1976). Evolution and the theory of games. *American Scientist 64*:41.

Maynard Smith, J. (1982a). *Evolution and the theory of games*. Cambridge: Cambridge University Press.

Maynard Smith, J. (1982b). The evolution of social behavior—A classification of models. In King's College Sociobiology Group (Eds.), *Current problems in sociobiology*. Cambridge: Cambridge University Press.

Mayr, E. (1963). *Animal species and evolution*. Cambridge, MA: Harvard University Press.

McIntosh, W.A., Fitch, S.D., Wilson, J.B., & Nyberg, K.L. (1981). The effect of mainstream religious social controls on adolescent drug use in rural areas. *Review of Religious Research 23*:54.

McLellan, D. (1973). *Karl Marx: His life and thought*. New York: Harper & Row.

Mehta, V. (1976). *Mahatma Gandhi and his apostles*. New York: Penguin.

Meissner, W.W. (1984). *Psychoanalysis and religious experience*. New Haven, CT: Yale University Press.

Mellen, S.L.W. (1981). *The evolution of love*. San Francisco: W.H. Freeman.

Menzel, E.W. (1975). Natural language of young chimpanzees. *New Scientist 65*:127.

Middleton, R., & Putney, S. (1962). Religion, normative standards, and behavior. *Sociometry 25*:141.

Miller, D.H. (1959). *Ghost Dance*. Lincoln: University of Nebraska Press.

Miller, J.W. (1982). In defense of monotheistic father religion. *Journal of Religion and Health 21*:62.

Miller, J.W. (1983). Psychoanalytic approaches to biblical religion. *Journal of Religion and Health 22*:19.

Minton, B., & Spilka, B. (1976). Perspectives on death in relation to powerlessness and form of personal religion. *Omega 7*:261.

Mollica, R.F., Streets, F.J., Boscarino, J., & Redlich, F.C. (1986). A community study of formal pastoral counseling activities of the clergy. *American Journal of Psychiatry 143:*323.

Moore, T.V. (1944). Religion, psychiatry and mental hygiene. *Psychiatry 7:*321.

Morphew, J.A. (1968). Religion and attempted suicide. *International Journal of Social Psychiatry 14:*188.

Morris, B. (1987). *Anthropological studies of religion: An introductory text.* Cambridge: Cambridge University Press.

Murphy, H.B.M., & Vega, G. (1982). Schizophrenia and religious affiliation in Northern Ireland. *Psychological Medicine 12:*595.

Murphy, J.M. (1976). Psychiatric labeling in cross-cultural perspective. *Science 191:*1019.

Nagy, M. (1948). The child's view of death. *Journal of Genetic Psychology 73:*3.

Natale, S.M. (1985). Confrontation and the religious beliefs of a client. In E.M. Stern (Ed.), *Psychotherapy and the religiously committed patient.* New York: Haworth Press.

Neisser, U. (1982). Preface. In, U. Neisser (Ed.), *Memory observed: Remembering in natural contexts.* San Francisco: W.H. Freeman.

Nelson, E. (1940). Student attitudes toward religion. *Genetic Psychology Monographs 22:*323.

Nelson, L.D., & Dynes, R.R. (1976). The impact of devotionalism and attendance on ordinary and emergency helping behavior. *Journal for the Scientific Study of Religion 15:*47.

Nelson, M.O. (1971). The concept of God and feelings toward the parents. *Journal of Individual Psychology 27:*46.

Nelson, M.O., & Jones, E.M. (1957). An application of the Q-technique to the study of religious concepts. *Psychological Reports 3:*293.

Nelson, S.H., & Torrey, E.F. (1973). The religious functions of psychiatry. *American Journal of Orthopsychiatry 43:*362.

Neumann, E. (1955). *The great mother: An analysis of the archetype.* London: Routledge & Kegan Paul.

Nicholi, A.M. (1974). A new dimension of the youth culture. *American Journal of Psychiatry 131:*396.

Niederland, W.G. (1959a). The "miracled-up" world of Schreber's childhood. *Psychoanalytic Study of the Child 14:*383.

Niederland, W.G. (1959b). Schreber: Father and son. *Psychoanalytic Quarterly 28:*151.

Noyes, R. (1980). Attitude change following near-death experiences. *Psychiatry 43:*234.

Oates, W. (1949). The role of religion in the psychoses. *Journal of Pastoral Care 3:*21.

Ofshe, R. (1980). The social development of the Synanon cult: The managerial strategy of organizational transformation. *Sociological Analysis 41:*109.

Olsson, P.A. (1983). Adolescent involvement with the supernatural and cults: Or new bottles for old wine. In D.A. Halperin (Ed.), *Psychodynamic perspectives on religion sect and cult.* Boston: John Wright Press.

Ostow, M. (1980). Religion and psychiatry. In H.I. Kaplan, A.M. Freedman, & B.J. Sadock (Eds.), *Comprehensive textbook of psychiatry* (vol. III, 3rd ed.). Baltimore: Williams & Wilkins.

Papousek, H., & Papousek, M. (1979). Early ontogeny of human social interaction: Its biological roots and social dimensions. In M. von Cranach, K. Foppa, W. Lepenies, and D. Ploog (Eds.), *Human ethology: Claims and limits of a new discipline*. New York: Cambridge University Press.

Pargament, K.I., Steele, R.E., & Tyler, F.B. (1979). Religious participation, religious motivation, and psychosocial competence. *Journal for the Scientific Study of Religion 18:412.*

Parker, G.A. (1974). Assessment strategy and the evolution of fighting behavior. *Journal of Theoretical Biology 47:223.*

Parkes, C.M. (1972). *Bereavement: Studies of grief in later life.* New York: International Universities Press.

Parkes, C.M., & Stevenson-Hinde, J. (Eds.). (1982). *The place of attachment in human behavior.* New York: Basic Books.

Patai, R. (1978). *The Hebrew goddess.* New York: Avon Books.

Pattison, E.M. (1966). Social and psychological aspects of religion in psychotherapy. *Journal of Nervous and Mental Disease 141:586.*

Pattison, E.M., Lapins, N.A., & Doerr, H.A. (1973). Faith healing: A study of personality and function. *Journal of Nervous and Mental Disease 157:397.*

Pattison, E.M., & Pattison, M.L. (1980). "Ex-gays": Religiously mediated change in homosexuals. *American Journal of Psychiatry 137:1553.*

Paul, S.M., Janowsky, A., & Skolnick, P. (1985). Mono-aminergic neurotransmitters and antidepressant drugs. In R.E. Hales & A.J. Frances (Eds.), *American Psychiatric Association annual review* (Vol. 4). Washington, DC: American Psychiatric Press.

Pettigrew, T.F. (1978). Three issues in ethnicity: Boundaries, deprivations, and perceptions. In J.M. Yinger & S.J. Cutler (Eds.), *Major social issues: A multidisciplinary view*. New York: Free Press.

Preston, R.J., & Hammerschlag, C.A. (1983). The Native American Church. In D.A. Halperin (Ed.), *Psychodynamic perspectives on religion sect and cult.* Boston: John Wright Press.

Proudfoot, W., & Shaver, P. (1975). Attribution theory and the psychology of religion. *Journal for the Scientific Study of Religion 14:317.*

Radcliffe-Brown, A.R. (1952). *Structure and function in primitive society.* London: Cohen & West.

Raphael, B. (1983). *The anatomy of bereavement.* New York: Basic Books.

Rayburn, C.A. (1985). The religious patient's initial encounter with psychotherapy. In E.M. Stern (Ed.), *Psychotherapy and the religiously committed patient.* New York: Haworth Press.

Rebhan, J. (1983). The drug rehabilitation program: Cults in formation? In D.A. Halperin (Ed.), *Psychodynamic perspectives on religion sect and cult.* Boston: John Wright Press.

Reiss, I.L. (1969). Premarital sex permissiveness among negroes and whites. *American Sociological Review 29*:688.

Reynolds, P.C. (1981). *On the evolution of human behavior.* Berkeley: University of California Press.

Reynolds, V., & Tanner, R.E.S. (1983). *The biology of religion.* London: Longman.

Richards, R.J. (1987). *Darwin and the emergence of evolutionary theories of mind and behavior.* Chicago: University of Chicago Press.

Rieff, P. (1966). *The triumph of the therapeutic: Uses of faith after Freud.* New York: Harper & Row.

Rizzuto, A. (1976). Freud, God, and the Devil and the theory of object representations. *International Review of Psychoanalysis 31*:165.

Rizzuto, A. (1979). *The birth of the living God: A psychoanalytic study.* Chicago: University of Chicago Press.

Robbins, T. (1969). Eastern mysticism and the resocialization of drug users: The Meher Baba cult. *Journal for the Scientific Study of Religion 8*:308.

Roberts, F.J. (1965). Some psychological factors in religious conversion. *British Journal of Social and Clinical Psychology 4*:185.

Robinson, D.N. (1986). *An intellectual history of psychology.* Madison: University of Wisconsin Press.

Rodinson, M. (1971). *Muhammad* (A. Carter, Trans.). New York: Pantheon Books.

Roheim, G. (1946). Saint Agatha and the Tuesday Woman. *International Journal of Psychoanalysis 27*:119.

Rohrbaugh, J., & Jessor, R. (1975). Religiosity in youth: A personal control against deviant behavior. *Journal of Personality 43*:136.

Rokeach, M. (1960). *The open and closed mind.* New York: Basic Books.

Rokeach, M. (1981). *The three Christs of Ypsilanti: A psychological study.* New York: Columbia University Press.

Roof, W.C. (1984). Religiosity in Middletown. *Science 223*:691.

Ross, M.W. (1983). Clinical profiles of Hare Krishna devotees. *American Journal of Psychiatry 140*:416.

Rossi, A.S. (1985). Change in the client and in the client's God. In E.M. Stern (Ed.), *Psychotherapy and the religiously committed patient.* New York: Haworth Press.

Rubinstein, B.B. (1980). On the psychoanalytic theory of unconscious motivation and the problem of its confirmation. *Nous 14*:427.

Rutledge, A.L. (1951). Concepts of God among the emotionally upset. *Pastoral Psychology 2*:22.

Sabini, J. (1981). *Armies in the sand: The struggle for Mecca and Medina.* London: Thames & Hudson.

Sabom, W.S. (1980). Near-death experience: A review from pastoral psychology. *Journal of Religion and Health 19*:130.

Salzman, L. (1953). The psychology of religious and ideological conversion. *Psychiatry 16*:177.

Salzman, L. (1966). Types of religious conversion. *Pastoral Psychology 17*:8.

Schafer, R. (1976). *A new language for psychoanalysis.* New Haven, CT: Yale University Press.

Schafer, R. (1978). *Language and insight.* New Haven, CT: Yale University Press.

Schoeneman, T.J. (1982). Criticisms of the psychopathological interpretation of witch hunts: A review. *American Journal of Psychiatry 139:*1028.

Schumacher, M., & Balthazart, J. (1985). Sexual differentiation is a biphasic process in mammals and birds. In R. Gilles & J. Balthazart (Eds.), *Neurobiology.* Berlin: Springer-Verlag.

Schumacher, M., Legros, J.J., & Balthazart, J. (1987). Steroid hormones, behavior and sexual dimorphism in animals and men: The nature-nurture controversy. *Experimental and Clinical Endocrinology 90:*129.

Schwab, M.E. (1977). A study of reported hallucinations in a southeastern county. *Mental Health Society 4:*344.

Schweitzer, A. (1948). *The psychiatric study of Jesus: Exposition and criticism* (C.R. Joy, Trans.). Boston: Beacon Press.

Sennett, R. (1981). *Authority.* New York: Random House.

Sensky, T., Wilson, A., Petty, R., Fenwick, P.B.C., & Rose, F.C. (1984). The interictal personality traits of temporal lobe epileptics: Religious belief and its association with reported mystical experiences. In R.J. Porter et al. (Eds.), *Advances in epileptology: XVth Epilepsy International Symposium.* New York: Raven Press.

Senter, D. (1947). Witches and psychiatrists. *Psychiatry 10:*49.

Sexton, R.O., & Maddock, R.C. (1980). The missionary syndrome. *Journal of Religion and Health 19:*59.

Shapiro, D. (1965). *Neurotic styles.* New York: Basic Books.

Shaver, P., Lenauer, M., & Sadd, S. (1980). Religiousness, conversion, and subjective well-being: The "healthy-minded" religion of modern American women. *American Journal of Psychiatry 137:*1563.

Shimano, E.T., & Douglas, D.B. (1975). On research in Zen. *American Journal of Psychiatry 132:*1300.

Shirer, W.L. (1979). *Gandhi: A memoir.* New York: Washington Square Press.

Shneidman, J.L., & Levine-Schneidman, C. (1983). The Albigensian Cathari. In D.A. Halperin (Ed.), *Psychodynamic perspectives on religion sect and cult.* Boston: John Wright Press.

Siegel, R.K. (1980). The psychology of life after death. *American Psychologist 35:*911.

Siegman, A.W. (1961). An empirical investigation of the psychoanalytic theory of religious behavior. *Journal for the Scientific Study of Religion 1:*74.

Simmonds, R.B. (1977). Conversion or addiction: Consequences of joining a Jesus movement group. *American Behavioral Scientist 20:*909.

Simpson, G.G. (1953). The Baldwin Effect. *Evolution 7:*110.

Slater, E., & Roth, M. (1969). *Clinical psychiatry.* London: Bailliere, Tindall & Cassell.

Smith, A. (1981). Religion and mental health among blacks. *Journal of Religion and Health 20:*264.

Spellman, C.M., Baskett, G.D., & Byrne, D. (1971). Manifest anxiety as a contributing factor in religious conversion. *Journal of Consulting and Clinical Psychology* 36:245.

Spencer, J. (1975). The mental health of Jehovah's Witnesses. *British Journal of Psychiatry* 126:556.

Spero, M.H. (1982). The use of folklore as a developmental phenomenon in nouveau-orthodox religionists. *American Journal of Psychoanalysis* 42:149.

Spero, M.H. (1983). Individual psychodynamic intervention with the cult devotee: Diagnostic and treatment procedure with a dysautonomous religious personality. In D.A. Halperin (Ed.), *Psychodynamic perspectives on religion sect and cult*. Boston: John Wright Press.

Spero, M.H. (1985). The reality and the image of God in psychotherapy. *American Journal of Psychotherapy* 39:75.

Spero, M.H. (1987). Identity and individuality in the nouveau-religious patient: Theoretical and clinical aspects. *Psychiatry* 50:55.

Spilka, B. (1977). Utilitarianism and personal faith. *Journal of Psychology and Theology* 5:226.

Spilka, B., Hood, R.W., & Gorsuch, R.L. (1985). *The psychology of religion: An empirical approach*. Englewood Cliffs, NJ: Prentice-Hall.

Spilka, B., Stout, L., Minton, B., & Sizemore, D. (1977). Death and personal faith: A psychometric investigation. *Journal for the Scientific Study of Religion* 16:169.

Spinetta, J.J., Rigler, D., & Karon, M. (1974). Personal space as a measure of a dying child's sense of isolation. *Journal of Consulting and Clinical Psychology* 42:751.

Spiro, M.E., & D'Andrade, R.G. (1958). A cross-cultural study of some religious beliefs. *American Anthropologist* 60:456.

Spitz, R.A. (1965). *The first year of life*. New York: International Universities Press.

Starbuck, E.D. (1897). A study of conversion. *American Journal of Psychology* 8:268.

Stark, R. (1964). Class, radicalism, and religious involvement in Great Britain. *American Sociological Review* 29:698.

Stark, R. (1971). Psychopathology and religious commitment. *Review of Religious Research* 12:165.

Steffenhagen, R.A., McAree, C.P., & Nixon, H.L., II. (1972). Drug use among college females: Sociodemographic and social psychological correlates. *International Journal of the Addictions* 7:285.

Stern, E.M. (1985). Psychotheology of religious commitment. In E.M. Stern (Ed.), *Psychotherapy and the religiously committed patient*. New York: Haworth Press.

Stevens, A. (1983). *Archetypes: A natural history of the self*. New York: Quill.

Stevenson, I., & Greyson, B. (1979). Near-death experiences: Relevance to the question of survival after death. *Journal of the American Medical Association* 242:265.

Stone, O.M. (1962). Cultural uses of religious visions: A case study. *Ethnology* 1:329.

Stone, S. (1934). The Miller delusion: A comparative study in mass psychology. *American Journal of Psychiatry* 91:593.

Strunk, O. (1959). Perceived relationships between parental and deity concepts. *Psychological Newsletter* 10:222.

Sullivan, H.S. (1947). Psychiatry and the need for religion. *Psychiatry* 10:335.

Sulloway, F.J. (1979). *Freud, biologist of the mind: Beyond the psychoanalytic legend*. New York: Basic Books.

Swanson, G.E. (1960). *The birth of the gods*. Ann Arbor: University of Michigan Press.

Symons, D. (1979). *The evolution of human sexuality*. New York: Oxford University Press.

Tart, C.T. (1975). *States of consciousness*. New York: Dutton.

Tavris, C., & Sadd, S. (1975). *The Redbook report on female sexuality*. New York: Dell.

Thomas, J.M. (1932). Fragments of a schizophrenic's "Virgin Mary" delusions. *American Journal of Psychiatry* 12:285.

Tiger, L. (1979). *Optimism: The biology of hope*. New York: Simon & Schuster.

Tinbergen, N. (1976). Ethology in a changing world. In P.P.G. Bateson & R.A. Hinde (Eds.), *Growing points in ethology*. New York: Cambridge University Press.

Tooby, J., & Cosmides, L. (1989). Evolutionary psychology and the generation of culture: Part I. Theoretical considerations. *Ethology and Sociobiology* 10:29.

Trevarthen, C. (1979). Instincts for human understanding and cultural cooperation: Their development in infancy. In M. von Cranach, K. Foppa, W. Lepenies, & D. Ploog (Eds.), *Human ethology: Claims and limits of a new discipline*. Cambridge: Cambridge University Press.

Trivers, R. (1971). The evolution of reciprocal altruism. *Quarterly Review of Biology* 46:35.

Trivers, R. (1974). Parent–offspring conflict. *American Zoologist* 14:249.

Trivers, R. (1978). Parental investment and sexual selection. In T.H. Clutton-Brock & P.H. Harvey (Eds.), *Readings in sociobiology*. San Francisco: W.H. Freeman.

Trivers, R. (1981). Sociobiology and politics. In E. White (Ed.), *Sociobiology and human politics*. Lexington, MA: Lexington Books.

Trivers, R. (1985). *Social evolution*. Menlo Park, CA: Benjamin Cummings.

Troeltsch, E. (1931). *The social teachings of the Christian churches*. New York: Macmillan.

Tucker, D.M., Novelly, R.A., & Walker, P.J. (1987). Hyperreligiosity in temporal lobe epilepsy: Redefining the relationship. *Journal of Nervous and Mental Disease* 175:181.

Turner, V.W. (1968). *The drums of affliction*. New York: Oxford University Press.

Tylor, E.B. (1913). *Primitive culture*. London: Murray.

Ullman, C. (1988). Psychological well-being among converts in traditional and nontraditional religious groups. *Psychiatry 51:*312.

Ungerleider, J.T., & Wellisch, D.K. (1979). Coercive persuasion (brainwashing), religious cults, and deprogramming. *American Journal of Psychiatry 136:*279.

Vaillant, G.E. (1983). *The natural history of alcoholism: Causes, patterns, and paths to recovery*. Cambridge, MA: Harvard University Press.

Vergote, A. (1988). *Guilt and desire: Religious attitudes and their pathological derivatives* (M.H. Wood, Trans.). New Haven, CT: Yale University Press.

Vergote, A., Tamayo, A., Pasquali, L., Bonami, M., Pattyn, M., & Custers, A. (1969). Concept of God and parental images. *Journal for the Scientific Study of Religion 8:*79.

Vernon, G.M. (1968). The religious nones: A neglected category. *Journal for the Scientific Study of Religion 7:*219.

Vitz, P.C. (1988). *Sigmund Freud's Christian unconscious*. New York: Guilford Press.

Wack, D.J. (1968). The image of God in psychotherapy: A study of cases. In A. Godin (Ed.), *From cry to word: Contributions towards a psychology of prayer*. Brussels: Lumen Vitae.

Wallace, A.F.C. (1959). Cultural determinants of response to hallucinatory experience. *Archives of General Psychiatry 1:*58.

Wallace, A.M. (1985). Initial encounters of religious and priests with psychotherapy. In E.M. Stern (Ed.), *Psychotherapy and the religiously committed patient*. New York: Haworth Press.

Wallace, R.K. (1970). Physiological effects of Transcendental Mediation. *Science 167:*1751.

Wallace, R.K., Benson, H., & Wilson, A.F. (1971). A wakeful hypometabolic physiologic state. *American Journal of Psychology 221:*795.

Walters, O.S. (1964). Religion and psychopathology. *Comprehensive Psychiatry 5:*24.

Wapnick, K. (1985). Forgiveness: A spiritual psychotherapy. In E.M. Stern (Ed.), *Psychotherapy and the religiously committed patient*. New York: Haworth Press.

Warner, R. (1983). Recovery from schizophrenia in the third world. *Psychiatry 46:*197.

Wasserman, M. (1982). Madness as religious experience: The case of Allen Ginsberg. *Journal of Religion and Health 21:*145.

Watson, S.J., Kelsey, J.E., Lopez, J.F., & Akil, H. (1985). Neuropeptide biology: Basic and clinical lessons from the opioids. In R.E. Hales & A.J. Frances (Eds.), *American Psychiatric Association annual review* (Vol. 4). Washington, DC: American Psychiatric Press.

Weber, M. (1930). *The Protestant ethic and the spirit of capitalism*. New York: Scribner's.

Weber, M. (1963). *The sociology of religion* (E. Fischof, Trans.). Boston: Beacon Press.

Weber, V. (1983). Modern cults and gnosticism: Some observations on religious and totalitarian movements. In D.A. Halperin (Ed.), *Psychodynamic perspectives on religion sect and cult*. Boston: John Wright Press.

Weibe, K.F., & Fleck, J.R. (1980). Personality correlates of intrinsic, extrinsic and non-religious orientations. *Journal of Psychology 105:*181.

Weigert-Vowinkel, E. (1938). The cult and mythology of the magna mater from the standpoint of psychoanalysis. *Psychiatry 1:*347.

Weininger, B. (1955). The interpersonal factor in the religious experience. *Psychoanalysis 3:*27.

Wenegrat, B. (1984). *Sociobiology and mental disorder: A new view*. Menlo Park, CA: Addison-Wesley.

Wenegrat, B. (1988, May). *Religious delusions with temporal lobe activation: A case report*. Paper presented at the American Psychiatric Association Annual Convention, Montreal, Quebec.

Wenger, M.A., & Bagchi, B.K. (1961). Studies of autonomic functions in practitioners of Yoga in India. *Behavioral Science 6:*312.

Wenger, M.A., Bagchi, B.K., & Anand, B.K. (1961). Experiments in India on "voluntary" control of the heart and pulse. *Circulation 24:*1319.

West, L.J., & Singer, M.T. (1980). Cults, quacks, and nonprofessional psychotherapies. In H.I. Kaplan, A.M. Freedman, & B.J. Sadock (Eds.), *Comprehensive textbook of psychiatry* (Vol. III, 3rd ed.). Baltimore: Williams & Wilkins.

Westermeyer, J., & Walzer, V. (1975). Drug usage: An alternative to religion? *Diseases of the Nervous System 36:*492.

Westermeyer, J., & Wintrob, R. (1979a). Folk criteria for the diagnosis of mental illness in rural Laos: On being insane in sane places. *American Journal of Psychiatry 136:*755.

Westermeyer, J., & Wintrob, R. (1979b). Folk explanations of mental illness in rural Laos. *American Journal of Psychiatry 136:*901.

Williams, R.L., & Cole, S. (1968). Religiosity, generalized anxiety, and apprehension concerning death. *Journal of Social Psychology 75:*111.

Wilson, D.S. (1980). *The natural selection of populations and communities*. Menlo Park, CA: Benjamin Cummings.

Wilson, E.O. (1975). *Sociobiology: The new synthesis*. Cambridge, MA: Belknap Press.

Wilson, E.O. (1978). *On human nature*. Cambridge, MA: Harvard University Press.

Wilson, W.P. (1972). Mental health benefits of religious salvation. *Diseases of the Nervous System 33:*382.

Winnicott, D.W. (1971). *Playing and reality*. New York: Basic Books.

Wintrob, R.M. (1973). The influence of others: Witchcraft and rootwork as explanations of behavior disturbances. *Journal of Nervous and Mental Disease 156:*318.

Wolf, A.P. (1966). Childhood association, sexual attraction, and the incest taboo: A Chinese case. *American Anthropology 68:*883.

Wolf, A.P. (1968). Adopt a daughter-in-law, marry a sister: A Chinese solution to the problem of the incest taboo. *American Anthropology 70*:864.

Wolf, A.P., & Huang, C. (1980). *Marriage and adoption in China, 1845–1945.* Stanford, CA: Stanford University Press.

Wolff, P.H. (1978). The biology of morals from a psychological perspective. In G.S. Stent (ed.), *Morality as a biological phenomenon.* Berlin: Dahlem Konferenzen.

Wood, B.G. (1980). The religion of psychoanalysis. *American Journal of Psychoanalysis 40*:13.

Worsley, P.M. (1959). Cargo cults. *Scientific American 200*:117.

Wrangham, R.W. (1982). Mutualism, kinship and social evolution. In King's College Sociobiology Group (Eds.), *Current problems in sociobiology.* Cambridge: Cambridge University Press.

Wyer, R.S., & Srull, T.K. (Eds.). (1984). *Handbook of social cognition.* Hillsdale, NJ: Lawrence Erlbaum.

Wyer, R.S., & Srull, T.K. (1986). Human cognition in its social context. *Psychological Review 93*:322.

Yager, J., & Strober, M. (1985). Family aspects of eating disorders. In R.E. Hales & A.J. Frances (Eds.), *American Psychiatric Association annual review* (Vol. 4). Washington, DC: American Psychiatric Press.

Yalom, I.D. (1980). *Existential psychotherapy.* New York: Basic Books.

Yap, P.M. (1960). The possession syndrome: A comparison of Hong Kong and French findings. *Journal of Mental Science 106*:114.

Young, H.F., Bentall, R.P., Slade, P.D., & Dewey, M.E. (1987). The role of brief instructions and suggestibility in the elicitation of auditory and visual hallucinations in normal and psychiatric subjects. *Journal of Nervous and Mental Disease 175*:41.

Zilboorg, G. (1935). *The medical man and the witch during the Renaissance.* Baltimore: Johns Hopkins University Press.

Zilboorg, G. (1941). *A history of medical psychology.* New York: W.W. Norton.

Zilboorg, G. (1958). *Freud and religion.* Westminster, MD: Neuman Press.

Zilboorg, G. (1962). Psychoanalysis and religion. New York: Farrar, Straus & Cudahy.

Index

About the Author

Brant Wenegrat is Assistant Professor of Psychiatry and Behavioral Science at Stanford University School of Medicine and Chief of Psychiatric Clinical Services at the Palo Alto Veterans' Administration Medical Center. He is the author of *Sociobiology and Mental Disorder,* which was the first systematic treatment of mental illness from a sociobiologic viewpoint. *Sociobiology and Mental Disorder* won a "Book of the Year" award from the *American Journal of Nursing.* Doctor Wenegrat has been a consultant to the American Psychiatric Association's Committee on Psychiatry and Religion. He has lectured and written about religious psychology and religious cults.